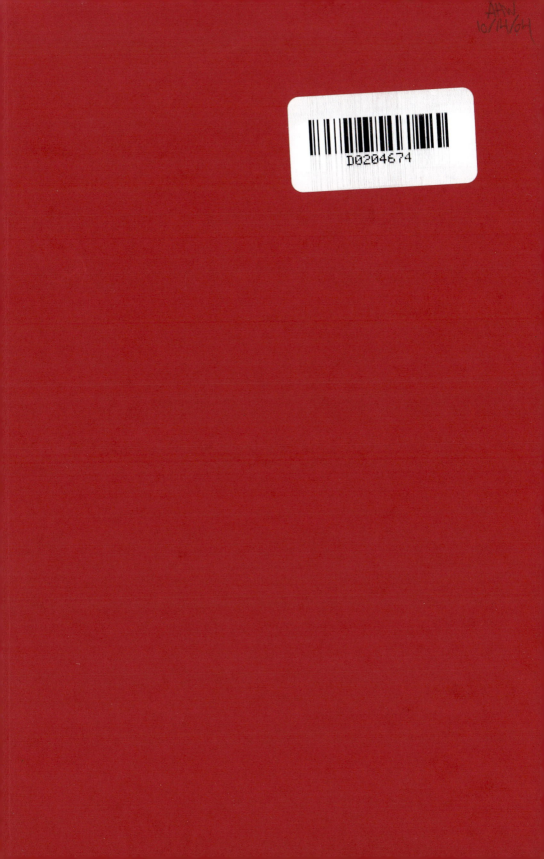

WAR WITH IRAQ

Winning—there is no substitute.

*Minimum loss of life—there is
no compromise.*

WAR WITH
IRAQ

Critical Lessons

★★★Gen. Buster Glosson, USAF (Ret.)

Library of Congress Control Number: 2003102029

ISBN: 0-9729117-0-7

CONTENTS

ILLUSTRATIONS

ACKNOWLEDGMENTS

In any historical account, accuracy and objectivity are of paramount importance. I am therefore forever grateful to three fellow flag officers who granted me access to their personal journals and recollections, namely,

Major General Larry Henry, USAF (Ret.)
Major General Dave Deptula, USAF
Brigadier General Rick Lewis, USAF

That Generals Henry, Deptula, and Lewis played an integral role in this account is only appropriate since they were instrumental in all phases of the planning and execution of the Gulf War. Their exemplary leadership and "out-of-the-box" solutions made our successes possible. For their service, I, and the country, will always be indebted.

In addition, I am indebted to the hard work and loyalty of those who worked with me in the "Black Hole" and whose names are found on the following page.

I also want to acknowledge the assistance of biographer and historian Howard E. Covington Jr. of Greensboro, North Carolina, who helped in the final preparation of this book. Anne Theilgard and her colleagues at Kachergis Book Design in Pittsboro, North Carolina, conscientiously pulled all the pieces together and brought the entire process smoothly to publication.

GENERAL GLOSSON'S "BLACK HOLE" AIR CAMPAIGN PLANNERS

———————→

Brigadier General Larry Henry

Brigadier General Ahmed Sudairy

Brigadier General Glen Profitt

Colonel Tony Tolin

Colonel Bob Osterloh

Lieutenant Colonel Khalid Bin Abdullah

Lieutenant Colonel Sam Baptiste

Lieutenant Colonel Dave Deptula

Lieutenant Colonel Phil Faye

Lieutenant Colonel Rodgers Greenawalt

Lieutenant Colonel Bob Kershaw

Lieutenant Colonel Rick Lewis

Commander "Duck" McSwain

Lieutenant Colonel John Meyer

Lieutenant Colonel "Joe Bob" Phillips

Lieutenant Colonel Jim Pritchett

Lieutenant Colonel Bert Pryor

Wing Commander Mick Richardson

Commander "Fast" Eddie Smith

Lieutenant Colonel John Turk

Lieutenant Colonel Bill Welch

Major Faris Al Mazroui

Major Gary Alexander

Major Charley Allan

Major Abdulhameed Alqadhi

Major Kevin "Jeep" Dunleavy

Major Bob Eskridge

Major Harry Heintzelman

Major Scott Hente

Major Dave Karns

Major John Kinser

Major Ernie Norsworthy

Major Mike Oelrich

Major Jefferey L. "Oly" Olsen

Major Mark "Buck" Rogers

Major Michael P. "Chip" Setnor

Major John Sweeney

Major Al Vogel

Major Dave Waterstreet

Major Russ Wellbrock

Major Cliff Williford

Captain Turki bin Bandar bin Abdulaziz

Captain Bill "Burners" Bruner

Captain Chris "Hoser" Connelly

Captain Mike "Cos" Cosby

Captain John Glock

Captain Jim Hawkins

Captain Eric Holdaway

Captain Kirby Lindsey

Captain Randy O'Boyle

Captain Rolf "Bugsy" Siegel

Flight Leftenant Callum Steele

SSgt Heidi Pacheco

Sgt Mike "Preach" Prichard

"For those who have fought for it—FREEDOM has a taste the protected will never know."

(Vietnam Fighter Pilot maxim)

PREFACE

"The future belongs to those who prepare for it."
—*Emerson*

I entered the Air Force as a second lieutenant from North Carolina State University in 1965. I retired 29 years later as a three-star general. By the time that happened, I'd been fortunate enough to serve as the senior Air Force general responsible for the Air Force's interface with Congress, and to be the Deputy Chief of Staff for operations, plans and requirements.

How it all ended is a story I'll spare you, except for this comment: It was my personal decision to retire in 1994. As I always said at retirement ceremonies, you enter the Air Force with only one thing: your family. If you are blessed by God, you leave the Air Force with that same family.

As for how it began, I'm going to skip over all that, too. I won't tell you the story of my formative years in Piedmont North Carolina; my high school and college exploits; the experiences—and the scar tissue—I acquired as a fighter pilot in Vietnam. I'll skip over my cherished memories of commanding the Air Force's premier squadron, the 414th Fighter Weapons Squadron at Nellis Air Force Base in Nevada, then the 347th Tactical Fighter Wing at Moody Air Force Base in Georgia, and the 1st Tactical Fighter Wing at Langley Air Force Base in Virginia. These opportunities and the firm hand and loving foundation provided by my parents are a story for another day.

The real story I want to tell you now covers just seven months, from August 1990 to March 1991. I was a brigadier general and I was given the opportunity in Desert Storm to plan, execute, and command all Air Force fighter wings in an offensive air campaign like no other before it. It was a war that demonstrated how air power had become the dominant element in our military operations and it was a war that set us on a winding path toward September 11 and beyond.

I am always mindful of the message on a plaque that hung beside the exit to my fighter squadron in Vietnam. It said war is an ugly thing, but not the ugliest of things; the decayed and degraded state of moral and patriotic feeling, which thinks that nothing is worth war, is much worse.

A man who has nothing for which he is willing to fight, or nothing he cares about more than his own personal safety, is a miserable creature who has no chance of being free, unless made and kept so by the exertions of better men than himself.

War sometimes is a necessity. But there are many ways to wage war. The only sane one is the one that accomplishes our national objectives with the minimum loss of life.

I abhor brute force frontal attack and I always have. I'm even one of those few people that are critical of certain early military tacticians, the ones everybody thinks are so bright. You can go all the way back to Hannibal and there's never been a military leader that didn't acknowledge in his writings or his discussions the importance of surprise and deception. Yet even though they would acknowledge it, they would only use surprise and deception to a degree, and then they would end up with a frontal attack and kill thousands of people. I always thought that was absolutely insane.

That doesn't mean that I don't believe that sometimes you're going to have significant loss of life, no matter how much you try to optimize your strength and take advantage of the enemy's weaknesses. In war, sometimes you're going to have those points of confrontation that basically boil down to nothing but force on force. You want to keep those to an absolute minimum.

I am aggressive and ruthless when I need to be. But I always fundamentally believed that when you say we're going to fight a certain way and lose this many people, you are copping out because you don't have the intellectual capacity to figure out a way to do it that won't lose those people.

This was my intuitive belief. War can be fought without brute force on force. You hit the "vital centers" and you destroy what needs to be destroyed, but you're smart about it. You conserve force—don't send everyone rushing in for a big maneuver war when you don't need to. Don't bomb every telephone exchange or piece of industry if you don't need to.

Air power has the flexibility to go beyond brute force. Of course it must be employed correctly. Air power, if not applied in a timely fashion, is still just brute force. The only thing that makes air power stand apart is that it can bring mass to a point in a timely fashion. Air power can adjust and move from one point to another point while other commanders are still contemplating change. That's what separates airmen from everybody else.

Billy Mitchell saw that first. If you take Mitchell's basic thesis, he saw that air power would grow to shape and dominate war itself.

It so infuriates me when I read critics who try to rip up his views. I don't really care where he got the views. If he got the views during World War I from Trenchard of Britain's Royal Air Force, well, that's okay. But one thing for certain, Mitchell knew how to take those views, articulate them, and he also knew how to apply them in time of war.

When Mitchell was in command of U.S. air operations in Europe in late World War I, he made the right decisions for the technology and the capabilities that he had. He made the right statements. He knew how to support Pershing's plans and how to get the most out of the forces under his command. He was smart enough to be able to see how air power was going to remold the way we fought.

Look at the war against Iraq in 1991. That was almost seventy-five years after Mitchell was in France. Yet it was an example of his philosophy and his vision being 100 percent accurate. It wasn't just about the rise of air power; it was a change in the way wars should be fought.

Operation Desert Storm was the watershed change. Mitchell had it right, only he did not have the technology to make it happen. I did.

WAR WITH IRAQ

THE PERSIAN GULF

I'd been in the Persian Gulf less than a month when Iraq invaded Kuwait on August 2, 1990.

Maybe it was the grace of God, but I ended up in the right place at the right time. Certainly the Air Force hadn't planned for me to be in the middle of the biggest military conflict since Vietnam. No, my assignment as Deputy Commander of the Joint Task Force Middle East was intended to subtly terminate my career.

A year earlier, in March 1989, I was a one-star general working in the Pentagon as the deputy to David Gribben III, the Director of Legislative Affairs for the Office of the Secretary of Defense. George H. W. Bush was our new President and after a fiasco with Senator John Tower, he had selected Dick Cheney, a Congressman from Wyoming, to be the new Secretary of Defense.

Cheney was tough and respected and he came to the Pentagon in no mood to take any nonsense from generals. That's when Air Force Chief of Staff Larry Welch wandered into his sights. Welch was pursuing a deal for procurement of the Midgetman and MX missiles. Before he made a recommendation to Cheney, Welch decided to meet with several key members of Congress such as Senator Al Gore, Jr. and the chairman of the House Armed Services Committee, Representative Les Aspin. Welch was "pulsing the system," or at least that's what he told the *Washington Post*.

Cheney saw it differently. In his very first press conference as Secretary of Defense, he came down hard on Welch for "free-lancing." "I think

1

it's inappropriate for a uniformed officer to be in a position where he's in fact negotiating an arrangement," said Cheney. "I'll make known to him my displeasure. Everybody's entitled to one mistake."[1]

The whole Air Force leadership was skating on thin ice for weeks afterwards. I was drawn into the mess by trying to help. One of Cheney's assistants commented to me that General Welch could do himself a favor if he sought a meeting with Cheney to explain what had happened and show contrition. That sounded like a good suggestion to me, so I passed the comment along to Welch, via another general I knew.

Somehow, Welch came to the conclusion I was disloyal. Although I'd worked for Welch in the past, as a colonel, that incident was it for me in Welch's eyes. I became "persona non grata."

"There are very few people in uniform that the Chief despises as much as you," General Bob Russ told me privately. I trusted his assessment. He was not only a personal friend but also the four-star head of Tactical Air Command.

Several months passed, and it was time for Welch to send me to a new assignment. One day, as I was walking toward Cheney's office, there was Welch coming down the dark green marble stairs from the fourth floor. He approached me in a friendly way.

"I've been meaning to chat with you about your assignment," he said. "The Generals' group wanted me to let you go and be the commander of intelligence down at Keesler (Air Force Base in Texas)." I knew that the all-powerful General Officer Matters Office typically brought the Chief a choice of potential new jobs for generals. Welch paused. "I didn't want to do that. I wanted to send you to something where you were going to have the opportunity afterwards to go do something else and continue on with your career. I thought that Keesler was a dead end for you."

Something did not track. Pass up command? Keesler was the center of the Air Force's most sophisticated intelligence analysis—their work was so secret most did not even know what they did. There is no question, Keesler would not be the first assignment choice of any flag-officer fighter pilot with a brain. However, the old adage of being number one is always better than being number two was still applicable.

Instead, Welch was sending me to be the Deputy Commander of the

1. George C. Wilson, "Air Force Acts to Break ICBM Impasse, New Options offered on MX, Midgetman," *Washington Post,* March 24, 1989 and George C. Wilson, "Cheney Scolds Air Force Chief For Hill Contacts on Missiles," *Washington Post,* March 25, 1989.

Joint Task Force, Middle East. As I listened to him, I was sure he was basically intending to terminate my career with this assignment. But he didn't have the guts to tell me that to my face.

I again talked to Russ. "We better not try to outmaneuver Welch," Russ said. "You should go to the Gulf and let me worry about your next job." Russ was a man of integrity and loyalty. I figured if he was unable to affect my next assignment, then after my stint in the Gulf, it would be time to retire and do something else.

Then two things happened. Welch himself retired, and General Michael Dugan replaced him as Chief of Staff in June 1990.

Next, the doctors handed me a perfect excuse to get out of the Joint Task Force assignment. A few months before, I'd had back surgery for a ruptured disk. The neurosurgeon who operated wanted to disapprove the assignment for medical reasons. He said I risked further problems climbing up and down the ladders aboard the command ship USS *LaSalle*, where I would be working.

"Is it going to permanently damage anything?" I asked.

"You're going to have to be very careful," he replied.

If Dugan was not willing to change the assignment—and he wasn't, even after it was brought to his attention—then I was not going to opt out for medical reasons although it would have been easy to do. So I was off to Bahrain.

Meeting General Schwarzkopf

The Joint Task Force, Middle East, was established in the late 1970s, when people were concerned about growing Soviet influence in the region.

It now was under the command of General Norman Schwarzkopf, Commander in Chief (CINC), United States Central Command or CENTCOM. Central Command spanned the globe from the eastern United States all the way to the Middle East and part of Africa. The Navy was busy in the region escorting oil tankers, but it was not a theater for a major war. Schwarzkopf's headquarters were not even in the region but in Tampa, Florida, at MacDill Air Force Base.

The first thing I wanted to do was meet my new boss. If my first personal principle of war was to abhor brute force, my second and equally important principle was that personalities and command relationships meant everything.

I learned this young. When I was a first lieutenant, with just three years in the Air Force, they sent me to Squadron Officer School (SOS) at Maxwell Air Force Base. It was an experiment. They normally sent captains, but they were all in Vietnam that year, so they tried out a group of lieutenants. At SOS, I read and studied different air conflicts. It was the first time I'd read General Billy Mitchell's work in depth.

Reading air power history convinced me that personalities and relationships were far more important in war than historians ever made out. All you have to do is look at the classic case of Douglas MacArthur and George Kenney in the Philippines. Kenney was MacArthur's air commander in the southwest Pacific and they had a great relationship. Together they used air power to hold off the Japanese in New Guinea and then to take Japanese-held islands one right after another. MacArthur trusted Kenney. They understood each other, and because of that relationship Kenney got the most out of air power and made a big success of his command. In Korea, it was altogether different. MacArthur and his air deputy did not get along in the same way. MacArthur's problems in Korea are well documented.

Those senior commander relationships are critical. Pershing and Mitchell, Eisenhower and Tedder, Bradley and Quesada—there's a long list, but you don't have to go any further than that.

When I was assigned to the Task Force, right off the bat I said there's only one person here that's really important to me in the leadership chain of command and that's Schwarzkopf. You must have the backing and trust of the person who is the decision-maker or else your views will never see the light of day.

So at my first opportunity, I was off to MacDill.

Schwarzkopf had taken over Central Command in the summer of 1988. The word in the Pentagon was that Schwarzkopf was on his final assignment and set for retirement. Supposedly he had a hot temper and no one got along with him.

My first impression was completely different. Schwarzkopf was at ease with himself. He was very sincere, very bright, and very tough. He was smart in his understanding of the Middle East. He was focused, but also caring, especially for the people that worked for him. He knew his strengths and weaknesses. Once he heard all the options and made a decision, he didn't want his staff to revisit the issues. He just wanted the decision executed. We were alike in that way. From the first meeting, I saw there was a certain toughness to him, and I found it attractive and refreshing. His personality would not be a problem for me, I believed.

When Schwarzkopf and I talked in late June 1990 neither of us had any idea of what was about to happen. We discussed the overall mission of the Joint Task Force and the politics of the area. Soon my courtesy call was over.

"Buster, I'll see you from time to time in the region," Schwarzkopf said. "Make sure you go visit my friend Sheikh Mohammed Bin Zayed down in the UAE (United Arab Emirates) occasionally. He's a very good man. You need to get to know him. I'm sure there'll be enough happening that will at least make it interesting and challenging."

No one expected there to be much action in the Gulf. I remember Schwarzkopf saying as I left: "There's always a chance Saddam Hussein will do something stupid." It was just a throwaway line, I thought to myself, a passing comment.

Little did we know.

The USS *LaSalle*

I arrived in Bahrain on July 21, 1990. It was a short drive from the airport to the pier.

The Task Force commander was Rear Admiral William Fogarty. When not embarked on the USS *LaSalle* he had his headquarters in Bahrain, where the Navy had been ensconced since the 1950s. In the Navy facility in Bahrain you could drink alcohol, shop in the Post Exchange, and participate in the social swirl of a Navy base if that's what you wanted to do. The mission of the USS *LaSalle* was to serve as the floating command post for a Central Command operation. However, she spent much of her time tied up at the pier. When at sea, the USS *LaSalle* had been in the thick of the tanker war of the late 1980s. The USS *LaSalle* had state-of-the-art communications for the Task Force, since that was her mission, but the ship herself was not near the top of the priority list for the Navy. Her captain, John B. Nathman, a naval aviator learning to drive a ship, said the USS *LaSalle* was scheduled for a long spell in dry-dock.

Living and working aboard ship was a new experience for me. As a general officer, my quarters were comparatively spacious. But what I found on the USS *LaSalle* just underscored one pronounced difference between the Navy and the Air Force. In the Navy, a flag officer's office and living quarters are one and the same. To an Air Force senior officer, that

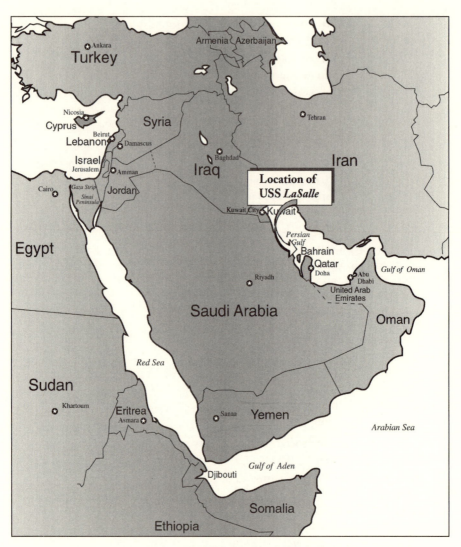

FIGURE 1

takes adjustment. Air Force officers either leave the house or leave the tent or leave the trailer, and work on the flightline or at the headquarters. For me, the ship seemed like a cocoon. I felt so isolated and confined that the only thing I could do to stay abreast of everything was to read constantly.

As it turned out, I spent one night on the USS *LaSalle* and the next morning, Schwarzkopf called me from Tampa. "I want you to go down to the UAE," he said. "Saddam Hussein's threatening the Emirates. Go down and comfort our friend Sheikh Mohammed and take a look at the operation. We're going to send some tankers over there and do some refueling under the guise of training."

Saddam was threatening to attack the Das Island oil wells. I didn't know whether to take it seriously or not. With somebody as radical and unpredictable as Saddam, you never knew what he might talk himself into doing. He'd already done plenty over the years: brutalizing and killing his own people on a daily basis, gassing Iranians and Kurds, almost sinking the USS *Stark*, threatening to incinerate Israel.

The most troubling part was that we didn't have anything in the region to help the UAE defend against the Iraqis. The UAE was on its own if Saddam attacked their oil facilities. In response, Operation Ivory Justice deployed Air Force tankers to the UAE. They wanted to get more of their fighter pilots checked out in air refueling, so they could patrol for longer periods of time. That was the real purpose of Ivory Justice.

I hadn't given the war plans for the region more than a cursory glance. My intention was to settle in aboard the USS *LaSalle* and go through the contingency options in a systematic way, but now there was no chance to do that.

I did as Schwarzkopf instructed and spent time acquainting Sheikh Mohammed with the military exercise. He listened to the communications link between the tanker crews and his fighter pilots to stay abreast of the training. Schwarzkopf had been astute about Sheikh Mohammed; he was very bright, and we needed his counsel in what was to come.

At the time, I wondered why the UAE immediately took Saddam's July posturing much more seriously than did the Kuwaitis. While Kuwait attempted to move matters to an "Arab dialogue" mode and only asked for U.S. forces as the Iraqis were on the ground in Kuwait city, the UAE Chief of Staff persuaded his country's leadership to immediately request a well-publicized "exercise" involving USAF tanker aircraft. It was only after the war that the picture became clear.

It seems the Iraqis had placed a general officer "liaison" in their embassy in Abu Dhabi (which was located right behind the official residence of our own military representative.) At some point in his tour, this officer warned his UAE counterparts (who had undoubtedly "worked" him to their side) that Saddam would eventually turn on his Arab brethren in the Gulf, whose financial support during and after his struggle with Iran had not added up to the Iraqi dictator's expectations. Shortly afterwards, the Iraqi embassy notified the UAE that the officer had died of "natural causes" in the Embassy, and the Iraqis would be sending the body home without any local formalities.

This event, coupled with Saddam's aggressive performance at the May 1990 Summit, persuaded the UAE that Iraq was a serious threat.

Additionally, the UAE sent several strong messages to Kuwait during the pre-invasion crisis—including dispatching the Deputy Air Force Commander—warning them to take Saddam's threats seriously, obviously to no avail.

On August 2, I was still in the UAE working Ivory Justice. Suddenly I got word that a C-12 airplane would be down to pick me up within two hours. I asked what was going on. I was only told: "Be at the airport. That's all you need to know." As I boarded the plane, I asked one of the pilots what it was all about. "Iraqi forces are going into Kuwait," he said.

Iraq Invades

Saddam's attempt to make Kuwait the nineteenth province of Iraq took us all by surprise. In July, after my visit, CENTCOM staff ran a war game against Iraq. Schwarzkopf had actually briefed the Joint Chiefs of Staff on contingency plans just hours before Iraq invaded Kuwait on August 2.[2] When word of the invasion came, Schwarzkopf hurried back to Washington to brief President Bush and the National Security Council. He told them the U.S. could do nothing to stop Iraq but "we could make certain moves with our air and sea power to demonstrate U.S. determination and, if necessary, punish Iraq."[3]

An oil embargo was one of those moves. When I returned to the USS *LaSalle*, I was totally focused on the oil embargo and maritime interceptions.

2. General Norman Schwarzkopf, *It Doesn't Take a Hero* (New York: Bantam, 1992), p. 295

3. Ibid., p. 298.

Schwarzkopf, on the other hand, had bigger fish to fry. On Saturday, August 4, he and CENTCOM's air component commander, Lieutenant General Charles Horner, helicoptered to Camp David to brief the President and a small team of cabinet officers and discuss options. Schwarzkopf again told Bush and his counselors that "air power was the option most immediately available."[4] But even that would take time. CENTCOM had already turned the aircraft carrier USS *Independence* back toward the Gulf. Air Force fighters and their tankers were on alert to deploy. Small units from the 82nd Airborne Division from Fort Bragg in North Carolina could arrive soon, but Schwarzkopf would have no real attack options for several weeks. Two weeks would give him a few hundred aircraft and rapid-reaction Marines, Special Forces, and Army ground units. What the CINC really wanted was "tank-killing" equipment, from Apaches to A-10s to U.S. tanks. To defend Saudi Arabia, he estimated he would need "three months to mass enough combat power to be absolutely assured of beating back an Iraqi attack." If the President wanted to kick the Iraqis out of Kuwait—which no one had discussed yet—Schwarzkopf told him it would take eight to ten months to build up the forces.[5]

After Camp David, the next step for Schwarzkopf was a trip to Riyadh, Saudi Arabia, with Defense Secretary Cheney to see King Fahd. When the king agreed to host U.S. forces, Schwarzkopf ordered Horner to stay in Riyadh, get the tactical fighter squadrons moving, and be the CENTCOM Forward Commander in charge of the joint force deployments and the defense of Saudi Arabia. Schwarzkopf handled Washington and made preparations to transfer his headquarters to the theater.

Horner and I had talked on the telephone a few times about bringing F-15s in to help with air cover for the Navy's oil embargo operations. On August 17, I flew up to see him in Riyadh.

Horner and I had known each other for a long time. He was a good commander to work for. He was the wing commander at Nellis Air Force Base while I was commander of the 414th Squadron there. He'd been on the staff at Tactical Air Command at Langley Air Force Base while I was working programs and resources in the Pentagon. We'd socialized together, spent time in each other's homes. For me, it was not like walking

4. Ibid., p. 300.
5. Ibid., p. 301.

in to meet a commander I didn't know. Horner and I had a more comfortable relationship.

Now, he had an enormous challenge on his hands. He was under a lot of pressure dealing with the Arab nations as the forward U.S. commander, trying to bring in forces. Additionally, as the Joint Force Air Component Commander he was responsible for planning how to use our big air power advantage to the fullest.

"I'm available to help," I told him.

"I need to check with Schwarzkopf. I certainly could use your help," he said.

My mind was racing. I dearly wanted to be involved. On my way back to the ship, I started a little diary in a spiral notebook. *'Horner upset about planning activities in Washington, no more Vietnams, war will be planned and fought in theater. I totally understand this issue,'* I wrote. That was Horner's perspective and I agreed with him one hundred percent. Then, mulling it over, I added: *'Need to give some thought to offensive air effort: retaliatory prelude to ground action.'* Horner seemed to be focused on defensive air, in line with Schwarzkopf's top immediate priority of defending Saudi Arabia. I could not resist thinking about it more. The U.S. might take a stand and fight to free Kuwait.

'If Horner's correct and I get the opportunity my priorities will be massive offensive air, across the entire spectrum of the country.' I also wrote three key words to remind myself: Vietnam—Mitchell—Israel.

If I got the chance, I would apply air power my way!

Staring at the sheets of paper, I started to think about my convictions. Which of these three was most important to me? By a wide margin, it was Billy Mitchell's theories and Mitchell's approach, using air power at its maximum.

Mitchell's theory as I saw it was this: Use air power before you even consider resorting to any other use of military force. Through air power, you can take action with the highest potential for the least loss of life. And although I beat home the loss of life and saving lives a lot more than Mitchell ever did, it certainly was inherent in what he wanted to accomplish; I believe he deplored brute force, the useless loss of life, as much as I did.

Also, I did not want to make the mistakes I'd lived through in Vietnam. For the most part, fighter pilots were treated as long-range artillery assigned to service targets. "Never ever again," I vowed. I made this promise to myself more than once.

As for Israel, the success in the Beka'a Valley in 1982 after the disaster of the Yom Kippur War in 1973 was a classic case study for airmen. During the Yom Kippur War, the Israelis fought it like the last war while in the Beka'a Valley they thought of the future and used tactics and technology that surprised the enemy.

Beyond these three thoughts was one other vivid imprint. Wars are fought with technology and wars are won with people!

It was late and my mind was spinning down. I stopped for the night.

First Sketch

The next morning, August 18, I awoke with a campaign plan starting to take shape in my mind. Horner and I had talked in very general terms about a potential air campaign.

For now, I was alone with my thoughts. I pulled out a long piece of yellow stenograph notebook paper to continue where I'd left off the night before. These and the notes made on my trip back from Riyadh were the first entries in what became my wartime diary, and, twelve years later, the source for this book. Never before had I kept notes or a diary. I didn't want to risk it being misinterpreted. Once you retire you can be more candid.

The first thing on the paper—and in my mind—was the political objective. No ifs, ands or buts about it, the President would dictate his objectives, we would follow them. It was naïve to think this wouldn't have a political as well as a military dimension. *'I've got to stay on top of that,'* I jotted down, *'because if I don't, then I may make a mistake in either the pace or the degree with which I go about trying to develop a military plan that's consistent with the political objectives.'* Horner had shared the guidance from his Camp David meeting with the President. It boiled down to a few clear points.

- Our national interest is at stake
- Iraq must leave Kuwait
- Iraq must be contained
- We will use whatever force is necessary

Those were the President's views.

Then I thought about Iraq. Iraq's strengths were:

- Leadership—which could easily be a plus or a minus.
- Chemical and biological weapons, which we were sure they had, plus an advanced nuclear research program that we knew little about.

• The Republican Guard, a loyal, well-equipped and battle-tested force.
• The "Arab mentality"—their patience.
• Surface-to-surface missiles like the Scuds.
• The Arab brotherhood, a fraternity among the Gulf region states that made them loath to fight each other.

Iraq also had glaring weaknesses. Again, leadership headed the list. Also worth noting was their lack of flexibility in military tactics and training. Their forward-deployed forces were exposed in the desert terrain.

I had a fundamental belief that if Saddam and his family left tomorrow, the whole country would instantly turn around. The Iraqi people were just in a bad situation. If Saddam was the number-one center of gravity, I thought the second one was the military, specifically, the Iraqi Air Force fighters, the Scud missiles, and the elite Republican Guard. Iraq had a large army but its core was the Republican Guard Forces Command: about six divisions, half motorized infantry, half armored. They'd determine how successful Saddam could attack from the ground. Later, I changed that listing, and put Iraq's nuclear, biological and chemical (NBC) capability as the number two center of gravity—the thing that made Saddam who he was, and made Iraq who they were. Infrastructure was next, but it was a throwaway. At that point, early on, "you don't know what you don't know" about the infrastructure. Some of it can be very critical and some of it is "so what?" However, my belief was we should go after the support base or underpinnings for the real centers of gravity, such as leadership, NBC, Republican Guard, etc. Of course, a single infrastructure target may become important suddenly, in psychological operations, for example. But overall, the idea of attacking infrastructure is not to attack it for its own sake but to get at the underpinnings and make a key force element impotent.

The next factors in my embryonic campaign outline were CENTCOM, CENTAF (the Air Force component of CENTCOM), Washington, the intelligence agencies, and the Coalition. I needed to try to "lead turn" their ideas and suggestions and set up a process where they could be blended into my planning without disruption.

My first operational instinct was, 'this will be a night operation.' Our ability to fight at night completely outweighed Iraq's and gave us the widest margin of our strength over Saddam's weakness.

On balance, the U.S. had far greater strengths, starting with our leadership, at every level from the President to any flight lead in any squadron. We had technology on our side—from the F-117 stealth fighter and its precision guided munitions to other aircraft and satellites. We believed in flexibility. We placed value on the importance of individual life. Alexis de Tocqueville was correct, I jotted down. *'America is great because America is good. America will no longer be great when it is no longer good.'*

In the past, when confronted with a challenge and mounting obstacles, Saddam had always resorted to bold and unpredictable action. *'Let's make sure his success doesn't continue,'* I resolved. Yet I also wondered: *'What will be his next move?'*

All the above was just speculation for now. I was still on the USS *LaSalle.*

Three days later, on August 20, Horner called. "Get your ass up here now," he said. "Tell Fogarty you won't be back."

To Riyadh

I flew to Riyadh early the next day without even packing my things. Just over two weeks had passed since Iraq's invasion and CENTCOM was a hurricane of activity. Schwarzkopf needed two things: a way to defend Saudi Arabia and the ability to strike back at Iraq if Saddam made a crazy move. We all remembered the Tehran hostage crisis. What if Saddam ordered his forces in Kuwait to seize the U.S. Embassy and start killing Americans? What if the Iraqis launched a chemical weapons attack as they had done during the Iran-Iraq war? If the U.S. wanted to retaliate, Schwarzkopf later said of this time, "CENTCOM had little to offer short of a nuclear strike on Baghdad."[6]

The fortunes of war! I couldn't help but think that last week, I was a visitor stopping by to see Horner as a professional acquaintance, not knowing where our discussion would lead. *'But now, for better or worse, I am being handed the largest challenge of my military career. Yes, I am excited, and I am confident, but the enormity of the task at hand ensures humility is ever present especially during private moments,'* I wrote in my diary.

My old friend Brigadier General Larry Henry met me at the airport in Riyadh when I landed a little before six in the evening. Henry was a tall, lean Tennesseean who'd been sent over to Saudi from his job at Tac-

6. *It Doesn't Take a Hero,* p. 313

tical Air Command (TAC) because he was an expert in electronic war-fare. Henry was the warrior personified. The closer he got to hand-to-hand combat the better he liked it. "It should always be up close and per-sonal. That way you never forget how bad war really is," he often said.

As we drove to the Royal Saudi Air Force headquarters, Henry updat-ed me on the lay of the land at CENTAF from the fertile soil to the "pot-holes and sink holes," as he put it. In the sink hole category was an Air Staff briefing presented by Colonel John Warden, which Horner and Henry had seen the day before. Henry told me how Horner had picked apart many of the key assumptions just on practical grounds and sent Warden home.

Henry and I called on Air Force Major General Tom Olsen, Horner's deputy. Horner then invited us to join him for dinner. He had his hands full running the deployment and getting his small CENTAF staff to pull together a plan for immediate defensive action if Iraq moved on toward Saudi Arabia. Amazingly, Horner was not showing the wear and tear like everyone else. He was focused, but outwardly he looked confident and relaxed.

The Washington briefing came up again over dinner, causing a tense moment, as did our discussion of the fact that we were all basically sitting ducks vulnerable to any Iraqi move.

After dinner, Horner and I went back to his office at the Royal Saudi Air Force headquarters for a private meeting. The first thing on his mind was that the Air Staff back in Washington was trying to dictate to him how he was going to run the campaign. He ranted and raved about it.

He had his reasons. With Horner in Riyadh, Schwarzkopf had reached out to the Air Staff to put together some planning options. Warden's brief-ing the day before was the result. Schwarzkopf and Powell had seen the briefing and reacted well—it was all they had by way of attack options—but Horner realized it was barely a start on a full-fledged offensive cam-paign.

As the forward commander, Horner's first responsibility was to be ready to act if Iraq attacked or did something stupid, like use chemical weapons in Kuwait or harm U.S. Embassy personnel. Horner realized very well the significance of future campaign planning. The last thing he wanted was for someone else to come up with a plan, then issue it to him. But he couldn't give full time to acting as CENTCOM Forward Com-mander and mastermind the planning. He wanted to get rid of one of these two tasks immediately. If he could take the planning off his radar screen, so to speak, he could focus on trying to make sure that the bed-down of forces went right and that we had some sort of defensive capability in position to deal with any unexpected actions by Iraq.

So that's why Horner called me to Riyadh. Horner later said, "I was in a fog about who to pick. Then, just like in cartoons when the light bulb comes on over somebody's head, it hit me. Buster Glosson!"[7] He knew that I would take control and keep others at arm's length.

As we talked, Horner's directions to me were specific. Get the Warden briefing. Get the defensive plan from Colonel Jim Crigger, Horner's deputy for operations. Then send the Warden crowd home.

"After we get the CINC's okay on a two- or three-day Air Tasking Order (ATO), you can work on an offensive plan if we get the opportunity to decide when the shooting starts," Horner said. Schwarzkopf was due to arrive in days so Horner wanted to see my first cut of the initial ATO fast. He gestured to the door adjoining his office and said, "You can use the conference room."

Now it was my turn. I respected Horner as a combat leader—bright, tough, with good instincts. He did not have all the answers on air power and most important, did not pretend to. We had different views on air power, but I thought they would be compatible. Still, I wanted to get some of the issues out on the table right away

I took out my yellow notebook sheet just to remind me of the points I wanted to cover with him. I wanted to make sure he and I were more or less in agreement on the centers of gravity. I also wanted to make sure that he understood where I came down on the forces needed. I was sure we would have a few differences of opinion. Horner was not high on the F-117. He was a little bit more of the old school than I was on the importance of stealth. I think he did not believe that stealth would be as effective as it was, so he wanted to take a more conventional approach. But for the most part, we were thinking along similar lines. Horner was satisfied to leave the planning to me.

"This is your problem, go solve it," Horner said to me. "I don't have time to focus on this. Now, get out of here. I'll see you Sunday, if not before." In a totally different tone, he added, "I'm glad you are here."

Looking back, I've often thought that probably no other person in

7. Tom Clancy and General Chuck Horner, *Every Man A Tiger* (New York: G.P. Putnam's Sons, 1999), pp. 265–66.

uniform would have given me the freedom that he did. I don't think there's a parallel for that anywhere in the history of the United States Air Force. Horner was the Joint Forces Air Component Commander (JFACC)—it was his command—but he let me have unprecedented freedom to plan, and ultimately to command the fighters, and still keep the planning hat. It was unique. He had total confidence that I would do the right thing and, more impressive, the confidence in himself to delegate.

That night, he had one caveat: "Make damn sure everything is done here. Everybody works for you and you can get rid of all those guys that came over with Warden. Put them all on an airplane tomorrow and get them out of here. I have already sent Warden's ass back to the Pentagon."

Instant Thunder

The next morning, I awoke with a thought: Build a briefing for Schwarzkopf that shows the CINC how we will use air power. "A picture is worth a thousand words," I told Horner.

"When will it be ready?" Horner wanted to know.

"Three weeks."

"You have one," he said.

That afternoon, I arranged to see the Washington briefing.

As for Horner's dismissal of the briefing, I thought he was over-reacting to his resentment of Washington interference and the way he'd been treated by Warden. Warden was a very bright academician, but every time the Air Force gave him an opportunity to command, he failed. Horner had no respect for Warden because of his inability to command. I always viewed Warden as a super staff officer but not a commander. I've always believed that if you are going to send people into combat, you need to have done two things. First, you need to have been in harm's way yourself, and, second, you need to have shown you can succeed in command. If someone doesn't meet those criteria, I'm only interested in what they have to say as it relates to ideas for me to consider.

Warden was a case in point. I'd known him in Europe, before Desert Storm, when I was Director of Plans and Programs for the U.S. Air Forces in Europe, my first job as a one-star. Warden had been moved out of a plum assignment as commander of an F-15 wing due to the unit's low morale, and the stigma never left him as far as the operational community was concerned. However, some in the Air Force leadership tried to sweep his failures of command under the rug. But that stigma had a life of its own.

After hearing the reactions from Henry and Horner, my first task was simply to keep an open mind about the Instant Thunder briefing. John Warden was intellectually honest—by which I mean, in his briefings, he laid out all his assumptions very clearly. (I could never shake my conviction that he ripped off Billy Mitchell, who is not credited in Warden's book). As I prepared to see the briefing, I did not want to be so influenced by Horner's negative view that I would not take advantage of what ideas might be there. Also, I was on a recruiting mission. Quite candidly, I was looking at the four who'd come over with Warden as potential people that would stay and work for me.

The briefer was a Lieutenant Colonel Dave Deptula, whom I'd never met before. He was tall, with dark brown hair, an intelligent mind, and strong convictions. He wore a Fighter Weapons School patch, a good sign. Three others were with him. The only one of the Washington group I knew slightly was Steve Wilson.

As I listened to Deptula give the briefing, I thought, *here's a pretty good think piece.* They had excellent intelligence on the targets selected; it was better than what we had in theater. The briefing had only 84 targets but that was 84 more than we had planning folders and photographs for at the time.

As for the estimate of finishing the campaign in six to nine days, they were smoking dope on that one. I needed an air campaign plan for a full 15 rounds, not two or three ending up with just giving Saddam a bloody nose.

My understanding of the target base for the Republican Guard and NBC alone was that even if every bomb was 100 percent successful, there was no way to finish in six-to-nine days. Not even if you left the leadership targets out. I mean, it was a very good way to go bash the Iraqis in the head for a week and see if they might decide to withdraw or sue for peace—if that was the objective. But to destroy their military capability, that time estimate was insane. The plan only included 84 targets. *'You've got to be shitting me,'* I wrote in my notes. It was just neophyte thinking. In a word, dumb. This plan, called Instant Thunder, was a good academic effort but I needed a much more diverse option. Horner had been right. There were some good ideas in the briefing, but too many naïve ones. And we could not waste air power on naïve ideas.

It was a long day. *'Once again, John and I show our true colors,'* I wrote that night. *'He loves war and I abhor it.'* My notes continued: *'need God's help—courage and vision.'* I knew what I had to do and I wrote it down: *'I will develop the air campaign as I think correct; if the CINC and Horner do not agree they can get someone else. I will not be part of needless loss of life!'*

Instant Thunder turned out to have two very distinct uses for me. First, it brought me some talented people, which I desperately needed.

"Believe me, the talent pool on the CENTAF staff is very limited," Henry told me. "You're going to have to break some of those bright people in," he added, referring to the briefers from Washington.

After two days in Riyadh it was apparent to me what a tough spot Horner was in—and now I was in it with him. *'Everyone fighting each other; no wonder Horner is fit to be tied,'* I wrote. Horner knew what he wanted, but he was getting little help. Crigger in operations was strong; as was Colonel Bill Rider, in charge of logistics; and Major Harry Heintzelman, the lawyer. But aside from these and a few other bright spots, I assessed the staff overall as mediocre at best. Not only did Horner have a talent shortage at CENTAF, he had ringers from Washington. Instant Thunder was just the straw that broke the camel's back. I wrote: *'While the Warden effort has merit, the people involved don't have any concern about Horner's position or desires . . . they are all marching to their own drummer or have their own little agendas.'*

I decided to ignore the infighting and accept all the help initially until I could build my team. Deptula showed the most potential of the group. *'Bright, aggressive—needs directional control,'* said the first note in my diary about him.

Second, the Instant Thunder groundwork, as I was about to find out, would help fill Schwarzkopf's most immediate need.

Conversation with Schwarzkopf

I learned this in what was for me maybe the most important single conversation of the entire war. On August 22, I headed back to Bahrain to collect my things and then return to Riyadh for good. That night, my last on the USS *LaSalle*, Schwarzkopf called the ship. Admiral Fogarty was not aboard so I took the call. To this day I am not sure whether Schwarzkopf was trying to reach Fogarty or me.

The first thing out of his mouth was about the embargo, and the maritime rules of engagement. "Don't go hunting trouble or trying to get him to do something stupid. Everyone must stay calm," Schwarzkopf commanded. He did not want U.S. ships firing on the Iraqis and setting off a war right at that moment. I assured him Fogarty and I were making sure everyone understood that.

Schwarzkopf launched into a fresh tirade. "The Pentagon's going to try to run this. That's not going to happen. I'm not going to relive Vietnam." I listened in silence. This was no time for me to interject that I'd just seen a briefing from Washington, no matter if Schwarzkopf had been the one who sent it over!

"You know Horner wants you to come up and help him," Schwarzkopf said in a calmer tone. Then he told me: "Don't forget you're still working for me." He continued, "I know that you can do this," he said, "but you make sure you understand that you still work for me." I felt he said that because he wanted to make sure that I would come talk to him and get guidance from him, especially if I thought things were heading in the wrong direction.

I was very appreciative of what Schwarzkopf was saying. He gave me a direct line to him whenever I might need it. In the months to come, it served both of us extremely well.

There was more. The conversation became very emotional. "I have no other alternatives," he said. "I have got to have something I can tell the President we can do. What if they start executing people in Kuwait City in the embassy tomorrow? What can I do about it? I need something to give the President if Saddam acts crazy."

As we talked I felt the emotion in his voice. I felt empathy for where he was and the pressure he was under.

Schwarzkopf told me he was briefing Colin Powell, the Chairman of the Joint Chiefs, and Secretary Cheney that week on a four-phase theater campaign plan. "I'll need your help with the theater plan when I get there." He reiterated that he did not want the Air Staff involved. "Use what they've done to help us get started," he said. *Horner will like that*, I thought to myself. "You go ahead and help Horner," Schwarzkopf said again, but "remember you work for me."

When I got Schwarzkopf's guidance that night the course open to me was very straightforward. Instant Thunder would be cleaned up and serve as our "El Dorado Canyon" retaliatory plan, in case Saddam started executing hostages.[8] Then, with the team in place, we'd get to work on a full air campaign.

8. El Dorado Canyon was the code name for the 1986 strike on Libya in retaliation for Moammar Ghaddafi's involvement in terrorism.

CAMPAIGN TO DEFEAT IRAQ

I need to write a book after retirement, I mused to myself on the return flight to Riyadh. *I'll title it:* Navy Mind. *They think and plan as they move, at 15 knots. Another learning experience I will always remember!*

Ahead lay more serious issues. CENTAF had no focus—and wouldn't until Horner could relinquish the CINC's hat. Long before then, I had to remove the Warden stigma and get the planning shifted into gear. *Air Staff effort is in many respects a sophisticated El Dorado Canyon . . . just as the CINC perceives but almost opposite to what Air Staff is trying to project!!*

After that, I needed to construct a campaign to defeat Iraq.

This was not World War II. We would not spend years winning air supremacy, then roll up the enemy along a broad front.

The President's goals gave us a set of objectives fundamentally different from what we'd seen in earlier twentieth-century conflicts. Our mandate was to free Kuwait, make sure Iraq didn't have a military that could threaten the region, and pick apart the worst of Saddam's arsenal of missiles, chemical and biological weapons, and nuclear research programs. Defeating Iraq did not mean occupying Baghdad. It meant working through the above list.

The way I wanted to defeat Iraq was to craft our joint air power to do as much of the job as possible so Schwarzkopf would not have to throw Coalition soldiers and Marines across the line unless he absolutely had to—and if they did go in, I wanted it to end up looking like a police action, not like Patton vs. Rommel.

The first place this new idea had to take hold was among the airmen. With the new technology in hand, we did not have to wait to hit the top priority targets. This wouldn't be one bit like Vietnam. We could strike any target from day one and work against the Iraqi army and Iraqi fixed targets in the order we chose.

I believed if we planned the right campaign, executed it well, and gave it time to work, we'd essentially defeat Iraq from the air. That did not mean follow-up ground action would not be required. It did mean any ground action would be quick, with minimum loss of life. But I had a long way to go to build the team and the plan to make this happen.

Finding bright, experienced people was the first challenge. The lack of a strong planning staff was our own fault in the Air Force—not that we wanted to admit it. The truth was we didn't send our best and brightest to the staffs of the numbered air forces in those days, even though these "numbered" air forces, like the Ninth, became the Air Force element of the combatant command in time of war. Many officers at CENTAF had already been passed over for promotion. Now here they were as the forward air component for what might be a major battle. I was a long way from having the right people with the right experiences and intellectual capacity to think outside the box.

This bothered me greatly. We could not be rigid. The standard, default mindset of the Air Force staff planner was to start at the edge of the enemy military mass and beat down defenses and eventually get where you have total control. Only then could you focus on what you were really going to take away from the nation-state that you were fighting against. It was believed that getting total control of the air would take a fair amount of time, so until you had that, you didn't do anything toward your real objective. It was the same mindset as the Eighth Air Force in World War II. I'm not criticizing them—that's the only choice they had. But I sure didn't have to go down that road, because technology had changed things in the intervening fifty years. I was not going to follow the same blueprint and mold they had been following in previous wars.

We'd go back to basics. Apply Billy Mitchell's vision via our technology, avoid Vietnam's mistakes, aim for the spirit of the Beka'a Valley breakthrough campaign and above all, keep Schwarzkopf's trust and confidence.

War is both political and military, I reminded myself. *Successful combat leaders keep both in sync.*

Almost every successful combat leader also has an indispensable individual by his side, his aide-de-camp or executive officer. Mine was Lieutenant Colonel Rodgers Greenawalt, who was working in the planning shop when I arrived. Greenawalt was an RF-4 pilot who'd flown many dangerous missions in Vietnam, going back to key routes over and over again to take reconnaissance photographs while being shot at. He was loyal, very conscientious, and an unmercifully hard worker. I asked him to be my Executive Officer. As my immediate assistant he was the officer closest to me at all times for the next eight months. He kept me organized, placated and fed, and found time to write us some rousing warrior poems along the way.

Retaliatory Plan

Most people believe that we started out with the idea of building a strategic plan. That's just absolutely wrong. It's a figment of their imagination.

Picture the situation: Schwarzkopf's only guidance for the first several weeks of Operation Desert Shield (as this part of the operation came to be called) was to shield the kingdom from further attacks. His instructions were to deter and defend. We hoped Saddam would not be so foolish as to cross the Saudi border, but it was a real possibility—an Iraqi defector brought over a plan in late August showing a three-pronged drive into Saudi Arabia.

CENTCOM had only a thin line of ground forces in theater. The bulk of the combat force was air power. The Air Force had squadrons arriving daily, and the Navy had its carriers in the Gulf. The only move CENTCOM could make would be to strike back against Iraq while trying to help the Saudis hold a defensive line.

We also thought that mischief by Saddam was even more likely than a potential invasion. That's why Schwarzkopf wanted a retaliatory air option above all else. As Horner put it in his assignment to me, it would be a concept of operations—an attack plan we could execute no later than September 13, 1990. Horner sweetened the deal by promising me an operational role before the shooting started, probably as his Deputy for Operations.

Back in Riyadh, Horner indicated that in the longer term Schwarzkopf was thinking of a four-phase plan for a campaign against Iraq. He was settled on the outline; he was ready to brief Secretary Cheney and Chairman Powell on August 25.

The plan matched what Schwarzkopf said to me, but the way he divided up the air phases troubled me at first. I didn't quite understand his logic.

"Why would we have more than three phases? I don't understand," I said to Horner.

"Well, the CINC perceives it as a four-phase plan," Horner replied. "Three phases of air, divided up as a strategic campaign, winning air supremacy, preparing the battlefield, and then a ground action."

To me, the first two phases, a strategic air campaign and air supremacy, were all one thing.

"As far as I'm concerned," I said, "we're going to do the strategic part and if that doesn't reach the objectives we want to reach, the next thing we're going to do is basically all the little things that you need to do that you may not have done for the ground forces to move forward. Last, but always most critical we support the ground forces. Now how could there be another phase here?"

"The CINC is hung up on this air supremacy issue," he explained again. "The one thing he fundamentally believes and knows from his own army experience is the U.S. Army is never going to get in trouble as long as nobody's overhead to attack them. They can hold their own with or without any kind of support, as long as they can't be attacked from the air."

The bottom line was that Schwarzkopf already had a clear view of a full-scale theater campaign, if that became his mission. But a theater campaign was still a long way off. President Bush had told the world "this will not stand" but the U.S. and its allies needed time to decide what to do. It would also take time to deploy ground forces and build a plan for them. Given the situation in Iraq, there was just no logic to starting a theater-wide air campaign before ground forces arrived. Several Republican Guard divisions were within striking distance of the Saudi border. If they suddenly got on the highway and started south, we could harass them, but we didn't have enough air assets to stop them all. Without ground forces, we'd end up with A-10s up there protecting our own airbase instead of conducting a strategic air campaign.

For the time being, the best we could do was to develop a good retaliatory option. The full theater campaign would have to wait.

Desert "Something"

The retaliatory plan had to make the most of the air assets in theater. Air was the only weapon we had for reaching Iraq itself and attacking what mattered most to Saddam.

That's why Instant Thunder was helpful—but for a different purpose. Its authors intended it to be a war-winning air campaign—which it wasn't. To me, it was a useful draft targeting list because it selected targets across Iraq. For building a retaliatory option, it was very useful indeed.

I actually liked the name Instant Thunder. It was meant to erase the legacy of Vietnam campaign Rolling Thunder, the on-and-off bombing of the North that applied air power so weakly and created so many POWs.

Horner couldn't stand the name. It blew all his circuit breakers. Instant Thunder sank beneath the waves. As for a new name, Horner made clear that the four-stars, Schwarzkopf and Powell, would be the ones picking the actual name.

"It'll be Desert something," Horner conjectured.

For now there was nothing to name anyway. On my second day in Riyadh I jotted down in my diary: *'Nobody's taking this seriously.'*

My immediate task was to put together a team and get them out of the defensive-planning mindset (in the case of CENTAF) or the win-it-all naiveté of Instant Thunder (in the case of the Washington crowd). That team soon gave itself the nickname the Black Hole—because like the stellar phenomenon, the gravity of the place was so powerful that not one word of what we were doing escaped and anyone that entered would never leave.

CENTAF could hardly be blamed for being on the defensive. All the air planning done in theater so far had been defensive planning, out of necessity. Horner himself arrived August 5, and immediately took up wide duties as CENTCOM forward. He turned over the air planning to Major General Tom Olsen, his deputy, who arrived on August 8 and began setting up the organizational framework necessary to generate air power should it be needed to head off an Iraqi offensive. By August 13, more than a week before I showed up, they were generating a daily Air Tasking Orders (ATO) to coordinate air defense sorties and exercises. Some long-range planning was underway, too, but it centered mainly on defending Saudi airspace. The product was even nicknamed the "D-Day

1. *Every Man a Tiger*, pp. 252–254.

ATO."[1] This response to an Iraqi attack on Saudi Arabia was the only thing in CENTAF's playbook.

But if we kept up this approach, we'd practically be guilty of sitting and waiting to be attacked. I needed to shake things up if we were going to put together a campaign to defeat Iraq.

My first tactic was a little devious. I let the staff keep working toward building a strategic campaign—without telling them their real first product would not be a strategic campaign, but Schwarzkopf's retaliatory plan. Aside from Horner, the only other person who knew the real objective was Larry Henry.

No doubt this runs counter to every book on good management I'd ever read, but the staff genuinely thought they were planning the strategic air campaign itself. And I let them think that. I wanted them to think that.

My reasoning was this: Nothing was more important than getting those first 24 hours sharpened and ready. Why dilute their focus? Everything was there. All I had to do was take the Instant Thunder targeting material and manipulate that somewhat and expand it, and it was a perfect match for a sophisticated retaliatory plan.

I didn't need to make life more difficult for myself by saying, "Okay team, this is not a strategic air campaign. We'll get to that later. Just do this now so we can bash Saddam if he executes hostages." I didn't want to have tension and I didn't want to have infighting—for example, if I split some of them to work on the retaliatory plan and others to begin the air campaign plan itself. Not until my first 24 hours were locked. I wanted them focused on what I wanted them focused on. I gained nothing by changing their attitudes or making them focus on this in a more restricted way.

Also, I did not want to let the Instant Thunder brouhaha become a distraction. In the eyes of my planners, Horner had set off a controversy by throwing Warden out of the theater. There was a lot of hoopla. I didn't want to get hung up in all that crap, involved in it, or in any way distracted by it.

What we were setting out to do was so much larger than the pettiness associated with this bullshit over Warden and his briefing. *Just let it run off your back like water does off a duck,* I told myself.

Core of the Campaign

My real dilemmas were the shortage of targeting intelligence and the lack of awareness.

'*We have a disaster waiting to happen,*' I noted as we dug deeper into the planning on August 24. '*We need to connect to the Pentagon and Checkmate for support or we will fail.*' CENTAF's intelligence section did not have the equipment, software or understanding of our objectives. We'd have to get Washington to push us raw targeting data such as satellite and U-2 reconnaissance photographs, and the analysis to go along with them.

Henry pitched in to help me out. "I don't care where it comes from as long as it is timely and accurate," I told him.

Intelligence was critical for precision targeting and that would be the assignment of the F-117s that I knew would be the key to the campaign.

Arguing for this philosophy put me to the test within my own service, because not everyone believed in the F-117 like I did. That day Horner told me he did not think the F-117s would work the way I thought they would. Every instinct I had told me he was dead wrong. '*Mass is a thing of the past,*' I scribbled in my notes. '*We are in a precision world.*'

Horner, on the other hand, thought there would be a full-scale ground offensive that would require a significant amount of effort in the classic sense. He, like many others in the Air Force, was dubious about the value of the F-117. Horner truly did not believe that the F-117 could be as effective as I thought it could. He thought that I was going to get surprised and have to turn to brute force. He focused on supporting the engaged force. It was a difference of degree in our thinking, but a significant one.

Precision was at the core of all my plans. I couldn't emphasize this enough. Precision was going to let me carve and dice Iraq's strategic capabilities and do it fast. With precision, I wouldn't have to wait to batter down defenses and chip away at targets. I could hit what I wanted and destroy what had to be destroyed faster and more efficiently than air power had ever done before.

Breakthrough technology in the F-117 was part of what would help me plan this air war to do the job without brute force. After Vietnam, it was pretty obvious that we had shortcomings. As the Air Force started to correct that with better individual pilot training, accuracy of weapons, the Red Flag warfare exercises, and so on, we also got the breakthrough with the potential for stealth technology, which was a quantum leap.

I first learned about stealth when I was on the Air Staff in Washington during the early 1980s and needed to move money to support something called the Have Blue program. General Chuck Cunningham came to me and said, "I need you to help me with a classified program. For right now, what you need to know is it's a prototype, but it's very, very promising and is based on radar cross-section reduction." I didn't have any idea how good it was; I just knew the basic concept and the millions of dollars that were going to be necessary to get there from here. We had to work it secretly with committees on Capitol Hill and enter that money in the budget in ways that were not obvious. It was awfully expensive, but you had to either not believe in the technology or you had to be oblivious to warfighting not to see the benefits. Have Blue became the F-117.

By 1990, the F-117s were out of the secret world and had been flying in the Nevada desert for many years. Their ability to penetrate defended airspace and drop precision weapons was going to be more useful to me than a thousand F-16s. The non-believers made their case early and often. On August 29, I briefed Major General Royal Moore, commander of Marine air units arriving in the Gulf. Another brute force advocate, he believed the F-117 had failed in Panama and would miss its targets again in the Gulf.[2] I told him time would tell.

The victory of Coalition operations was never in question. We'd win. The only issue was the price we were going to pay. I never built up the Iraqi military capability to be ten feet tall. I resented the fact that the Army and the press perpetuated that myth. Was Iraq a formidable foe? In some respects, yes, if we didn't deal with them correctly. But if dealt with correctly, they were a nation led by a tin-horn, Third-World dictator who did not have very much imagination on anything other than how to harass his neighbors, survive, and try to establish his own place in history. Saddam's ability as a thinker and war-planner was non-existent. It was just a matter of how many lives—but that meant everything to me.

Impending Disaster

With all the different ideas flying around, I wasn't sure we were going to make Horner's deadline for the first cut of a two- to three-day ATO. I was having a hard time getting the staff to see how I wanted this campaign built. *'If attitudes don't change, Deptula and crowd are history!!'* I vented in my diary notes late at night on August 25. *'They are thinking and acting like an SOS war gaming seminar.'*

2. Michael Gordon and Bernard Trainor, *The Generals' War* (Boston: Little, Brown and Company, 1995), p. 98.

The F-117 and the Tomahawk cruise missles had to be the focus of the retaliatory option; not A-6s, F/A-18s, F-15Es, F-111s. Only the stealthy F-117 and the Tomahawks had the survivability and precision to get to the immediate targets right away. If the shooting lasted just a few days we had to be sure to hit targets like the nuclear, biological and chemical sites. The Tomahawk Land Attack Missile (TLAM) would plaster communications nodes and air defense sites. We'd fill in with other platforms from there.

Late at night on August 25, I gave in to the inevitable and wrote in my diary, *'ATO brief for Horner will be a disaster, but a necessary step. At least I'll have everyone's attention after he explodes.'* Right then, if someone had magically given me three average CENTAF planners not tainted by the war-game mindset, I'd have sent all of Warden's bunch home like Horner directed me to do at the outset.

Instead, everyone stayed up all night working on the brief. By 5:30 the next morning I was ready to fire the whole CENTAF staff. I threw myself into it, all the more so because Schwarzkopf himself was arriving later that day, meaning the September 3 target date for briefing the CINC was now for real.

I had to build the plan one step at a time. *'Do not have resources to plan any other way,'* I noted.

Here's how I laid it out. The retaliatory plan would use the Air Staff's Instant Thunder as a base. Next, I'd take my retaliatory plan and turn it into the skeleton for a full offensive air campaign. CENTAF's initial defensive plan work would be the first input to what Schwarzkopf called Phase III—destruction of Iraqi field army units. When the Army got ready to think about its ground option, we'd develop a plan to support the ground campaign from scratch.

I decided to plan for that whole package of phases to last about two months—and to pray it would only take three weeks.

Who was going to do this planning? I penciled in Deptula as a primary assistant for the first two tasks, Crigger and Baptiste for the attacks on the Iraqi army and the support of our ground forces. I thought about who else I could bring in to assist. I needed people who understood warfare and the seamless nature of the attacks we were planning. *'For better or worse,'* I wrote, *'I'm going with Deptula, Baptiste, Lewis, Cash, Joe Bob and Tolin.'* I wouldn't be able to get them all to the theater for several months but that list, with a few additions later, would be my core group.

For the next few days, the weight of it fell on Deptula. I gave him direct guidance: 200 aircraft minimum for the first night attack; no second passes on the same targets, not even by the F-117s; use F-117s, F-111s and F-15Es, in that order, F-16s and F-18s were just filler; and F-111s were to be fragged for attacks on the Iraqi power plants. My priorities for targets were non-negotiable. We'd hit air defense sector operations centers, leadership (including Saddam, if we were so lucky), communications, and NBC targets.

Somehow, we got the slides together, and I briefed Horner on August 26. His reaction was just the fireball I'd expected. Actually, it was the only time I ever witnessed him grandstanding. I could not help but feel sad.

Horner was very concerned that, by the way the briefing sounded, we'd end up talking over the CINC's head with technical air power details. Maps and pictures would help. Overall, he criticized the plan as too mechanical, without enough flow, and impossible for an Army mind to comprehend, and really, he was right.

As for substance, Horner and I were at cross-purposes on some key issues like the importance of strategic attack. Another closely related sore point was the F-117. There was not a shred of doubt in my mind that I was going to put as much dependence on the F-117 as I possibly could and let them carry the brunt of the air war. I was going to do this at night and I was going to do this with precision weapons in a way that the world had never seen before. Strategic attack would lead the way.

I never once thought that there would not be Marines in Kuwait City, or ground troops in Iraq, if only to confirm the Iraqis were withdrawing. At the very minimum I thought some sort of police action would be necessary. How much ground action there would be in this campaign depended on what the air phases accomplished. But we needed to pay close attention to the strategic attack phase—not least because it formed the heart of a retaliatory plan. Also, in a wider campaign to reduce Iraq's danger to the region, there were going to be things that only air power could accomplish. How else would we tackle the weapons arsenal?

In the hallway outside Horner's office, Henry turned to me. "You know how I'd describe that briefing?" he said.

"How?" I replied.

"Ill-prepared, poorly presented, and violently received," said Henry.

I knew Horner was under extreme pressure and I felt empathy for him. From now on, I had to make sure I did not add to his tension. When we got back to the Black Hole area everyone was waiting to find out how the briefing had gone. Henry broke the bad news. I then told Deptula, who'd flipped the slides for me during the briefing, to give everyone a de-brief.

Henry and I went off alone to think it through again. "Let's re-do the briefing so that we start out with a map of Iraq and overlay all the attacks on it," Henry suggested. His crucial formatting change broke the logjam of ideas and enabled us to build a vivid briefing with a smooth flow.

The plan had to cover the main strategic centers of gravity. I listed them and Henry agreed.

• Destroy the leadership, NBC targets, Republican Guard, Air Force and Saddam's security forces, in that order.
• Disrupt C3 (communications, command and control), industrial infrastructure, and other military facilities.

I'd split these into two groups while talking with Henry partly to de-lineate what we could do in just a few days. For example, I didn't want to waste precious time attacking military industry if we were executing a re-taliatory option.

The staff didn't understand that, and I paid the price for keeping them in the dark. *'There's no trap so deadly as the one you set for yourself,'* I wrote in my notes. The staff would come to me with suggestions for tar-gets that were logical if you were doing a strategic air campaign. Howev-er, there were some things I wanted to do more quickly up front, so it could be executed as a stand-alone option. I gave them no hints. I'd just say, "NO, you're taking too long to do that, I want that done in the first week, or the first four days." I'm sure they thought I was a little too dicta-torial, to say the least.

There was a much bigger issue at work, too.

Most previous air wars had started out by taking all the time needed to roll back enemy air defenses so targets could be struck without too much attrition. That's what they did in World War II. The raids of 1942 and 1943 were all about defeating the Luftwaffe: attacking factories that supported it, shooting down fighters in the air. Eighth Air Force had to do that before they could strike hard at bridges in France prior to the Normandy invasion or hit German industry centers.

For the first time, as we faced Iraq, we had much more lethality and if we built it right, much less vulnerability. It wouldn't take us months or years. We could hit strategic targets from the first moment while simultaneously knocking out air defenses.

The difficult issue initially was the distinction between destroying and disrupting selected targets. Some targets, such as nuclear capability would have to be killed, dead, gone. My intent for the El Dorado option was to destroy certain things in that four-day period. I wanted to destroy or kill the leadership, NBC targets, selected Republican Guard units, and Saddam's security forces. Not just hit and paralyze them, but destroy them. Other targets I wanted to just disrupt. But, if I was only to have four days, that's what I wanted to do, and I was not concerned about disrupting other targets from some broader strategic campaign list. I wanted the main ones killed.

This was an extremely important point, and one that caused strife among my planning staff on more than one occasion over the next several months.

By the next day I'd cooled off enough to give the plans developed so far a dispassionate report card. The overall concept was sound—but not outstanding. Our operation order—in case we truly had to execute this four-day plan—was good, but far from excellent. The target list? Who knew, with intel experts wiggling around over the information. The ATO needed more work; the tanker plan that went with it was okay for now. Overall, as of August 27, I gave our efforts a "C."

With just a few days to go before taking the briefing to Schwarzkopf, the pressure was on again. The new briefing following Henry's format now suited my personal style: the air picture, the attack flow, with a lead-in section on how we got where we are. Horner, I believed, was now also willing to tolerate a little strategic discussion on the operational art of air warfare, so I worked that in, too. The bottom line? I briefed Horner again two days later, with no problems. Next up would be Schwarzkopf.

On August 28, I took time out to call my wife, Vicki, and my daughter, Tanya. I'd left them in Washington, D.C. when I was assigned to the USS *LaSalle*. Our farewells had been said many weeks earlier but under much different circumstances. Now we were in a war zone, and there was no question, I was missing them greatly. '*I really miss both of them,*' I wrote in my diary. '*I'll be glad when this is over.*'

The rest of that day was tough and long as we struggled to improve the planning and to deal with a host of other issues. We weren't making progress fast enough. The attitude from the squadrons arriving in theater was very positive, and that buoyed me somewhat. However, at the headquarters, we saw big-picture problems. Fuel was one. Even in the midst of the richest oil reserves on earth, we had to get JP-4 jet fuel precisely where it was needed and that wasn't always easy. Munitions were a bigger worry. Major General Mike Ryan, the Deputy for Operations at TAC, was doing his best to supply us the munitions stockpiles we'd need plus the limited-quantity weapons like HARM—the high-speed anti-radiation missile we'd use for latching on to Iraqi surface-to-air missile radar and knocking them out.

The good news was that every day that passed sunk Saddam deeper into the mess he'd created for himself by invading Kuwait. *'One more week and Saddam will have waited too long . . . He'll be in deep trouble,'* I entered in my diary. Our munitions, fuel, aircraft, target folders, crew workups, etc. were moving steadily. We were far from having the perfect theater campaign but we'd at least have an executable option for Schwarzkopf.

In the midst of this I made the decision to send all of the Warden planners home, keeping only Deptula—he was proving invaluable, way up in the top 1 percent of officers. He was both a thinker and a doer. *'I don't know how this would have turned out without him,'* I wrote, *'but one thing for sure . . . it would not have been as good.'*

Effects vs. Destruction

On August 30, I sat down to review the Master Attack Plan. For three hours I scrubbed every target and sortie. At the end, I noted that I was still disturbed by the issue of "effects-based" targeting.

Balancing effects and destruction was an absolutely critical point. Philosophically, I believed in effects. You don't have to kill every target for a campaign to succeed. In fact, you are wasting time and resources if you only focus on total destruction of every target. There are situations when knocking out a target for a time—screwing up the enemy's ability to use a radar or communications gear or to drive a truck convoy without blowing every last piece of it to bits—can be effective. Also, I didn't believe that every target that must be killed necessarily has to have eight bombs on it and be turned into rubble that would satisfy the most cold-blooded Air Force targeting geek.

But effects have to be based on some set of criteria. It's not enough just to put one or two bombs on every critical target without asking yourself, how dead does this have to be? What was the specific reason for stunning a target or even temporarily paralyzing a target set? Maybe you wanted to pin down forces while your army moved up (which was the case in World War I.) Maybe you wanted to prevent shipment of supplies. Maybe—as in our case—you wanted no electricity in Baghdad.

To balance effects and destruction, you have to think several steps ahead and decide what you ultimately want to achieve. Some targets need to be thoroughly destroyed. You must evaluate what level of destruction you need to achieve for every target based on its type, function and importance in the system of which it is a part. Some targets will need bomb after bomb, even when those bombs are hitting exact coordinates, because they were built to withstand conventional bombs. Nothing short of a nuclear weapon was supposed to penetrate the hardened structures.

We needed to rethink the definition that I was permitting Deptula to use in targeting, and fast! For leadership, communications, aircraft shelters and general facilities, the concept of a few bombs to cause paralysis, not destruction, was okay.

For other targets, this approach was very definitely not okay. NBC sites, bridges, mobile assets—all these needed a hard kill, not an "effect." I could see that either Larry Henry or I was going to have to personally monitor this slice of the campaign to be sure that targets I wanted hit hard were being hit hard enough.

For now, just getting targeting data was a challenge. Intelligence was my number-one problem. Personalities, antiquated systems, Cold War mentality—the obstacles were too long to list. CENTAF intelligence at the time had no capacity and no understanding of how to go about planning. It was absolutely the worst situation a human could imagine. The only thing they knew how to do was to brief Horner on the latest intelligence that had been wired over to them electronically in the previous 24 hours. They would say, "Iraq flew so many sorties yesterday." Whatever Washington intelligence gave them, they spouted out for Horner.

That was the sum total of their capability. They didn't know how to think. They didn't know how to plan. They didn't even know what we were trying to accomplish. No matter how graphic I make it, no matter how emotional I make it, no matter how I choose my words, I cannot say how bad it was. I had never seen anything in my entire military service that was a parallel to the incompetence of CENTAF intelligence. Never.

With the intelligence piece so poor, it was hard to focus properly on everything else. CENTAF intelligence had no real leadership. The Navy on the USS *LaSalle* made CENTAF look like amateur hour. Here I was in Riyadh, assigned to put together a premature attack and build a strategic air campaign, and I didn't even have the intelligence support that a small operation like the USS *LaSalle* provided. It was criminal.

Lieutenant General Jimmie Adams, Deputy Chief of Staff for Plans and Operations at the Air Staff in Washington, came to my aid. In a telephone call, he asked me what I needed.

"Let Warden push anything he wants to over here because I'll ignore what I don't need," I told Adams gratefully. "If he wants you to send stuff direct to me, I would appreciate it, because I don't need all this crap going through Horner." I knew Horner and Adams did not have a smooth relationship and I didn't want information from Warden to be short-stopped by Horner. Yes, it was a little bit of a sleight of hand. But the fact was, I was desperate for more targeting material and welcomed Adams' offer to push forward what he had from Checkmate. It became one of my most valuable resources.

Parochialism vs. Jointness

No planning for an air retaliatory option would have been possible without an impressive deployment—Operation Desert Shield. From mid-August to mid-September, the Navy had at least one carrier in the Gulf, and for most of August, they had two. The Marines had sent over 100 strike aircraft to the theater by the end of August. Air Force fighters started to arrive on August 8. They had 11 fighter squadrons comprising over 250 aircraft on the ground by August 24.[3]

With forces arriving in theater, everyone wanted a piece of the action, and sorting out real capabilities and shortfalls was a big challenge.

In late 1986, Congress had passed the Goldwater-Nichols Act and it was just beginning to take effect. It strengthened the Chairman's job, made the CINCs the lead executors of military operations, and one level down, began to put meat on the bones of the concept of a joint commander for each component, air, maritime, land, etc. Except for Panama, which was a quick operation, no one had really tested it out. Schwarzkopf was the first CINC to truly wear that mantle in combat. I was keenly

---

3. Department of Defense, *Conduct of the Persian Gulf War* (US Government Printing Office, April 1992), pp. 384–388.

aware that it would be historically significant and it was going to set precedent.

Aviators were dealing with a worse legacy, our parochial mindsets. In theory Horner, as the Joint Force Air Component Commander for CENTCOM, was going to have control of all the air forces: Navy, Marine, Air Force and through the Coalition, the allies who joined us. But the reality was we'd never done it that way. Horner was adamant this would be a joint effort and we would not have the fractured set-up of Vietnam all over again with the Navy and the Air Force flying separate routes. But one thing for sure, service parochialism was alive and well.

In fact, parochialism began at home.

In the heat of preparing for the first disastrous briefing to Horner on August 26, I'd noted in my diary *'parochialism's out of control.'*

To be honest, the first problem was with my own staff. Deptula, I was discovering, was a very bright, very talented individual but so parochial that it inhibited his thought process at times. I was confident I could help him grow out of this problem. Letting go of the academic mindset and staying in a warfighting mindset without reverting back to innate parochialism was difficult for some.

That said, there was a yawning gap between warfare styles. In 1990 the Navy and Marines trained to fight as a team, one supporting the other. They trained to fight in tune with the carrier deck operations cycle and the battle group resupply cycles. Their ability to operate in a continuous manner was limited, unless you got two or three carrier battle groups working together as a single unit. Eventually that's what we did: one carrier battle group operated for two days, and we'd shut it down, then the next carrier battle group would operate for two days, then shut it down. The optimum was three or four carrier battle groups, because every third day we'd shut one down.

Every unit had operational limitations but what bothered me even more were the limits in mindset. For planning air warfare, the Navy and the Marines at the time had only one mindset: start at the very front of enemy defenses and roll it back. If your adversary has a defensive system set up where there is one AAA battery 40 miles in front of everything else, the first thing you do is take out that AAA battery. It was regimented. That's not the way I wanted this campaign to unfold.

However, the Navy had a very valuable resource I wanted to use: the A-6, with its laser designator capability. The A-6 was not stealthy or fast but it had legs and precision and I wanted to assign the A-6s to a couple of targets on the outskirts of Baghdad. The Navy component commander, Admiral Hank Mauz, was skeptical. They put pressure on their representative, Admiral Tim Wright. Lucky for me, Wright was a total warrior—the kind of man who never blinks. I told him to force the Navy component to tell us what they could really do, and we would back them out of everything else. At the same time, he broke the news to them that there would be no strike on Iraqi naval bases in the first three days. That took guts.

The Navy, Marines and for that matter, our Air Force F-16 units also wanted a lot more SEAD—Suppression of Enemy Air Defenses. I told them all that Henry and I would decide on the number of strike aircraft and what SEAD support they got. After that, the units could decide everything else.

In part this was because Henry was the only one who had a complete picture of the Iraqi defenses and how to use our electronic warfare assets against them. With the plans Henry was cooking up, we'd spoof enemy radar operators and debilitate their centralized system. The SEAD requirements would be entirely different from what a roll-back campaign of destroying every surface-to-air missile (SAM) would have dictated.

Mixed in with the relentless activity—reviewing every element of the master attack plan, going over munitions shortages—was a larger concern about not getting enough original, critical thought. Working at that pace threatened to create an activity trap that would cause us to miss a weak spot, or a vital opportunity. As everyone became more and more satisfied with the plan, I became concerned we were reading our own press clippings. *'Must be more critical,'* I wrote in my notes.

One such failing became clear on September 2, when we met with squadron commanders and weapons officers from the units that would be flying. As we talked through the plan and listened to their comments, all I could think was, *why didn't I do this before?* I was mad at myself for failing to think of it sooner. Their comments and suggestions were right on target.

I was short of intelligence materials and I was short of people whom I could trust to understand the kind of seamless campaign we needed to build.

War is defined by danger, physical and mental fatigue, intelligence, and friction. Combat experience lubricates all the machinery of war, as

Clausewitz warned us. I had to remember that my staff were confronting war for the first time. It would take them time to shift into gear. I wrote it down in my diary so I would not forget. *'My people are primarily inexperienced with combat—I must not forget—they'll make mistakes.'*

Briefing to Schwarzkopf

The next move was up to me. On September 5, I briefed the CINC on our plans.

This was my first face-to-face discussion with Schwarzkopf in theater—the first chance to brief him on his retaliatory plan. I knew he and I were on the same wavelength; he'd made it very clear to me what he wanted. Not an in-depth briefing on a big strategic campaign at this moment, but a retaliatory option, something to give the President, something we could execute soon.

I gave him the briefing in the most professional way I could. I stood in front of the screen while Deptula flipped the acetate charts on the overhead projector. Horner was present, along with Major General Bob Johnston, CENTCOM Chief of Staff; Admiral Grant Sharp, J-5 (Policy and Plans); Army Brigadier General Jack Leide, the CENTCOM J-2 (Intelligence); Air Force Major General Burt Moore, the CENTCOM J-3 (Operations); and the CINC's ever-present Executive Assistant, Army Colonel B.B. Bell. I gave the briefing emphasizing the here and now, because I knew that's what he wanted to know. The question in his mind had to be: "What are you going to be able to do next week?"

Schwarzkopf listened quietly and didn't say much. His body language told me he was very pleased.

At one point he commented that he was going to put the Army in their chemical gear at the start of Phase I. I reiterated that the key was for Saddam to have no tactical warning of the strikes. Admiral Sharpe raised concerns about logistics shortfalls; we were hurting for munitions such as HARMs, GBU-24s and GBU-27s, I acknowledged. "Let me know when you need help with that," Schwarzkopf said.

As I talked through the campaign—unfolding around the centerpiece of the F-117s—the CINC nodded approval. B-52s would hit the Republican Guard, with an impact averaging one strike every hour, starting during the second 24-hour period.

"That is what I've been waiting to hear," Schwarzkopf exclaimed.

He was also impressed with the target imagery we showed him—

although I thought it was bare minimum, from a fighter pilot perspective.

When I reached the last chart, he looked up.

"Super. Most impressive war plan I have ever seen. This is exactly what we need."

After a brief discussion, Schwarzkopf thanked me and stood up, indicating the meeting was over. As everyone departed, he walked up to the big map and put his arm around me.

"Words don't describe my appreciation for what you've done. This is great," he said.

I knew that he was sincere. From Schwarzkopf's demeanor that evening I knew that we were on the same wavelength and I could tell that my initial feeling at our Tampa meeting was correct. The chemistry was right and the personalities were compatible. But I also tried to put myself in his position, and I said to myself, *Okay, if there's an attack tomorrow, he will be held responsible for whatever happens, and as we go forward, he's going to ultimately be held responsible for success or failure and the loss of lives.*

Our private conversation touched on several more issues. Schwarzkopf said he believed Powell would find this plan "too bloody." What he meant was, he thought the Chairman would be skeptical of the air campaign because of the direct potential for loss of life on the Iraqi side. Therefore, we will have a problem getting the Chairman's approval.

I have to admit, when I left that room that night, I certainly was on a high because I had been successful in convincing him that he could trust and depend on me to get the job done. His support was total as indicated by his statement: "Anything you want to do, you do it and anywhere you need my help, just let me know what it is. I don't care what service it is. Everybody works for me in this theater."

Schwarzkopf was deeply concerned about saving lives—he was always very critical of any Army planning, or anybody's planning, that did not put saving lives at the forefront and consider the cost of any option. But he had a warrior mind. Later, Schwarzkopf got some bad publicity about the ground planning. Others tried to take credit for his ground scheme of maneuver ideas and other ideas that were really his. It was his intellectual capital behind the final plans.

His other questions to me after the meeting that night said volumes about Schwarzkopf the man.

"How many aircraft do you think you are going to lose?" he asked.

"Not more than 10 in the first 24 hours," I told him, "and perhaps 30 in the first three phases of the air campaign."

"Well, you know you've got to make this joint," he said. "You've got to have everybody on board."

I told him I was working on that very hard.

We also discussed my plan to use Special Operations Forces (SOF) to take out early-warning radar on the Iraqi border. That one soon got me in hot water with Schwarzkopf.

As I briefed him on September 5, I pointed to four or five radar sites and I said "I'm going to take those out using special ops." I meant I was going to take them out by putting the special ops over there on the ground with their buggies to take them out. Schwarzkopf apparently thought I was going to take them out with air.

A week or two later, when I signed off on a request for special ops to bring in all their vehicles and equipment, Schwarzkopf absolutely exploded. He called me and told me to get my ass over there.

And he said, "I never approved this!"

I said, "Sir, let me tell you, remember when we walked up to the map?"

"Yes!"

I said, "Well, remember I told you we would take that radar out with special ops?"

"But you didn't say you'll put forces over there!" he retorted. "I can't send forces across the border until the President gives me permission to!"

Having calmed down slightly, he asked, "Can you take these out with helicopters."

"Sure. I can use the HH-53s and let them lead the Black Hawks in and take them out that way," I replied.

"Let's do it that way."

Now, there are those who have said the only reason he made that request was because he wanted to get the Army involved in the air war in some way, but I'm not that cynical. By using the helicopters, it kept that part of the plan more consistent in his mind with the way we were planning to do things. He was running this campaign—no doubt about it.

As I left the room that night after our first meeting, Schwarzkopf again reminded me: "Don't forget you work for me."

———————————————————————————➤

BRIEFING THE PRESIDENT

"Both you and the CINC were on a high," Horner teased me as we reviewed the briefing to Schwarzkopf over dinner that night. I agreed. For my part, though, it was really more relief than euphoria. I passed on to Horner what Schwarzkopf had said to me privately. Horner was glad Schwarzkopf now had an option that could be executed. "I could not believe how accepting he was of everything you said," Horner mused. "Even some of your B.S.!"

After the briefing to Schwarzkopf, I was committed to having the plan ready to execute on 36-hours notice by September 13. I requested more F-4Gs, more F-117s and more tankers. Each week, more aircraft arrived in the Gulf.

An Eagle's View

I had spent over two weeks locked away in Riyadh working on the air planning. Now I wanted to visit the units.

Assembling in the desert were fighter squadrons that would eventually be organized under the 14th Air Division (Provisional). As depicted in Figure 2, they included air-to-air fighters, like the F-15C, along with dual and multi-role fighters such as the F-15E and the F-16. The tank-killer A-10s were also arriving. The prize, of course, were those fighters with precision: the F-117 and the F-111. Through all of Desert Storm we had only about a dozen F-15Es with the new LANTIRN infrared targeting pod that enabled them to drop laser-guided bombs.

Since Horner had told me I'd be the Deputy for Operations if we

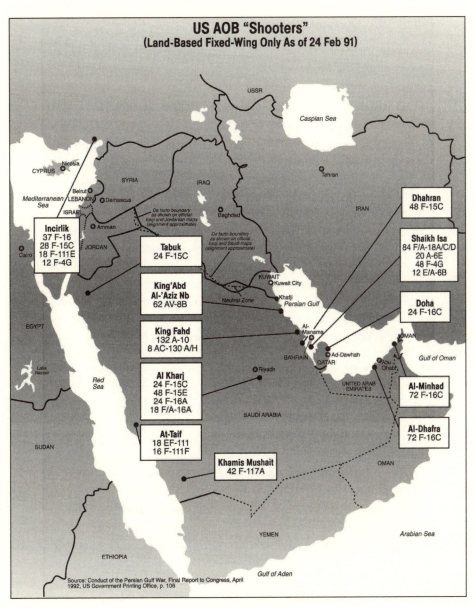

US AOB "Shooters"
(Land-Based Fixed-Wing Only As of 24 Feb 91)

USSR

Caspian Sea

Nicosia
CYPRUS
SYRIA
IRAQ
Tehran

Mediterranean Sea
Beirut
LEBANON   Damascus
ISRAEL
Baghdad
IRAN

Dhahran
48 F-15C

Incirlik
37 F-16
28 F-15C
18 F-111E
12 F-4G

Amman
JORDAN
Cairo

De facto boundary
as shown on official
Iraqi and Jordanian maps
(alignment approximate)

De facto boundary
as shown on official
Iraqi and Saudi maps
(alignment approximate)

Tabuk
24 F-15C

Shaikh Isa
84 F/A-18A/C/D
20 A-6E
48 F-4G
12 E/A-6B

**King'Abd
Al-'Aziz Nb**
62 AV-8B

KUWAIT
Kuwait City
Neutral Zone
Khafji   Persian Gulf

Doha
24 F-16C

EGYPT

King Fahd
132 A-10
8 AC-130 A/H

Al-Manama

Al Kharj
24 F-15C
48 F-15E
24 F-16A
18 F/A-16A

BAHRAIN
Ad-Dawhah
QATAR
Abu Ohabi
OMAN
Gulf of Oman

Lake Nasser
Red Sea

Riyadh

UNITED ARAB EMIRATES

Al-Minhad
72 F-16C

SAUDI ARABIA

At-Taif
18 EF-111
16 F-111F

Al-Dhafra
72 F-16C

SUDAN

OMAN

Khamis Mushait
42 F-117A

YEMEN
Arabian Sea

ETHIOPIA

Gulf of Aden

Source: Conduct of the Persian Gulf War, Final Report to Congress, April
1992, US Government Printing Office, p. 106

FIGURE 2

went to war, I wanted to visit the fighter units because it was likely they'd fall under my control. I wanted those in the combat units to have as close as I could give them to an eagle's view of the battle ahead—to know what we were planning from the start.

Like a lot of other people, I was still carrying the scar tissue of Vietnam. In Vietnam, I was a flight commander in the F-4. We fighter pilots rarely knew why we were flying sorties. I abhorred that war in many respects because of the way it was run out of Washington and the way it was executed and planned—or not planned, as the case may be. The Air Force was over some of the shortcomings of the Vietnam War. Our technology was far better, and so was our training of aircrews. The one area I still worried about was planning and execution. At the campaign level, this drove my obsession with saving lives. As a commander, I did not want to keep the aircrews in the dark the way I had been. I did not want them to live through the mistakes I lived through in Vietnam when I was a captain. We bombed targets at the same time every day, with never an explanation as to how the missions fit into the overall plan. We flew under restrictions that did not make sense. Our leaders were so far removed they might as well have been commanding from Washington.

In this war, I wanted each fighter wing commander to believe and to think that he and his people were truly a part of planning the campaign they'd be asked to execute. So I asked each wing commander to send me two aircrew members from their wing to be part of the planning center. The air campaign needed to be *their* plan, not just a plan being issued to them.

No warrior with a Western mind wants to be dictated to by higher commanders. I was responsible for putting the air campaign plan together. Although I was working for the CINC and Horner, I didn't want Washington dictating to me. I didn't even want the CINC's staff getting into my business. My view was I'm the operator and I'm the guy that's going to put the air campaign together.

I frequently reminded myself that all the levels below you think the same way. The wing commander doesn't want to be dictated to. He would like ideally for you to tell him what you want him to accomplish and then let him figure out the "how" to accomplish it himself.

Aside from laying the groundwork for planning, I needed to light a fire under the aircrews. We might execute the retaliatory plan in a week if Saddam did something rash.

So on September 7, I visited several of the bases. I didn't want them to think they had two to three months to just lollygag around and get their act together.

I told the units bluntly that it wasn't going to be their choice when they went to war. "The only two people that determine when we are going to have to execute are either President Bush or Saddam Hussein. I sure don't know what Saddam's going to do, but if he does something, President Bush will react," I told them.

"Within a week from now, I'm going to be expecting you to execute what your people and I have put together. I'm not going to accept excuses. Make sure you keep your act together."

Then, I asked them, "Now, what do you need to be able to execute the first three or four days that I have laid out? What do you not have that maybe I don't know about?" I had the logistics experts brief me every morning on the status of every wing and what portion of the plan could be executed by that wing that day.

My visits also gave me a chance to assess the aircrews and their leaders. There's no one right way to command a wing. Successful combat leaders often have different styles; all of them start to focus on the fight ahead at their own pace. Some of them never quite make it. They get caught in an activity trap and lose sight of the jobs only the commander can do; or it turns out that despite years in the cockpit, they just don't have the aptitude for war. Others have the hard edge from day one. Still, others push their people too hard—but get the payoff with excellent combat results.

Part of my job was to know the strengths and weaknesses among my commanders, and what the units needed—often due to circumstances beyond their control. For example, the 388th Tactical Fighter Wing (TFW) was leaning forward; however, when I visited, the 388th had no bombs. Neither did the 401st TFW.

My key F-111 unit under Colonel Tom Lennon, a hard taskmaster, was integral to my plan; but they had rushed to their base at Taif lacking a few items in their kit bag. They did not have coolant for the Pave Tack precision targeting pods—which to me, meant no hard-target kill capability until the coolant arrived. They also needed 5,000-gallon fuel bladders since there were no refueling trucks at Taif.

Hal Hornburg at the 4th TFW pressed me for better intelligence information on the Scuds, which I surely wished I could give him. Tip Osterhaler's 35th TFW had lots of new leadership to break in, and worse, only a three-day supply of HARMs.

I also visited Colonel Don Beaufait's Marines in the 3rd Marine Air Wing (MAW). We were a joint force under Horner on paper, but the specifics needed to be worked out. For our retaliatory plan, Beaufait and his Marines agreed to depart a little from their playbook and strike fixed targets, such as airfields and bunkers, plus troops and bridges, with 2000-pound bombs. They agreed to hit the Republican Guard. I agreed to give them two or three KC-10 tankers—my best—to refuel their aircrews.

Some units, like the 363rd TFW under Colonel Ed Eberhart, had no limiting factors. My assessment was they had the best pilots up front and in Eberhart, a commander who was the best of the best.

Perhaps the most important visit for me was to the F-117s at Khamis Mushat Air Base, south of Taif and only 30 miles from Saudi Arabia's border with Yemen. We stationed the F-117s as far back as we could from potential Scud attacks. The unit, commanded by Colonel Al Whitley, was ready and eager, except that they wanted better imagery. Later, Whitley sent a message to Russ about it, saying their intelligence was non-existent, just like I'd been telling everyone for a month.

Behind the gung-ho attitude of the F-117 pilots, I noticed that they were still smarting from their disappointing combat debut less than a year earlier in Operation Just Cause, the invasion of Panama. Two F-117s had been assigned to drop precision bombs on a barracks housing troops loyal to Panamanian dictator Manuel Noriega. Due to complications, the bombs had missed. The first information given out about the F-117 attacks was fuzzy, and by the time the Air Force clarified what had really happened, the reputation of the F-117 was tarnished. They were all eager to change that image.

For me, the F-117s were the focus of the campaign. I told them, "Our success or failure rides with you." It was that simple in my mind.

To prove it, Henry and I structured a test for the F-117. I directed Major Bob "Bullet" Eskridge, one of the F-117 wing representatives, to fly a special profile the next time he took an F-117 up. September 15 was the day. Bullet left the tanker track and headed for the Iraqi border. Fifteen nautical miles out, he shut down communications and slipped into the F-117's clean configuration as if for an attack. Then, two nautical miles from the border, he turned and flew parallel to Iraq's border for 20 nautical miles before heading due south, for 30 nautical miles.

The Iraqis didn't react. As far as they knew, the F-117 had never been there. I swore Bullet to secrecy. For now, only Bullet, Henry, Horner, and I needed to know.

Too Much Air Power?

At Taif, on September 7, I got a phone call from Schwarzkopf. He had been called by Powell, who was annoyed about the way air power was being portrayed as the 'answer to the problem.'

However, Schwarzkopf was sold, and he had told Powell that after seeing my September 5 briefing. "Have we got a bombing plan for you," Schwarzkopf said to Powell. "If you want to execute an air attack by itself, we're ready."[1]

This was a hot issue because, now that Schwarzkopf had been briefed, we were planning to present the briefing to Powell and Cheney during their upcoming visit to Riyadh. As Schwarzkopf explained to me, Powell was concerned that the air effort not be "Air Force only." He worried that we might be too interested in Baghdad and not attack the Iraqi army, especially the Republican Guard. Schwarzkopf confided that Powell had had his doubts ever since he saw the Air Staff briefing a few weeks earlier.

"I'm comfortable with our air plan," Schwarzkopf reiterated to me on the phone that day. "You might emphasize the Army, Navy, and allies a little more for the Chairman." He went on to say that Powell believed the Air Staff in the Pentagon wanted to make the campaign an Air-Force-only show. As I listened, I thought this perception came from the Air Force not being astute about the way they portrayed the campaign. Schwarzkopf said he'd reminded the Chairman that I worked for him; that he promised my guidance for planning the air campaign; and that the Air Staff was not involved.

"I'm sure you have a handle on this," Schwarzkopf half assured me. It was a common throwaway line of his, a courtesy. His main message came next.

"Buster, be prepared for him to probe a little in this area," Schwarzkopf counseled. Over the last few days he'd had two or three telephone conversations with Powell concerning the air planning. The same issues always came up. Powell maintained that "air thinkers will drive us down the wrong road." Ground troops will occupy Kuwait, not airplanes. This campaign will be joint, or it won't happen.

---

1. *It Doesn't Take a Hero*, p. 354.

"After we give him our air campaign briefing," Schwarzkopf continued, "I'm sure his concerns will disappear." Schwarzkopf sounded frustrated with Powell. Usually he did not ramble like this. Schwarzkopf ended the call abruptly, saying to me, "Thank you for your time." That was unusual, too. I took it as a sign that Schwarzkopf wanted to make extra sure the meeting with Powell did not have any surprises.

The call gave me a sinking feeling. I'd thought Schwarzkopf was totally comfortable with the air campaign, and now I did not feel as certain. Maybe I had not been spending enough time making sure that the CINC understood the plan well enough to defend it with Powell when I was not around. I made a mental note to rectify that. In my diary I wrote and underlined: *'I must not permit the Chairman's doubts to undermine this.'*

Soon after I returned to Riyadh I had to ask Schwarzkopf for a favor. Air Force Chief of Staff General Mike Dugan was coming to the theater and Schwarzkopf had laid down the law that "Buster will not give him any kind of briefing." This put me in an awkward spot. I'd worked for Dugan and we had friends in common, but we did not know each other well. Dugan was our boss, too—even though Horner and I worked for the CINC. In practice, any service chief was accorded great respect because he was the head of the military organization in which you served. We couldn't stiff him.

I went over to see Schwarzkopf and said, "I need your help on something." I made the case for why I needed to give Dugan at least a cursory briefing. "It's terrible," I said. "This is the Air Force Chief of Staff—put yourself in my place. I need to at least explain to him what we're basically doing," I continued.

"Alright, I understand," said Schwarzkopf. "I'll agree that you can brief him but only on the first 24 hours. Nothing past the first 24 hours."

When the Chief of Staff arrived, I gave him a briefing on the strategic objectives of the campaign and the tactical execution of the first 24 hours. He seemed removed, and his reaction was difficult to read. There was nothing negative in his reaction, just a bland attitude that was far from what I expected. All Dugan said when I finished was: "That's pretty good ATO for the first 24 hours." I couldn't believe his detached attitude.

Dugan stated he also did not believe that execution of the plan was likely anytime soon, if at all. Regardless of what he thought, I made a short comment for the record that we would be ready to execute in a couple of days. The meeting was not a high point. I was still smoldering a few days later when I wrote in my diary, *'Thank heavens he's in Washington, D.C., not Riyadh.'*

Briefing the Chairman

As I prepared to brief Powell on September 13, several joint issues reared their ugly heads. The Marines had been complaining that the retaliatory strikes and Phase I of the campaign did not leave their air assets available for other tasking direct from the Marine Expeditionary Force (MEF). In line with their doctrine and how they saw their role, they wanted to strike Iraqi ground targets in their sector. They finally settled down, and accepted that in this phase of the plan I needed to concentrate on communications, leadership, NBC targets, and more.

Then the Navy informed me that they wanted to back out of planned strikes near Baghdad. I told them they had to go or I would cancel the whole Red Sea package entirely.

My briefing with Powell was scheduled for 45 minutes. Powell's intent was to review the four-day retaliatory strike option.

Going into the briefing I mulled over the crisis of confidence imposed on us by our Vietnam memories. It was still affecting our view of ourselves as a military force and our capabilities. I believed we had to get that off our backs. Churchill once wrote, "The terrible ifs accumulate." Not this time. I wanted to make Powell confident about the plan. I also made a note to myself to discuss biological and chemical weapons—bugs and gas—with him to get a sense of where he stood. Finally, as an airman, I had to stress weather: Right now, it was perfect for an air campaign.

I'd worked with Powell on occasion during my assignment as the Deputy Director of Legislative Affairs in the Office of the Secretary of Defense. That was my first chance to watch him function in meetings, see what he had to say, and get to know him. He was charismatic, the kind to go out of his way to greet colleagues, and make junior officers feel at ease. Now, however, we were in an entirely different setting.

Powell began asking detailed questions as soon as I started the briefing and the meeting stretched to an hour and a half.

Powell's major concern that day was about TLAMS. He was obviously a skeptic of TLAMS; in fact, he made it pretty clear that he wanted me to be able to do everything I needed to do without using them. Otherwise he had no major changes.

I wrapped up the briefing by telling the Chairman that we were ready to execute Phase I as a retaliatory plan now. "Very impressive," Powell said. Then he asked me about Instant Thunder.

"Buster have you seen the Washington crowd's plan?"

"Yes," I said.

"It's about as far from joint as you can get. Keep this in the AOR (area of responsibility)," Powell said. "You don't know how pleased I am to be able to tell the President he has an executable option."

Powell thought we would execute—the question was when. "Stay ready," he told us. "1 October is still my personal opinion," Powell speculated. "However, that's the President's decision."

Powell was talking, of course, about executing our version of a sophisticated El Dorado Canyon retaliatory plan. I was pleased. I had given the CINC exactly what he asked for and Powell accepted it. He could go back to Washington and tell President Bush he can execute this if he needed to. When Powell said 1 October, he didn't mean 1 October for a massive ground campaign. He meant that the President might choose to execute this as a separate, stand-alone entity, for four or five days.

Finally this retaliatory option had jelled. That's why they were all so satisfied. Other people misinterpreted this and thought that the plan I'd briefed as executable was the strategic air campaign that could lead up to the ouster of Saddam from Kuwait. Misperceptions were rife. Most of the Air Force people in Washington and in the region thought this was the strategic plan.

To a certain extent, the confusion was my fault. The day following Powell's briefing, I promised the CINC that his strategic air campaign plan would be ready for prime time within three weeks (Phase I, II, III and IV). He said, "Make sure we keep the Phase I retaliatory plan ready to execute within twelve hours." I assured him we were ready if he gave the command.

When I briefed Powell, we did not have more than a thumbnail sketch of phases II and III of the campaign. None of that was on the table that day. The analysis to figure out levels of attrition for the Iraqi ground forces and all that type of work (which made up the bulk of the campaign) came much later. I didn't even have all the forces needed in theater for the full campaign—just what I needed for a retaliatory option.

Over the next few days I went back to dealing with munitions, intelligence, and other shortfalls. There were still a million details to iron out. For example, I decided the Rules of Engagement (ROE) for the initial sweep of fighters against Iraqi aircraft would be simple: If it moves, shoot it. They'd all be looking northward and we had so many advantages unknown to us in Vietnam such as AWACS with its massive air search radar and other ways for pilots in the jets to identify the enemy and avoid each other. This ROE was *'totally my decision . . . no Vietnam B.S,'* I noted.

Analyzing the possible reaction of Iraq's air force took up a lot of our time. Air defenses were a big concern. On September 18, I noted that one of our Black Hole intelligence gurus, Captain Eric Holdaway, had provided us with the first real intelligence analysis of the KARI system that controlled Iraq's air defenses. Hard data on the importance of the integrated operations centers caused us to change some of the F-117 targets. I also let a group head out to visit the border. With Larry Henry supervising, Deptula, Captain John Glock and Captain Randy O'Boyle headed out to talk to some of our special operators.

O'Boyle was the emissary. A stocky, sandy-haired "smoke-eater" who could joke about anything, O'Boyle was a MH-53 helicopter pilot and our liaison to the secretive world of special operators. Although he never talked about it, he'd led several critical night urban assault helicopter missions during the Panama invasion in 1989 and won the Military Airlift Command Pilot of the Year award for it. O'Boyle always had his sidearm on prominent display. He frowned on any of the rest of us having guns, although in a war zone, some thought we ought to. In his view, we just couldn't be trusted with them. On this trip Randy took it upon himself to drive the crew up to the border. They came back with proof that some mobile Iraqi teams were passing information on our aircraft back to the integrated operations centers. To block out this information source, we'd have to work more closely with the SOF forces and A-10s.

More help came from a welcomed source: Major Jeffery L. "Oly" Olsen, a Marine F/A-18 pilot, provided to CENTAF as a liaison officer was assigned to the black hole. Oly was sandy-haired, a fighter pilot and a Marine through and through. He must have had something special because there in the midst of the desert, surrounded mainly by other sweaty men in flight suits, Oly nonetheless managed to find himself a beautiful wife. She was one of my administrative specialists, Staff Sergeant Heidi Pacheco. They got married in short order after the shooting stopped and proper arrangements were made.

For me, Oly was a genius with plotting how the Iraqis might use their air threat and disperse to alternate bases. The Iraqis had a sackful of fighters, mostly of Soviet and French origins. We thought some of them could carry chemical or biological weapons. Their airborne air defense posture called for flushing to alternate bases. I had no doubt we'd dispatch the Iraqi air force in a hurry, but they might well have time to get a few aircraft through. I estimated they'd be able to launch about 30 aircraft if we started an attack. Based on Oly's airfield work, I made some changes to the plan on September 19. I assigned a pair of F-15Cs to each Iraqi air force base from Baghdad on south that had the potential to launch chemical and biological attacks. The only aircraft north of that sweep would be the enemy or our own F-117s. I figured two F-15Cs per base should keep everything under control. I'd send the F-14s out west with the same mission—and a very liberal ROE.

In the midst of our intense preparations, on Sunday, September 16, Rick Atkinson of the *Washington Post* published an article on the front page under the headline, "US to Rely on Air Strikes if War Erupts." What a shock! Dugan had talked with reporters on his flight home. The lead paragraph said it all: "The Joint Chiefs of Staff have concluded that U.S. military air power—including a massive bombing campaign against Baghdad that specifically targets Iraqi President Saddam Hussein—is the only effective option to force Iraqi forces from Kuwait if war erupts, according to Air Force Chief of Staff General Michael J. Dugan." The article went on to quote Dugan on attacking downtown Baghdad.

Horner told me Schwarzkopf and Powell were furious about the leak. "It lays out Phase I in living color," Horner protested. Powell was so angry he at first directed all senior commanders to stonewall any reporter's questions by saying not just "no comment," but "I have no knowledge of what you are asking, period."

When I read through the article, what hit me was that it was a sad day for the people who had been working for weeks on just four hours of sleep and had protected the security of the planning with total professionalism to see the Chief of Staff blunder like this.

I was worried, too, about how Saddam might react to this widely published challenge. My assessment was that he might try to leverage the position of our people still in the embassy in Kuwait. At the least, he would increase his air defenses, making tactical surprise more difficult, which could mean higher losses for our aircrews if we executed the retaliatory plan. Now there would likely be more anti-aircraft fire around the fixed Scud launch site targets, for example.

My diary read: *'most unprofessional act I have ever witnessed by a senior air force officer.'* Cheney fired Dugan on Monday morning. It was the only thing he could do. On September 18, we had a new nominee for Chief of Staff, General Tony McPeak.

Fighting Complacency

If one thing bothered me, it was the risk of complacency now that we'd gotten approval all around for our first efforts. After the initial adrenaline rush subsided, there was a business-as-usual mentality taking over and it was dangerous. Since Saddam hadn't fired another shot since his invasion of Kuwait, we were starting to worry about things like giving people time off instead of defending ourselves. It was time to shake things up—put myself on the razor's edge, and pull a surprise on Horner, too.

I called together a few of my planners and said, "If I were in Saddam's place, I might figure out a way to just try to dump some chemicals or something on Riyadh, just to really create mass confusion and disruption." I asked them, "How would I go about doing that? I want you to do it in a way it would be a totally surprise attack. We won't know it's happening until all of sudden the canister hits. And I don't want to do it with a Scud missile."

When they came back in, I quizzed them. "Can this be executed? For certain?" When they walked me through it I said, "I love it." That might have been the end of the exercise, except that the very next day, I learned that someone had adjusted one of our combat air patrols (CAP) in a way that made Riyadh more vulnerable.

It irritated me so badly I had to do something. So my planners turned their "what if" study into a memo. Here's what the "Saddam brain trust" wrote, pictured in Figure 3.

Pretty good, I thought, even with the weapons school lingo. They even drew out the mission on a map and attached it to their memo.

I got into the act and scribbled at the bottom: 'P.S. I could have executed this mission on the 20, 21, 22, 23, 24 or 26 of September' and signed that one "S."

Then, below it, I put 'Note: We need to get people thinking vice being fat, dumb and happy!!!' and signed my own initial "B."

I took the memo into Horner's office. He wasn't in. I left the memo

Dear General Chuck Horner   26 Sep 90

    I am writing you personally, to advise of my ability to attack your precious headquarters at Riyadh. You will be well advised to take careful note that I possess the capability to deliver Biological and Chemical warfare cannisters at my will using the attached low altitude profile. A combat ready division of Mirage F-1s, based at Tallil, will fly around the AWACS coverage, (provided by the OER 41 track), penetrate the Patriot Sam Envelope centered around Riyadh, deliver 3 Bio/Chem cannisters per aircraft then fly directly back to the recovery base at my new As Salman Airfield.

    I'm sure you've noted that I have omitted the time and date of such an attack. There is no time like the present since my animals are getting hungry and the troops are getting restless.

Salaam,

Saddam

P.S. I COULD HAVE EXECUTED THIS MISSION ON THE 20, 21, 22, 23, 24 or <u>26</u> of SEPT.

S

NOTE: WE NEED TO GET PEOPLE THINKING VICE BEING FAT, DUMB + HAPPY!!!

B

FIGURE 3

on his chair and went back to my office, just through the doorway, to wait for the reaction. A few minutes later he came in.

"What is this?" Horner demanded, waving the paper.

"We just got attacked because the CAP was in the wrong position," I explained. Horner laughed. He got it. The CAP went back to the right place.

I was just trying to keep everybody intellectually vigilant because nothing is worse than having somebody outsmart you. It causes untold grief and casualties because you were just too dense to use your brainpower to think. And there's no excuse for that. But boy, Americans are notorious for getting focused and acting like we're operating in a little cocoon. When I first got to Riyadh they were doing nothing offensive and everything defensive. Now, our planning operation had become such a big deal to everybody that they'd dropped some of the defensive things they were focused on when I first got there.

However, we had a new threat: Word was that Abu Nidal, the notorious terrorist, had made a deal with the Saudis to target American servicemen in Saudi Arabia. Schwarzkopf gave the order to get everyone out of the hotels on September 24. I wished it could be more low-key, but I could understand his sense of urgency. Force protection was vital and the CINC's number one task. *'I'm sure he is thinking . . . Marine Barracks,'* I wrote in my diary. We certainly did not need another Lebanon.

The Ground War

Now that our strategic air campaign was ready, the next stop was to brief the Joint Chiefs and then the President on the campaign plans. I learned on October 5 that the briefings to the Pentagon and the White House were definitely a "go."

October 5 was quite a day. *'Saddam moving aircraft everywhere,'* I noted in my diary. This was the day they dispersed aircraft to forward sites, thereby complicating our strategy issues and making the tactical targeting more difficult for the strategic campaign.

Schwarzkopf was edgy that day, too, though I had no idea if it was due to the Iraqi Air Force. When he was edgy, it was normally with senior officers. He was great with the troops. I never saw him act edgy and temperamental with majors and below, or with enlisted troops. Lieutenant colonels and above were fair game.

Schwarzkopf was on the hook to brief a ground operation as part of the theater campaign plan. It consumed him. 'Ground, ground, ground,' I noted in my diary, summing up the CINC's frame of mind. 'If we do our job in Phase 1 to Phase 3 at least the ground action will be minimal.'

Schwarzkopf and I had been so focused on building a retaliatory option that all of our discussions focused on what we could do with air. Now the pendulum had swung and our discussions were dominated with ground campaign issues. Not that he wanted a ground war—none of us did—but he was certain that this was never going to end with just air alone. Schwarzkopf believed that Saddam would never move those troops until they were driven back out of Kuwait. I don't think he believed the airmen could make it so painful for the ground forces in Kuwait that Saddam would just move them back.

Schwarzkopf was sure that ground forces would finish off the war. I have to say, I agreed. The difference to me was that I thought the ground campaign would be little more than a sophisticated police action, whereas Schwarzkopf approached it as a full-blown operation against a numerically superior Iraqi army—an operation that might be lengthy.

Schwarzkopf had started to concentrate on planning for the ground campaign. The request to brief President Bush put him, in his words, "under considerable pressure from Washington" to devise a complete ground campaign plan overnight. It was just how I'd felt in late August. Schwarzkopf had called in a team from the School of Advanced Military Studies (SAMS) out at Fort Leavenworth and set them to work. On October 6, Lieutenant Colonel Joe Purvis, head of the team, briefed him on a plan constructed around one U.S. Army corps. This plan picked up key factors: relying on 50 percent air attrition of forces, isolating the Kuwaiti Theater of Operations (KTO) But, Schwarzkopf didn't like the plan much because it drove straight into Kuwait. [2]

The CINC's nerves were starting to fray from the constant Washington pressure. On October 7, I noted in my diary that 'Stormin Norman should be named Nervous Norman.'

As for me, I was in a bad mood for the opposite reason. I had an executable strategic air campaign (Phases I, II and III) and I believed the longer we waited, the more it favored Saddam. His trick with the airfields was just one example. Give him more time and he'd squirm more.

The forces I needed were building to a peak. The first lot of SCATHE

2. Robert H. Scales, Certain Victory (Washington: Office of the Chief of Staff, U.S. Army, 1993) p. 125.

MEAN drones, the BQM-74, were to arrive at King Khalid Military City (KKMC) airfield on Wednesday, October 9. To the Iraqi radar operators the drones would appear as an actual combat aircraft, and they'd fire their SAMs prematurely. The remaining BQM-74s will arrive not later than October 12. *'Drones are our asset to help manage attrition,'* I noted. With the assets in place for Henry's plan—which we called Poobah's Party—I was confident we could strike the first blow of the campaign anytime.

The October weather was beautiful. As a commander, I was itching to take advantage of it. I would be less than truthful if I didn't say that in fact, I desperately wanted to start this war in late October, early November. I just thought it was the right time and that we didn't need the Powell build-up we were later forced to take.

Based on the above and the continuing Iraqi dispersal of fighter aircraft, I felt we were reaching an optimal window for Phase I, II and III operation about October 12–15. After that, Saddam might actually benefit because he could continue to disperse aircraft and carry out his covert activity with his chemical-biological assets. The fighter pilots were ready and I thought we were dissipating our margin of safety.

I talked this over with Horner, who brought it up at a meeting with the CINC, but we didn't make any progress. It wasn't Schwarzkopf's fault—it wasn't his decision when to start. Oh, by the way, Schwarzkopf didn't agree with us. As far as he was concerned, he didn't have a margin of safety until he got another corps on the ground and a ground campaign plan that didn't drive into the teeth of Kuwait. Horner and I didn't push it.

The main event, of course, was to brief the President. Schwarzkopf wanted to go to Washington himself to present the offensive plans, but Powell decided that would be too much visibility. Schwarzkopf was seething at Powell's insistence on briefing the incomplete ground plan and his refusal to let him come back to Washington for the consultations.[3]

So I would brief the air plan, Purvis would brief the ground plan, and Schwarzkopf's Chief of Staff, Bob Johnston, would go along to deliver a final "CINC's Assessment."

Schwarzkopf called us in for guidance before we left.

"You are to brief my views. No personal opinions. If you violate this you won't only leave the AOR, you'll be out of the military."

---

3. *It Doesn't Take a Hero*, p. 358.

'Only the insecure make threats,' I wrote later. The CINC certainly wasn't insecure, so why? I concluded the CINC's tough talk was for the benefit of the younger SAMS officers. I intended to brief what I thought was right based on my personal integrity, not someone else's, and I was sure Schwarzkopf would be comfortable with that. In fact, he didn't even ask me to review my briefing with him. I understood him being nervous about personal opinions—especially when he was in Riyadh, thousands of miles and eight time zones away—but he couldn't expect anyone to just say, "I can't answer that," to the President.

At any rate, the preparations for the trip gave me an opportunity to see the Army ground plan up close. It was not very imaginative. In fact, the plan was very close to brute force. Schwarzkopf did not want the ground plan briefing to go to prime time but he had no choice. Powell insisted on the Washington briefing.

What really concerned me about our Washington briefing was the fragmentation of the air and ground planning, as if they were not linked. We had our air campaign briefing and the SAMS' one-corps ground option briefing being presented as two distinct pieces. Since August, Schwarzkopf had been talking about a four-phased campaign. I was concerned that the briefings to the Joint Chiefs and the President were not going to show four cohesive phases. I worried it would not show a significant effort on the strategic, fixed target sites. Finally, it was not going to show enough information on how air was going to attrit the Iraqi Army even before Phase IV kicked off. The way we left Riyadh, it looked like airplanes were just going to support the ground army, where in fact, Phase II and Phase III and even part of Phase I were aimed at trying to destroy as much of the ground capabilities as we could. The two briefings were not portraying the overall campaign with the clarity I thought was warranted when you're briefing the President.

I wasn't completely sure how the split had happened. Based on what Schwarzkopf said, Powell called the CINC and said he wanted the air campaign to be briefed and then the options for the land campaign to be briefed. They always divided the two in their conversations, which was too bad, because they should have only been talking about one campaign.

Schwarzkopf generously lent us his airplane for our trip back to the States. We landed at Andrews Air Force Base in Maryland the night before our first briefing at the Pentagon. I was by myself on the air side—just me, my briefcase, and the "map-based" charts with acetate overlays handcrafted by my special planning group in the Black Hole.

On October 10, I briefed the Joint Chiefs in their special briefing room known as the Tank. Seats were few in the Tank so a Tank briefing was always considered the highest-level brief you could give in the Pentagon. Secretary Cheney was there, along with his deputy, Donald Atwood, and Undersecretary of Defense for Policy Paul Wolfowitz. Powell was there with his Vice Chairman, Admiral Jeremiah. Three service chiefs attended: the Army's General Carl Vuono; Admiral Frank Kelso; and Marine Corps General Al Grey. General Mike Loh attended for the Air Force. Also attending were the J3, Army Lieutenant General Thomas Kelly, who was in charge of operations; the Director of the Joint Staff, Air Force Lieutenant General Mike Carns; and the J2, Rear Admiral Mike McConnell, in charge of intelligence.

I began the briefing with an overview of Schwarzkopf's strategic air campaign. Attempting to make Phases I, II and III seamless, I took them through the same briefing I'd given Schwarzkopf: attacks on the integrated air defenses and key strategic targets the first night; a continuing campaign to gain air supremacy; degrading the NBC targets; and hitting the Republican Guard and other fielded Iraqi forces to attrit them to less than 50 percent strength before Phase IV, the ground campaign. I flashed up pictures of key targets and maps of the links among the Iraqi air defense nodes to illustrate how we'd take them out. A separate slide showed Poobah's Party: the mass of drones followed by HARMs shooters that would blow the Iraqi air defenders into submission, even while we were striking deep targets. But I made sure everyone understood this air campaign was riding on the back of stealth and precision, specifically as brought to life by the F-117.

The tank briefing was well received. Secretary Cheney seemed in favor of a strong, strategic air campaign. Atwood probed with a good question about how Saddam could derail our offensive campaign. Wolfowitz appeared to be impressed with the capabilities we could bring to bear. Other views were *'along service lines,'* I noted—including those of Powell.

Yet I noted afterward that the meeting was *'okay, not great.'* I felt the Chairman had cut me off before I really had a chance to discuss Phase III. As a result, Cheney did not get a true picture of what air power was doing to the Iraqi field army in that phase in sufficient detail.

Powell had a few words for me in the hallway as we walked toward his office.

"You've got to make sure when we go to the White House tomorrow that we don't oversell the air campaign because some of those idiots over there may convince the President to execute this before we're ready."

Next I was taken aside by Carns. The Director worked for the Chairman, coordinating the staff's activities. Carns' job was to make double sure I understood Powell's concerns before the White House meeting. "Your air campaign is too good," he told me. "The Chairman is afraid the President will tell us to execute. He wants you to go through the plan much faster and not be so convincing," Carns coached.

I couldn't quite believe what I was hearing. My response was curt.

I went on to tell Carns that I would shorten the briefing as requested, but I was not going to mislead the President about the capabilities of the offensive air campaign or make it sound more difficult to execute than I thought it really was. My immediate thought was: "I'll not compromise my integrity for the Chairman or anyone else. If the Chairman wants to brief the President himself that's fine by me."

In case I hadn't gotten the message by now, I heard it a third time from Johnston about an hour later, after he was released from a private meeting with Powell. That was enough! I gave Schwarzkopf a telephone call to discuss Powell's comments. Schwarzkopf was very direct: "Give the President the briefing you and I discussed. Let me deal with Powell."

Next, I paid a visit to the office of the Secretary of the Air Force, Dr. Donald Rice, on the fourth floor of the Pentagon. I vented a little more of my frustration with Powell by relating his comments to Rice, McPeak and Loh. However, the Secretary was mostly concerned about our needs. I told him my number one shortfall was SEAD assets. He and Loh (McPeak had not yet been confirmed) promised to work the problem. Rice was very direct and supportive of my efforts to get a factual briefing to the President the next day. He asked me to debrief him after the White House session. "I'm going to give the President a factual briefing and let the chips fall where they may," I said to them.

Briefing the President

Briefing the President in the White House Situation Room about our country going to war is a sobering experience. The room itself, as I remembered from earlier meetings in the White House, was just off a hallway in the glassed-in area for White House military communications. It did not hold very many people and so those seated at the table were all familiar.

Present for the 3 p.m. briefing on October 11, were Vice President Dan Quayle, Secretary of State James Baker, and Cheney. Powell was there, of course, along with National Security Adviser Brent Scowcroft, Deputy National Security Adviser Robert Gates and White House Chief of Staff John Sununu. He worked a stack of budget papers during my briefing but managed to stay tuned in and asked a question now and then. Johnston and Purvis sat in chairs along the wall.

Then, of course, there was President Bush. He was focused, although he looked tired. I stood about six feet from the President, at a slight angle, so everyone could see the charts. Before I began I had decided that I would lay everything on the table and not pull any punches.

My objective was to give him a briefing of which I could say: "As near as I can tell you now, this is exactly what I'm going to do when you give us the order to execute." I briefed the air campaign assuming that the President was going to make the decision to execute. I was basically giving him the option to make that decision any time he wanted to after October 15.

Bush paid close attention. I hadn't gone far before I realized that he had an understanding of air power execution that not very many people in politics have. I am sure his insight was based on his own experience as a naval aviator and as head of the CIA. Once I began, his military and intelligence experience came back to him, as was apparent by many insightful questions.

The plan for the briefing was the same as the day before: threat assessment by Francona, followed by me, with Purvis and the ground options next, and Johnston to wrap up with the slide requesting a second corps. During Purvis' brief I sat next to Gates, along the wall, and made notes on the comments and questions during my briefing.[4]

I was into the airfield attacks when Sununu popped his head up from the budget papers to ask, "What's a GR-1?" I told him it was the British Tornado strike aircraft.

Next came a slide of an Iraqi sector operations center, which was on the list of targets for the first strike. Bush questioned the thickness, surprised at the level of hardness, especially in the thick walls built over the top of the bunkers.

Baker asked, "Why do you need so many KC-10s?"

4. As soon as I got back to Riyadh I had the notes typed up, and I've drawn this account of the meeting from them.

"Primarily [for] support to the carriers but also for Air Force and Marine assets," I answered. I explained that at the time the F-15Es would be flying 1,100 miles to Baghdad from their base in Oman.

"Why are they based so far away?" Bush wanted to know. "Why not move them closer to the border?"

"The Saudis didn't want us in those airfields. They are using them to forward deploy their fighters," I replied.

Powell added, "We probably don't want them any closer because of the threat."

"Why are the carrier battle groups so far back and the *Wisconsin* so close?" was Bush's next question.

"Primarily due to Navy concern for safety of the carriers," I said.

"Also, as you know, the *Wisconsin* can stand a lot more punishment than the carrier groups," Powell told him.

Baker then asked, "How do you know they won't pick up F-117s? Did you fly them over Iraq?"

"No, sir," I said, but I explained Bullet's mission a few weeks earlier. "After air-to-air refueling I let him go north approximately 50 miles with IFF on, from there he flew parallel to the border using stealth characteristics for about five or six minutes, no indications Iraqis were seeing anything." I also told the President that the recent *Washington Post* article reporting the French could detect the F-117s was incorrect and this mission proved it.

The group seemed satisfied with the abilities of the F-117 and the discussion moved on.

"Are you sure the royal palace does not have symbolic value to Iraqi people?" asked Bush.

"I do not believe it does. I'm certain that it has no religious value."

Bush asked Powell to ensure no targets of religious significance were on the list.

"We've removed most of the targets in close proximity to shrines," I assured them. "We've also restricted run-in headings and selected the most accurate systems to avoid religious targets."

"We've worked that problem from the beginning," Powell told Bush.

"When are you attacking the SAMs?" said Baker.

I explained, "Sir, these arrows represent a sizable number of aircraft that are shooting armed missiles while attacks are being conducted. For example, this one arrow, west of Baghdad represents 35 to 40 airplanes, so the total answer is we're taking the SAMs out simultaneous with the leadership and the military targets."

The President asked, "what about TLAMs?"

"Their accuracy or the collateral damage?" I had to inquire.

"What about it hitting something else," Bush clarified.

"Sir, we are told by the technical experts that if they make it to the IP, the TLAMs have a .8 to .9 probability of kill. They normally go out of control in the first 20 minutes if they have a problem."

"What confidence is there?" Bush continued.

"We're putting a minimum of three of them on each target," I said, "for example, the power plants."

"How long for a TLAM to get to its target?" asked Baker.

Here I had to say, "I don't remember exactly; obviously it depends on whether they launch from the Med [Mediterranean Sea] or the Gulf. I believe it's in the 50-minute time frame." (Actually, it turned out to be 70 to 90 minutes.)

"Are you planning attacks from Turkey?" was Baker's next question.

"No," I said, "that's not part of our current plan; however, we do have an option to use the F-111s in Turkey if we are given the OK."

"Would it help?"

"Yes, significantly, since we would be attacking from two directions and complicating his air defense problems. Additionally, the distance from Turkey to all of the targets from Balad SE northward would be much shorter," I replied to Baker.

The President's next question was about Saddam. "What will he be able to do after Phase I?"

I said, "He will not be able to effectively communicate with his people—he will lose C2 to his forces and he will have significant problems reinforcing Kuwait because of LOC (lines of communication) cuts. He will have to deal with disruption throughout the country."

Baker remarked that the phrase "decapitate Saddam regime" was misleading.

"The intent of the slide is to indicate that he will have difficulty communicating and controlling his military and his people, and his people and his country will be visibly in disarray," I said.

I kept my answers conservative. I did not want to risk overstating anything to the President concerning Phase I. If anything, I understated the daylights out of it because I wanted to make sure that the President understood this was the bare minimum he should expect. It was not the optimum, but the bare minimum, because I didn't want him making a decision based on Phase I as the grandiose answer to everything. So, I chose my words very carefully.

I was now up to discussing Phase III, attrition of the Iraqi army. Phase III would be a seven-to-ten-day operation, I told the group.

"Does that include Phase I?" Sununu asked.

"No, the Phase III timeline is seven to ten days; Phase I will be occurring at low intensity during that time to keep Saddam from regaining essential military capabilities," I explained.

Sununu wanted to know about the minimum weather for laser weapons.

"Degradation becomes a major concern when the visibility is less than three miles," I answered.

"Do you have a plan to take hostages out of Kuwait?" asked Sununu.

"No," I said.

Powell jumped in quickly and said, "We're working that another way." At the time, I figured he was referring to the CIA or something I didn't know about.

Baker steered the discussion back to the campaign as a whole. "What is the projected loss rate for Phase I, II and III?"

"We project a loss of 10 to 15 aircraft for the first 24 hours, averaging out to significantly less over the first six days," I said. "Total aircraft losses could be as high as 40 aircraft for the entire Phase I. Phase II and III could result in the loss of an additional 40 aircraft."

Then Baker brought up grand strategy.

"What's the difference between Vietnam and Iraq?" he asked.

"First of all," I said, "we're being permitted to use full force to deal with the problem, not just clipping branches, but cutting the trunk," I said.

"Also, the logistics are a lot different," said Bush. "He had China and other unloading ports."

"Yes, that's very true," I said. "We have a total embargo and likewise we're striking his major LOCs, not over-flying them like we did the ships unloading at Haiphong Harbor."

Then Bush asked me: "What do you say to people who say Saddam will rise up out of the rubble on national TV and say, 'Here I am'?"

"He might do that but it won't be on his television or radio network. It will be with outside help," I said.

"We've got to be ready for that. We can't let people think we'll get him for sure," Powell commented. He was right about that. We weren't developing the necessary actions that would ensure that we did get him.

Cheney reiterated, "We've got to be careful not to lead people to expect Saddam to be eliminated personally in Phase I." I agreed with that.

I sat down when my briefing was over and the principals continued their freewheeling discussion. "Why do you think the Iraqis are so good?" Bush asked Powell. "My friend tells me once Phase I starts he will give up and run. He's not a strong person when the going gets tough."

"That must be your Bangladesh friend," Powell said to the President.

"You're right," Bush replied, "but he went to school with Saddam and knows him."

Bush then asked the most important question of the day: "Why not do Phase I, II and III and then stop?" I thought to myself, *brilliant, what insight.* Bush was trying to cover the spectrum in his own thought process. It was a logical question for the Commander in Chief to ask. Could his national objectives be accomplished before he irrevocably committed ground forces?

Too bad I was now seated on the side, and could only join the discussion to answer a direct question.

Powell quickly answered the President by saying, "You've got to be ready to do Phase IV because your objective won't be accomplished." It was a non-answer but, as I'm sure he intended, it tabled the issue. It was a technique he used adroitly when he did not support the thrust of a question.

A more truthful answer would have been, "We could certainly make an assessment following Phase I, II and III to determine which of your objectives have been accomplished before we begin Phase IV," rather than just flatly saying, "Your objectives won't be met."

Powell pressed ahead to his main point, telling the President he'd need one more corps to execute a flanking attack plan.

"What you've been briefed on so far is what's necessary for us to have a defensive operation if we're attacked," Powell said. That statement struck me as misleading. The air campaign was an offensive plan; it was what we were going to do whether they attacked or whether we attacked. It was the land campaign that was not ready at that point. Schwarzkopf had a lot more refining to do, and so he wanted another corps in theater before he went on the offensive. But Powell would never have characterized his strategic air campaign Phases I, II and III as "defensive."

'White House briefing was okay,' I wrote in my notes. I thought it went well in making sure that the President understood what our capabilities were. However, I didn't think it went well from a standpoint of giving the President a cohesive view. Once again the Chairman's comments had forestalled full discussion of the impact of air on the Iraqi army, especially during Phase III. In that sense the military had not served the President well that day.

The October 11 briefing to the President was a defining point for Operation Desert Storm. The offensive air campaign, in three phases, was a go. CENTCOM would get a second corps and encouragement to build a very different land attack. Schwarzkopf's theater campaign would go through all four phases, unless by chance, Saddam surrendered. Most of all, it was clear the President was prepared to take military action.

I spent part of the rest of my time in Washington touching my legislative liaison roots. I visited key members of Congress such as House Armed Services Chairman Les Aspin and the ranking Republican on his committee, Bill Dickson. I knew that Senator Sam Nunn was not being vocally supportive of the President at that time, so I wanted to do my part to make sure the House support stayed on track. I gave Aspin and his Chief of Staff, Rudy DeLeon, a run down of what I expected the results would be. I didn't hold anything back with Aspin. Anything he asked, I answered. I think the briefing contributed significantly to Aspin's steady support for Operation Desert Shield and, later, Desert Storm.

Being in Washington also gave me the chance to see my wife, Vicki, and my daughter, Tanya. My son, Brad, was in college. 'Nothing ever becomes more important than family,' I wrote in my notes as the trip ended. 'It was absolutely great to spend a little time with Vicki and Tanya . . . they are holding up very well, at least outwardly!' Yes, it deflates the warrior ego, but the fact is our wives and families are used to not having us around. I suspect they take separation better than we do.

POINT OF NO RETURN

Deptula had also been back in Washington at his regular job in Secretary Rice's office for a few weeks. Rice agreed that I could take Deptula back to Riyadh on my aircraft on October 15.

It was good to be back in the desert. Now I totally understood why tactical decisions made from Washington during a war usually turned out to be the wrong decisions. Washington simply did not look or feel the same as "in theater."

Rice visited us for a briefing on October 17. He was a great Secretary, a powerful mind who could remember something you'd briefed him on a chart eight months before like it was yesterday. He didn't let you get away with anything. I was pleased the briefings to him went well.

One of the things we demonstrated for him was the mission planning system and the capabilities it provided to the air campaign.

This system was pretty much entirely the brainchild of Captain Mike Cosby, a young F-16 pilot whom I'd pulled down from his squadron in Germany. The mission planning system was a critical tool for each sortie. It was an improvement on grease pencils, but like many of our computer systems then, it was anything but user-friendly. Fairchild built the system and one of their company representatives mentioned to me that there was a Captain Cosby—"Cos" to his buddies—stationed up at Hahn who was absolutely a genius on this stuff.

I called General Bob Oakes, the Commander of U.S. Air Forces, Europe, and said to him: "I don't know this captain. You probably don't know this captain. But I'm told he is very good with computer mission planning. I need him here." Oakes said he'd make it happen.

When Cosby arrived in early September we had no, and I mean *zero*, automated mission planning capability. Cosby installed the Mission Support System 2 (MSS2) in the Black Hole plus all the fighter units—ten separate locations. We could send mission planning data back and forth from the Black Hole to the fighter units in the 14th Air Division. All because of Cos. *'One of a kind . . . the world will never know unless I give him credit he deserves,'* I wrote in my diary at the time.

Preparing for War

In my mind, since the White House briefing, we were at the point of no return. It was time to act like we were going to war.

CENTAF was busy setting up an alternate command post in case the Royal Saudi Air Force headquarters was taken out. Where was this command post going to be? In a tent.

They had a screw loose, seriously. It was unbelievable. Saudi Arabia did not lack for suitable sites for an alternate command post. At several locations throughout the kingdom, the Saudis had built hardened aircraft shelters, designed to withstand bomb blast overpressure, complete with living quarters and 30 days' supply of food and water. Any one of them would be much more suitable than a tent.

So I had Tom Lennon set up an alternate command post in one of his shelters at the F-111 base in Taif. One whole side of the shelter duplicated all of the mission planning and other support material we had in the Black Hole. We even assigned a person to stay down there to keep it warm in case we needed to switch to it in a hurry. One night, I went down there myself and slept in the shelter just to make sure it was set up right.

Hunkering down in a tent wasn't the only brain-dead thing we were doing. For example, CENTAF had all the AWACS clustered at the same airbase in Riyadh. Every one of them. How could we be so cavalier about Saddam's capability to attack with chemical and biological weapons? The AWACS on the ground made a juicy target. In Vietnam they called them sapper attacks where the North Vietnamese or Viet Cong would scout out an area and then attack, creating chaos and destruction. A couple of Iraqi suicide jets could attack that base and wreak havoc. The AWACS and EW aircraft were under the control of 15th Air Division; if I'd owned them, I'd have moved them.

We just weren't being careful. When airborne, we let AWACS fly the exact same tracks 80 percent of the time, with refuelings at the same time and with only two or four F-15s airborne to protect them.

It was crazy. Saddam probably would not attack first unless he thought we were going to attack momentarily, but we still ought to be able to deal with his best punch. *'Bottom line—lack of preparation for Iraqi attack is naive and dumb, bordering on criminal negligence,'* I wrote.

On October 19, at two in the morning, I decided it was time to stop and assess where we were. We'd progressed from a retaliatory plan designed to last less than a week to a full scale Phase I, and done so impressively. SCATHE MEAN, airfield attacks, the plan to take down the Integrated Air Defense System (IADS), critical NBC targets—all was falling into place. My overriding priority was fine-tuning Phase II and III, which were slowly coming together. Phase IV, supporting the ground forces, remained disjointed.

'Most think Phase I and II will end the war,' I scribbled down. *'Although I would like for that to happen . . . risk is too high to assume.'* Plan for the worst, pray for the best was my motto. *'Paying more attention to Phase III and IV was essential,'* I wrote in my notes. *'Marathon not a dash.'*

I needed a sounding board, someone that was bright and loyal, and I knew just the individual. Rick Lewis was a bright, taciturn fighter pilot who'd been raised in the Nevada desert. I'd known him before, back when we worked on tactical air power and theater warfare assessments in the Pentagon in the early 1980s. He was now a lieutenant colonel on the staff at Ramstein, but my needs were greater than any in Germany.

I called him at his office in Germany. He was excited. I told him to keep his mouth shut about it until I could talk to General Oakes. *'We are fortunate I can move him to help . . . he understands that planning and execution must be seamless,'* I wrote in my diary after talking to him. *'We are not servicing targets, we are planning a campaign from strategic to tactical . . . Rick is one of the few that totally understand—or at least, he and I are on the same wavelength.'*

Meanwhile, I told Lewis to get up to speed on the work we'd done so far by going back to Washington to see Checkmate, J-33, Air Force Studies and Analyses and the other intelligence shops. He made the trip in November, when Deptula was in Washington for a few weeks. I told

Lewis to go see him for a brief on the campaign plans. The two had never met. Later they told me a funny story: Deptula was flabbergasted when Lewis arrived at his Pentagon office wanting to talk about super-secret war planning. How had the word leaked out about the super-secret war plans? Deptula didn't know whether to brief Lewis or call the Air Force security police to investigate him. Finally, after invoking my name several times, Lewis convinced Deptula that he was trustworthy. I wish I'd been there to see the looks on their faces. They quickly got over the initial shock, of course, and a good thing too, for these were two people whose talents I needed very much.

50-Percent Attrition

Meanwhile, I'd asked Major Mark "Buck" Rogers to have Checkmate build a briefing to help show the effects of air in Phase III. We'd visited Warden's Checkmate cell on the Air Staff during my Washington trip. Also, after my conversation with Lewis, he reminded me that Checkmate had a model to evaluate air operations based on a simulation using inputs from sample air tasking orders and estimated threat data. In fact, this model had been Lewis' baby when he was a captain on the staff and he'd passed care and feeding of it on to Mac Sikes, a bright young major. Using this model, Mac had come up with all sorts of estimates, including air attrition on Iraqi forces in the Kuwaiti Theater of Operations (KTO).

The briefing laid out six days for Phase I, one day for Phase II and 15 days for Phase III. However, the significant element was that Checkmate highlighted 20–40 percent attrition of each of the dozen Iraqi divisions then thought to be in Kuwait. They weren't even looking at the Republican Guard yet. (Although the Republican Guard had led the invasion, they'd switched places later, pulling back to more strategic positions in an arc along the curved western and northern border of Kuwait. The Republican Guard was mostly in Iraqi territory.)

I wanted to figure out a way to articulate better the impact of air power in Phase II and III on the Iraqi forces—and I wanted to do it in language that could not be disputed.

So I visited Purvis on October 20. After the White House briefing, Schwarzkopf and his team of planners had new guidance to implement. Since October 15, Purvis had been leading the team sketching out a two-corps plan, and the next day he was scheduled to brief it to Schwarzkopf.

In the plan, a new, heavy corps would now attack from the west, while XVIII Corps raced around to the left, then both would turn east to hit the Republican Guard. They'd seal off forces retreating from Kuwait and block the road across the Tigris and Euphrates to Baghdad.

I had the Checkmate estimate of 20 to 40 percent attrition in mind. Was that what the Army wanted?

"When is a U.S. Army Division considered to be not combat-effective because of attrition?" I asked Purvis.

"There is no black and white answer," he told me. "We teach at Leavenworth and Carlisle that it may occur as low as 20 to 30 percent or as late as 60 percent, but I think most people agree it is between 40 percent and 60 percent."

Fifty percent appeared to be the number everyone would accept. Purvis said 50 percent was great. Later I wrote, *'I'm going to decree that we will attrit enemy ground forces 50% (people, armor, and artillery).'*

This would mean a ground campaign timed and based on the results of an air campaign. *'Army will never admit it after the war,'* I predicted in my notes.

Schwarzkopf liked the Purvis group's two-corps plan. He imagined the plan unfolding as the two corps: "I sit on Highway 8 . . . I've defeated him in his mind; I've threatened his Republican Guard, now I'll destroy it."[1]

It put the heat on the Republican Guard Forces Command (RGFC). "Unquestionably, the Republican Guard would be the center of gravity and the main objective," the Army history *Certain Victory* summed up later.[2] They briefed Powell who came to Riyadh on October 22 and 23 and he liked the new plan, too. "Tell me what you need," he said. Schwarzkopf was going to get the second corps.

After these meetings, it was a race to tab forces for deployment and finalize the plans. The two-corps ground war now loomed so large that I grew concerned that the ground-war focus was actually starting to limit the President's options. The mindset of the CINC was still ground, ground, ground. During Powell's visit, there hadn't been one single question about air, except for hand wringing about the poor intelligence on biological and chemical targets.

1. Richard M. Swain, *Lucky War: Third Army in Desert Storm.* (Fort Leavenworth, KS: US Army Command and General Staff College Press, 1997), p. 83.
2. *Certain Victory,* p. 128–9.

The two-corps plan might indeed crush the RGFC, but we might well be able to deal them a lethal blow before they ever got to Phase IV. I had to demonstrate that to Schwarzkopf. But I didn't have the right product to do it.

My instincts told me Checkmate and RAND, who'd done their own analysis, were being far too optimistic. Besides, the CINC was going to make his decisions (such as when to launch Phase IV) based on what I said, not what Checkmate or RAND said.

"This is just not right," I told Rogers. "What we need are the assumptions that were used." I had them radically change the assumptions and make them more conservative than was reasonable. We tinkered with the battlefield configuration of Iraqi forces and how densely they'd be spaced. Then, at the end of it all, I had them insert a final assumption dictating that one out of every four airplanes that took off just would not get to the target. It could be for any reason: weather, maintenance, attrition, whatever. I didn't care what the reason was. I told them to just assume they wouldn't get there. That didn't go over very well in the Air Force but it did inject realism in the model.

'Key is selling the CINC,' my notes said on October 24, 'assumptions must be conservative to the point of insane!'

Checkmate ran more cases, and sent me the result. By November 7, I had a product to brief to Horner, and he liked it. He told me to dig deeper analyzing artillery and to please not "poke the Army in the eye" by touting air power. We also decided to call Phase III "Preparing the Battlefield." We agreed that this was different than Phase I, which needed careful orchestration to take out IADS and NBC and other targets very quickly. With Phase III, as long as the Coalition ground forces weren't in the fight yet, we could take our time and work over the target set.

Or so we thought. Phase III would turn out to be a lot harder than we knew.

For now, we had a good plan. Even with conservative assumptions, the analysis showed Phase III should be impressive. In the worst case, the briefing estimated 50 percent of the armor destroyed in eight to nine days. The objective of destroying the Republican Guard should be well within reach of the theater campaign.

I got a nice piece of news about this time. I'd been selected for promotion to Major General—my second star. It was still a secret—general officer promotion board results were absolutely not supposed to be disclosed until Congress and the President had approved the list, which often took months. In practice, commanders generally made a discrete phone call to the lucky candidates the minute the board lets out. (No such courtesy to those who hadn't made it—for them, no news was bad news.) I couldn't say anything to anybody yet, but I did jot down in my diary: '$1 + 1 = 2$.' It felt good.

Warriors and Politicians

Part of the art of war is unity of command. No matter how hard we work it, there is often something critical that can slip through the cracks unless the hard questions are asked before the shooting starts.

As of late October, Schwarzkopf could order every aircraft, ship, and soldier in theater to attack, with one exception: He could not order the launch of TLAMs and CALCMs himself. I'd failed to point out this potential problem to Schwarzkopf in my briefings on Phase I. Under procedures in place at the time, all Schwarzkopf could do was notify the Joint Staff of an "expeditious request" for the TLAMs and CALCMs to be fired. That was a long way from Schwarzkopf being able to order it.

The TLAMs were becoming more and more critical. Since Saddam had dispersed his aircraft, we'd had to move some of the F-111Fs to those targets instead of using them to back-up the TLAM strikes. A delay in execution could be a disaster.

Horner agreed it was a problem but he was not optimistic that the CINC would force the issue with Powell. I disagreed.

So I went to the CINC.

"Today, you do not have the authority to direct the Navy to launch TLAMs," I told him.

"What do you mean?" he demanded.

"I want you to pick up the telephone and get the Chairman to tell somebody on his staff that you have the authority to release TLAMs and you don't need anybody else's approval. I want that available for you from day one, before we even start the air campaign."

Schwarzkopf called the Chairman, and was satisfied they would be launched when he directed. Another potential glitch avoided!

All that fall I was still itchy about Saddam's ability to be disruptive if he wanted to. On November 1, for example, two Iraqi Mirage F-1s and one MiG-25 Foxbat penetrated Saudi Arabian airspace. One of our F-15s was within 30 seconds of shooting when the Foxbat abruptly turned north.

CENTCOM's response to this incident annoyed me to no end. They decided to make the rules for our pilots more restrictive by laying out a no-shoot zone extending 15 nautical miles south of the Saudi border. I couldn't believe it. The Iraqi F-1s were not flying for fun. They were trying to learn how to do intercepts without their ground controllers—a new tactic for them, but one they'd be forced to use if we took out their air defenses. That wasn't something we wanted them to master. This was the eighth time in 11 days that the Iraqis had flown the exact same profile—and the third time they'd actually crossed the border. It didn't do us any good to treat them with kid gloves. Strength and action were the only things respected in this region. This was a case of warriors trying to be politicians.

The reverse happened, too: Politicians tried to be generals. In the swirl of planning, the "what if" was alive and working over time. On November 3, I got a call from Gary Trexler, an Air Force lieutenant colonel working in Atwood's office. He said Cheney wanted to know what would happen if we had the 82nd Airborne drop in to take the airfields at H2 and H3 and hold them. Could we support the paratroopers and prevent emergency extraction?

"Yes, until Saddam moves a couple of his Republican Guard divisions," I answered. You can't say that you can put in the 82nd Airborne, as light as they are, capture H2 and H3, and then have air power absolutely guarantee they wouldn't be in danger. If Saddam wanted to run enough of his armored Republican Guard divisions in that direction, eventually they were going to break through. We could have destroyed most of the Republican Guard with air power but I could not be 100-percent certain it would be enough.

'The above sounds like civilian politicians trying to become tactical generals again. Johnson administration trying to raise its head,' according to my diary. Cheney, frustrated with what he'd been presented in October, was giving the planners a good kick-start. *'Chairman probably does not know about this brainstorm to any extent. He deserves this problem because of the limited options he's provided Cheney,'* I concluded.

But then this whole transition to the two-corps strategy carried parochial and political overtones. After hints about a force build-up from both Cheney and the President, and a visit by Secretary of State Baker to get King Fahd's permission, Bush formally announced on November 8 the plan to deploy VII Corps to the theater.

Now we were all expected to build up our forces accordingly. Schwarzkopf had put it in a message on November 3: "Although there is no definitive theater campaign concept for a wide-ranging, large-scale military offensive against Iraq, it is prudent that we consider such an operation and look at associated requirements and capabilities as soon as possible."

Well, I had a wide-ranging offensive theater campaign plan called Phases I, II, and III. This irritated me. But the larger point, as I wrote in my diary that day, was that the Chairman was now going to force a massive force build-up immediately following the election. *'Probably will double Army/Navy/AF Forces . . . a waste . . . this is a force structure issue not an Iraq warfighting issue . . . although it will be portrayed as the latter!'*

I wanted all the things that could kill people or that could help me find out who I should kill. I didn't want to look good in the shower, which is what the F-16 was best for at that time. I wanted more F-117s, F-15Es and F-111s, but I was sure we'd get issued F-16s. I stalled as long as I could. On the 7th, Horner finally caught up with me and held my feet to the fire.

"We're going to have to request more forces, period. I don't care whether you want them or not. You decide what you want or I'll decide for you," he said ominously. "And start off with 48 more F-16s."

I figured Schwarzkopf was tired of listening to the reasons we did not need more forces and had finally told Horner to shut up and color on this issue. I'd have to do the same. *'Final answer: he's the CINC and you can only have one at a time. Just as it must be,'* I noted in my diary.

To make matters worse, something truly valuable was being taken away from me: Larry Henry. He'd been moved to a new job in charge of plans for our training command. His replacement would be Glenn Profitt. This was so dumb. We were drawing close to the start of a war and the Air Force, in its wisdom, wanted to rotate the mastermind of SCATHE MEAN and the SEAD support for Phase I and send him to train junior officers. I called the Chief to complain but he told me to let it go. "Profitt will be fine," McPeak said. I had no doubt that Profitt would be good, but Henry was 100 percent up to speed, and portions of Phases I, II, and III were his ideas. I regretted the move, writing in my diary *'. . . I must admit—the Army would never make such a move.'*

Theater Campaign

By November 7, Schwarzkopf was preparing his full theater campaign brief. I told my Executive Officer, Rodgers Greenawalt, to be sure to change all our slide titles to "Theater Campaign" in line with the CINC's brief. *'Everyone must have the correct focus,'* I wrote.

Schwarzkopf's essential outline of the theater campaign was just as he described it to me during that late August telephone call while I was still on the *LaSalle*. *'Never a change . . . I admire him for his vision and leadership . . . it is his refusal to accept the possibility that Phase IV just might not be required . . . that profoundly troubles me! Most likely it will . . . to some degree . . . but it is not a certainty.'* As it turned out, Schwarzkopf was correct in saying there were things that had to be done on the ground. And we had a lot to learn about executing Phases I, II and III, far more than we knew.

The next week, I flew out to the USS *Blue Ridge* to see Admiral Mauz, and keep him informed. Not long after, the Navy rotated Mauz and brought in Vice Admiral Stan Arthur. Stan was a gem: bright, a straight shooter, and easy to work with even on the toughest of issues.

My next step was to brief Lieutenant General John Yeosock, Commander, Third Army, on the plans for Phase III attacks on the Republican Guard and Kuwait. Yeosock's Third Army was also known as ARCENT, the equivalent to Horner's CENTAF.

From Yeosock I learned that the ground forces needed a minimum of 14–18 days to get in place for Phase IV after we started Phase I. Schwarzkopf insisted not a single truck or soldier could move into position until we'd taken out Phase I targets and blinded Saddam's view of the theater. Then, they'd need two weeks to cross the two corps into the starting positions for what they were calling the Great Wheel attack.

During this briefing to Yeosock, I had another agenda. I *had* to get the Phase II attrition brief to Schwarzkopf, preferably as the introduction to Yeosock's Phase IV ground campaign. How else could the CINC balance the effects of the two? I wanted him to see the destruction of Iraqi forces in Phase II as part and parcel of Phase IV. I didn't want to repeat the same mistake I felt we made in Washington by fragmenting the theater campaign too much.

Yeosock agreed to ask Schwarzkopf to add my briefing in as the preamble to Phase IV when the commanders met again to review the campaign planning.

I also learned around this time that Schwarzkopf had decided to appoint as his deputy a three-star army general. What had happened to "jointness?" I didn't really care if they made the deputy a Navy admiral with air experience or an Air Force person; I could even have accepted a Marine airman, but I could not accept the fact he put a ground Army guy in as deputy. It was just absolutely a mockery of joint operations.

My personal pique aside, the decision to appoint a deputy was significant because it meant Schwarzkopf had decided to retain the position of Joint Force Land Component Commander himself, on top of his role as CINC. It was a "tough decision" that "created numerous challenges and difficulties," as one of the Army histories later said.[3] Schwarzkopf's reasoning was that he didn't want to clutter the chain of command by adding yet another layer. However, this meant he'd have to focus hard on the employment of the land force in addition to his original duties as the Joint Force Commander. Easy enough in the planning stages, but would it work in war?

Breathing Fire

On November 14, Schwarzkopf called in his commanders at the division level and above and told them the prime objective of this new two-corps plan would be the destruction of the Republican Guard.[4] "I knew this would be my most important meeting of the war," he later wrote.

Twenty-two generals and admirals arrived in Riyadh for this top-secret session. Horner and I were there.

"We are going on the offensive and I want everyone thinking that way," he began. He warned us that he was "appalled" by the lack of operational security in Washington. No more Dugan-style leaks. "No flag officer or officer will discuss military operations, military capabilities, or answer what if questions," Schwarzkopf ordered. "I'll be brutal with anyone who violates this."

Schwarzkopf spelled out the national objectives as unconditional withdrawal from Kuwait, restoring the Kuwaiti government, and making sure Western hostages were released by Iraq. He identified the centers of gravity as Saddam, the chemical, biological and missile threats, and the Republican Guard. He assessed Iraq's strengths—their numbers—and their weaknesses, including centralized command and limited air capability. In his view, *our* strengths began with "superior air capability" plus technological edge and leadership edge—at all levels.

3. *Certain Victory*, p. 141.
4. *Lucky War: Third Army in Desert Storm*, p. 90.

Schwarzkopf listed his campaign objectives:

• Attack leadership and command and control
• Gain and maintain air supremacy
• Cut totally supply lines
• Destroy chemical, biological, and nuclear capability
• Destroy Republican Guard

He put the last one down as a Phase IV objective, causing me to write in my notes '*CINC is going to be surprised at who destroys Republican Guard.*'

Then Schwarzkopf went through each phase of his theater campaign plan. "If you saw a detailed briefing of Phase I, you would be proud . . . it is awesome," he told the group of mostly land force commanders. He graciously acknowledged both Horner and me for preparing the plan. He skipped quickly through Phase II, Air Supremacy in the KTO, emphasizing that it would achieve total freedom from air threats for air and ground movement. Phase III, Battlefield Preparation, he described as shaping the battlefield.

Then it was on to Phase IV, the ground attack. Here Schwarzkopf said he expected the Republican Guard to counterattack to the southwest. "As Churchill said, 'Even the most brilliant tactician must occasionally think of the enemy,'" Schwarzkopf quoted.

The Army generals were sitting on the edge of their chairs waiting to hear what their division's mission would be. It was a tour de force as he described the four-pronged attack with the Marines pinning the forces in Kuwait, the Coalition pressing toward Kuwait City, and the two U.S. corps driving north on the left then pivoting east for the kill.

"I am probably going to send the XVIII Airborne Corps very deep," he said. Lieutenant General Gary Luck would then hook around to the east to join the "main attack on the Iraqi Army." Franks commanded VII Corps. "I think it's pretty obvious what your mission is going to be," Schwarzkopf told him, "attack through here and destroy the Republican Guard."[5]

"Destroy" was the operative word. "Not delay, capture, drive-out, but destroy, destroy," Schwarzkopf thundered.

"Once the attack in the KTO is over," he said, "XVIII and VII must be

5. *It Doesn't Take a Hero*, pp. 382–3.

ready to drive for Baghdad. I don't think it will ever come to that, but we must be ready." He also stressed that Arab forces would liberate Kuwait City.

Logistics would be "the long pole in the tent," Schwarzkopf said. He told his ground commanders to start offensive training now and get the juices flowing. Between February 10 and 19 was the probable start date.

"As long as I am CINC we are going to do Phases I, II, III, and IV in that order," Schwarzkopf declared. "If I am told to go with Phase IV early I'll say no."

"Remember this one last point," he told us. "In order for this to succeed it is going to take killer instinct—bayonet in the teeth—by all our forces, especially the leaders. If you have one with killer instincts missing get rid of him now—there will be no probing—'we will get to the target' attitude is a must! Attack, attack, attack, and destroy every step of the way—the prestige of our nation is on our shoulders and we will not fail—we dare not fail; we cannot fail; we will not fail."

The ground commanders surged forward for a closer look at the 15-foot briefing map. Schwarzkopf had put high-voltage passion into it and the ground commanders would carry the electricity back to their own commands. It was a great pep talk. I liked that he'd finally acknowledged the necessity of air power.

The main thing I disagreed with in his assessment was the implication that the Republican Guard would move southwest and close in for a fight. I told him if the Republican Guard did that, they would all die in the desert. Moving armor was easier to hit. The best thing that can ever happen to us is if they tried to move across the desert.

Also, I noticed he'd put the Phase IV start date pretty close to the start of Phase I. That window was too close for comfort.

His briefing made it absolutely clear that the Republican Guard was the focus of the theater campaign. The plan at this stage envisaged the ground attack taking up to two weeks, with the potential for another four-week consolidation phase to wipe out the Republican Guard. When President Bush came to visit the troops over Thanksgiving, Schwarzkopf gave him a range of estimates for a war as short as three days or as long as several months—with an in-between position of about three weeks.

What still troubled me was whether Schwarzkopf would give air the time to work and be confident enough to rely on Phase III to shape his Phase IV. I wrestled with it in my diary: '100% certain CINC and I both *want minimum loss of life . . . issue is how to accomplish . . . we must delay ground campaign to maximum . . . Phase I/II/II disrupt-destroy—maybe retreat and surrender . . . God as my witness . . . my every action has been focused on one objective . . . No Force-On-Force Bloodbath of soldiers and marines . . . I must not change . . . I will not change . . . God, I ask for your guiding hand!'*

For me, the struggle centered on whether Schwarzkopf would take the time to let the air power in Phase I, II, and III unleash its full fury. The CINC was mightily aware that the Iraqis outnumbered the Coalition. Army doctrine called for an overwhelming force ratio for a successful attack, something on the order of 3:1 or even 4:1 against defending enemy forces. Even with a second corps added in, the Coalition ground forces would technically be outnumbered about 2:1. Yet there were mitigating factors. The CINC knew we had built a powerful air campaign. The Air Force would work on objectives the ground forces couldn't reach, such as NBC targets. It would also, according to all the analysis, dismantle Iraq's divisions in the field.

Did he really believe that at the end of Phase III we would be facing a much-degraded enemy? We might even hit them so hard they would give up. More than likely, we'd need ground action, but all my analysis showed, and I believed in my heart, it was not going to be an apocalyptic battle—not unless he rushed it.

No one—not among the senior officers, anyway—was trying to set-up some air vs. ground theoretical fight. We had enough on our hands. I just wanted to get beyond the fragmentation in our plans and to be sure Schwarzkopf really knew what we'd deliver. I believed Schwarzkopf could rely on the air component to more than even the odds, and I wanted to be sure he believed and embraced that, too. My purpose in taking this Phase III attrition briefing to him was to put in his mind a very vivid image of just what the air component was going to do to Saddam's army.

One person who was truly sensitive to the balance of air and ground was President Bush. I'd seen it at the White House when he'd asked if Phase I, II, and III of the theater campaign would do the job. Bush was asking the same questions on October 30 when Powell briefed him on the latest developments with the ground options. Bush asked about air power: "Are you sure that won't do it?" After the war, Bush said: "I never considered seriously the possibility of an 'air-only' campaign. There was much discussion about what an air campaign might accomplish—and that it might be enough to convince Saddam to pull out. But from the outset, I thought we should plan on the assumption that Saddam would resist to the end and develop our force requirements on that basis."[6] As was clear in the October 11 briefing, Bush wanted the balance right.

About this time it had become clear, on a daily basis, that I had another strong player on my staff. Sam Baptiste was already part of CENTAF and had deployed forward. He'd been helping me work the Republican Guard and KTO forces problem. Now I wrote in my diary: *'Baptiste should have been inner circle from day one. Massive mistake on my part. Superior mind. No agendas. He's a real warrior.'* Another thing I liked about Sam was he didn't live and breathe strategic attack. That was just what I needed. *'I have enough zealots,'* I wrote. *'Baptiste's understanding of air power across the spectrum of conflict is second to none. Plus he's a super people person . . .'* When the war started, Baptiste would be the head of targeting for the KTO cell.

On Sunday, November 18, I briefed Schwarzkopf on Phase III. I was still troubled about meshing Phase III and Phase IV. I was the lead-off brief before a small group session with his senior ground commanders. Schwarzkopf was still very much in the Patton frame of mind after the briefing to the commanders four days earlier. He started by berating everyone about their lack of progress on their schemes of maneuver, then turned to me and asked:

"Buster, what have you got?"

"I want to brief you on the expected results of Phase III," I said.

Here's what I briefed. I assumed each aircraft flying a sortie would kill one target. For example, an F-16 armed with three Mavericks and five cluster bombs would hit only one tank. The F-15E, F-111 and A-10 with their different armaments would still kill only one tank per sortie. The F/A-18 would kill just one artillery tube per sortie. And of the 600 aircraft we flew, a quarter of them would get no kills at all.

The results? The Iraqi forces in Kuwait would be attrited to 50 percent in 10 to 12 days. The Republican Guard would be attrited to 50 percent in four to five days. Total time for the two: about three weeks. The model had applied 600 sorties a day against the fielded forces.

"Those assumptions appear about right to me," Schwarzkopf deadpanned.

6. *The Generals' War*, p. 139–140.

Then he laughed. So I knew he believed. My conservative assumptions paid off. Schwarzkopf realized that if I had erred, I had erred in being too conservative. No doubt in his mind, because he would never have laughed if he hadn't.

After my briefing I wrote a little note, *'I was reminded once again a lot of truth is shown in jest.'* The bottom line was Schwarzkopf was comfortable with what I was telling him. He trusted my assessment.

"Phase III looks good," he said when I finished. "That's okay, no problem." That's what he usually said. At first I was pleased. I'd gotten through to him. Then I stayed for Yeosock's Phase IV briefing.

'Once again . . . unmitigated disaster' was what I wrote in my notes.

Schwarzkopf beat up his ground commanders pretty hard in an effort to get what he wanted. "The Arabs must have a larger role," he told Yeosock. Then came questions and commands: "Why are we fighting the main Iraqi force . . . let's go around. Books I've read say force on force only as a last resort. Go west . . . stop trying to force everyone into a narrow Kuwait approach."

Afterwards it was hard for me to understand why ARCENT was not listening more to the CINC's guidance. The fact was, Schwarzkopf had already thought out most of what he wanted long before Third Army started making charts. Schwarzkopf had talked to me personally on at least two occasions about having the 24th Infantry Division race north and east to block everything off so nothing could go back toward Baghdad. He already knew the 24th Division was going to go around. Schwarzkopf had also always planned to have a second corps go up at an angle and then turn right. The "high diddle diddle, straight up the middle" label from Washington was never his intent—but he hadn't been in Washington. Now, in mid-November, he just wanted a functional plan. His only concern was getting those two corps positioned and doing that cross-corps maneuver.

I could not deny it: Despite his positive comments, he wasn't going to rely on Phase III to make this job easier, at least not in front of his ground commanders. *'Comments of CINC still show he deeply doubts air capability,'* was my memorandum for the record.

Saudi Liaisons

The next day, I had a different audience: our liaisons to the Royal Saudi Air Force (RSAF), our hosts. Brigadier General Ahmed Sudairy was the Deputy for Operations of the RSAF. His boss, General Ahmed Al

Behery, was Horner's counterpart. Sudairy was mine. In the Black Hole we now had two younger RSAF officers. The audience that day was Sudairy, Colonel Saud Bedaiwi, Lieutenant Colonel Mohammed Al-Ayeesh, Major Abdul Hameed Al-Qadhi and Captain Turki Bandar Abdul Aziz. The two younger officers, Al-Qadhi and Turki, were now in the Black Hole with us.

I briefed them on Phases I, II and III of the theater campaign. They liked it. After the briefing, Sudairy had one comment.

"I am concerned that you will not finish this campaign and Saddam will still be in a position of significant military strength," he said quietly.

How prophetic he was. You have to call a spade a spade. The only thing Sudairy was concerned about was exactly what happened. They knew us and they knew the Arabs and they knew Saddam.

That day in November, Sudairy was hinting they'd be very supportive of us making sure we took Saddam out as long as we didn't make a big deal out of it and as long as we did it in a way where we didn't have a half a million Army troops in Baghdad. The Saudis weren't in favor of the U.S. taking Baghdad, but they were very much in favor of getting rid of Saddam.

After the meeting, Sudairy talked to me privately. "I believe the Soviets and French are providing information to Iraq," he cautioned. I wasn't as concerned about that as Sudairy was, but his comment caused me to take notice. For all his formal demeanor, Sudairy was a source of reliable information, and he was willing to share it to help the common cause. He could make things happen. I had a feeling I'd be seeing a lot of Sudairy in the weeks ahead.

That same day, I got an intelligence briefing that made my blood boil. It painted a picture of the Iraqi Air Force that was completely inaccurate. To listen to intelligence, you'd have thought the Iraqis were the Thunderbirds. They said their best, most experienced pilots were in the Mirage F-1s. True, but despite the recent border forays, they didn't fly enough to be good. It was also true the Iraqis liked to fly at 15,000 to 26,000 feet. Good for them. But I did not want our fighter pilots concentrating between 15,000 and 26,000 feet as they get hosed from above and below. I refused to even let this briefing go to the wings. It was counter to my whole strategy. I *wanted* the Iraqis to fly because I knew we'd shoot them down in a hurry. If they stayed on the ground in those shelters we'd have to go bomb them one at a time.

Pacific Wind

From November 22 through December 6, I was in Washington to get the latest on several highly classified "black" programs that might help in the upcoming campaign. Black programs were so named for the same reason we called our special planning group the Black Hole—nothing was supposed to get out. That was prudent in peacetime but if we were going to war I needed to know everything I could about those black programs.

At the Riyadh Royal Saudi Air Base, I literally passed Major General John Corder on the flightline. Corder was coming in to be the two-star Deputy for Operations to Horner. He was a warfighter, through and through, and a good choice. While I was gone, he'd look over the plans to date. For a moment I regretted that—I wanted to be there with him—then I realized that ego aside, it would be much better for Corder to have a fresh look, while I was out of the theater.

On the airplane flying back to Washington with me was a young F-15E pilot with a special mission. The commander of the special operations forces had received tasking on October 15 to put together a plan to rescue the American personnel at the embassy in Kuwait. The date struck me—it was four days after the October 11 meeting at the White House, when Powell had indicated to the President he already had a plan in the works. It may have been, but the first action was tasked by the Joint Staff four days later.

So we got to work on a plan called Pacific Wind. Major General Wayne Downing, the head of the Joint Special Operations Command, was absolutely one of the sharpest Army senior officers I'd ever met. He was very committed to special ops, and if we had listened to him earlier we would have had a lot more capability in theater. I'm very much a special ops advocate because special ops get results with a minimum loss of life. Anything that has that ability, I'm for it. Downing and I got along extremely well; never had a cross word on anything.

Downing had a plan to extract the hostages from Kuwait City using helicopters. The first time I met with his team on Pacific Wind I said, "You've got to tell me everything you want to do, and then you've got to let me give you my thoughts on how I can best help with the mission and save lives." He gave me the full brief.

"You see the hotel sitting right beside the embassy?" I asked. "What we need to do is put three 2,000-pound bombs in that hotel as the helicopters are coming in. And they must be dropped by F-117s."

Downing's team had not envisioned F-117s being involved in this.

"The reason we need F-117s is accuracy. So that means it also has to be done when the weather's good. So this is going to be a weather-contingent operation." They had doubts but I convinced them it was worth it.

"When the F-117s put three 2,000-pound bombs in that building, your people are not going to have to worry about security forces coming from that building. You're just not going to have to worry about it. In fact, I think we probably can do it with two 2,000-pound bombs but I want the third guy sitting out here watching, and if those two don't hit where we want them to, then he'll drop the third bomb."

Downing had a very good mind. Working together, we created some diversionary attacks a couple blocks away with the F-15Es going low-level down the boulevard throwing down cluster bombs and other ordnance just to create a diversion in front of the helicopters. Back in Florida, they created a mock-up of the embassy buildings so they could rehearse the mission.

My special passenger, the Strike Eagle pilot, was going to lead that portion of Pacific Wind if we got the order to execute. At least *one* of my fighter pilots had to be there to practice with the snake-eaters.

It was quite an ambitious plan. Downing and I were going to supervise it from the back of a special C-130 flying off the Kuwaiti coast. But the timeline was tough. The helicopters were too vulnerable. I think that Downing deep inside felt that, too. If the choice was to let the Iraqis start executing our people or taking the risk to get them out, I would have been all in favor of Pacific Wind. But it was definitely a high-risk mission. When you've got AAA and everything set up on the beach right in front of the embassy, and when you've got the security police in the next building and you've got the compound surrounded and the whole town's full of Iraqis and you're going to go in and rescue 28 people, no matter how you plan it, and try to make the odds come over to your side, there are just too many moving parts. It was high risk. Very high risk. Do I think we would have gotten in there and would have gotten the majority of the people out safely? Yes. Do I think we'd have lost people? Without a doubt.

On December 6, I wrote in my diary: '*Pacific Wind . . . I hope we never execute.*' Amazingly, that very day, Saddam announced he would release all Western hostages in Kuwait City.

As for the rest of my trip, it was filled with productive meetings at Defense Intelligence Agency (DIA), CIA, the Pentagon and several other places. I drove down the parkway to Mount Vernon to talk with my friend and mentor, retired General Bill Kirk. I had unbelievable faith in him and his warlike mind. He single-handedly revolutionized the way air power used electronic warfare during Vietnam. His thumbs-up gesture following our discussion was very comforting.

I briefly stopped in Cheney's outer office to say hello, as a courtesy. He was just on his way to another meeting and I took a moment to thank him for being hard-nosed about letting the war be run from the Gulf. I assured him that we wouldn't let him down.

I solidified my relationship with the Joint Chiefs J-2, Rear Admiral Mike McConnell in several long meetings. One of the many things we discussed was our capability in information warfare. There were resources we were going to exploit—ways to use computers, and so forth, that were quite new to warfare.

After three days of briefings on our most sensitive, highly classified intelligence and systems, McConnell teased me: "Buster, you are now the single most lucrative national security target in the free world. Don't you forget that!"

The truth was it was McConnell who was invaluable: 'He will never know how important he has been and will be to our overall success,' I wrote down on my way back to Riyadh. In Washington, I took no notes. I promised myself: 'Not one note until I returned to Riyadh . . . you think different when you are not in Theater!'

Precious Systems

One disturbing element of my time in Washington was that I found the Air Force a bit reluctant to let me use some of their most precious new systems. A case in point was JSTARS. McPeak took me aside to make sure I would only request JSTARS if it was absolutely essential, not just "nice to have." JSTARS was a phenomenal platform for tracking moving targets on the ground. It was still being tested, and the Air Force had only one, extremely expensive platform at that moment. No one was completely sure it would work, and the Air Staff certainly did not want to risk getting it shot up.

JSTARS could tip us off to any Iraqi ground force movement in strength and potentially save hundreds of lives. For me, that's where the discussion ended—it was essential! However, when I got back to Riyadh,

Horner mentioned JSTARS to me, and it was clear they'd gotten to him too, to persuade us not to request it. I hated to go against the Chief, but I had to have it, ready or not. I was sure the CINC would understand and support my desire to use it in the war.

Another new capability was the F-15E and I got hints that the Air Force would like me to keep the Strike Eagles in a soft environment. Again, they didn't want to lose any. I was curious to see just how good the F-15E really was. I arranged to visit Seymour Johnson Air Force Base in my home state of North Carolina to log a few hours in the F-15E simulator there, prior to flying an F-15E in theater.

I'd commanded the 1st TFW at Langley Air Force Base in Virginia, flying F-15Cs, but my own combat experience was in the F-4. We didn't have the F-15 until after Vietnam. Most of the current F-15E pilots had, like me, transitioned from F-4s. I wanted to put myself in their place and see how easy it would be for someone who had flown the F-4, in air-to-ground, to employ the F-15E. After one simulator mission, and a subsequent F-15E training flight in theater, I was convinced. The F-15E would be a very easy aircraft to fly in combat and we could expect outstanding results. The F-15E gave the pilot so much more information and helped you so much, and did so many more things for you than the F-4 did, it was unbelievable. Once I'd flown the simulator I knew this was the ideal airplane for the former F-4 pilots to take on targets in the Gulf. I was not concerned about it after that.

And there was once again an effort to convince me not to rely so much on the F-117. Even my mentor, Bill Kirk, warned that I was placing a lot of eggs in the F-117 basket. At the request of General Bob Russ, I stopped at TAC headquarters at Langley to take a briefing on F-117 vulnerability.

According to this briefing, the F-117s were dead meat. Major General Mike Ryan, the TAC Director of Operations who'd helped us deploy forces for Operation Desert Shield, had seen a briefing based on tests done at Nellis that said the F-117s were going to be more vulnerable than I thought they were. I talked to Russ about this ahead of time, before the briefing. Russ was not convinced that Ryan was right.

Russ told me, "Buster, I think that my personal view is closer aligned with your assessment than with my own people's. But you need to listen to them and hear it out and make up your own mind. I can live with whatever decision you make."

In Russ' operations center they showed me their briefing. They'd set up some tests in the desert with equipment similar to what the Iraqis had. Then they took the most talented guy we had in the Air Force and they told him from which direction the F-117s would be coming and they gave him altitude stratas, they gave him the optimum frequency, and let him tweak that Iraqi-type equipment in a way that you had to be gifted and well-trained to be able to do.

As the F-117s came in, sure enough this guy picked them up. Now he not only had to detect them, he had to engage them. Once he engaged them, he had to launch a simulated missile, and he had to hand-off the launch to the fire control system. They set it up accurately to duplicate the chain of events needed to kill a stealth aircraft. The bottom line was, with all of that help, all that coaching and advance knowledge, they shot down about one out of every seven to ten F-117s.

I didn't even sit and listen to all the briefing.

"Is this all you have?" I said after about an hour. "Are you now going to give me more detail on how this all came about?"

They said yes.

I said, "I appreciate your time very much. But I don't think I need to hear all of the intricate details of your test." After I thanked them, I got up and walked out.

Yield to that type of mindset and you will always fight a brute force war. Accept that, and you will fall back on what you know and you will always send F-15Es, F-16s, F-111s, and all the SEAD you can and you'd get a lot of them shot down and a lot of fighter pilots killed. To talk yourself out of using the stealth technology that the American taxpayers had paid for, and that could save your fighter pilots lives, was absolutely repulsive to me.

I went straight back over to Russ' office.

"Sir, I must tell you, I don't mean to be disrespectful, but I understand why you're a little uncomfortable with their analysis. It's a Nervous Nellie approach. We can't take the best, most highly trained military individual we have in this country, who exceeds any other military person on the face of the earth by a significant factor, and then tweak a system to a level that we know the Iraqis don't have the ability to tweak it to, and then get concerned because we're going to lose one out of ten airplanes.

"Nobody guaranteed anyone that we would never lose an F-117. However, I want to make a commitment to you right now, unless we have a mechanical malfunction, the Iraqis will not put one hole in an F-117. They won't hit it. They just don't have the capacity to do it. There are only two possibilities that could cause us to lose an F-117: either we have a mechanical malfunction and therefore we lose the stealthiness, or the weather traps us and they get a visual shoot down."

"I told you beforehand that I'm closer to your view than to my staff's," Russ reminded me. Then he said, "You decide what you want to do and I will totally support you. Do not be concerned about that. I will help with the leadership in Washington. Do it however you think is the right way to do it."

That was a significant vote of confidence and one I appreciated greatly. He didn't have to say that.

I just didn't intend to lose many aircraft, period. McPeak estimated we'd lose about 150. "If I lose 150 airplanes, I hope you'll encourage Schwarzkopf to replace me," I told the Chief.

December

"It's about time you showed up," Horner said when I got back to Riyadh. "You are now the commander of the 14th Air Division. Now see if that plan of yours is as great as you think it is."

December brought a shift in command arrangements. Horner gave me command of all the U. S. Air Force fighter units deployed to the Gulf region. In this capacity I worked directly for Horner. This made it more difficult for Schwarzkopf to keep reminding me that I worked for him, or so Horner thought. In reality, it did not change anything in Schwarz-kopf's mind or actions.

I was delighted to be commander of the 14th Air Division. Horner's point of view was it's one thing to plan something, it's another thing to command it. We'd planned the use of all assets—Navy, tankers, bombers, and fighters—and now I'd command a significant chunk of the assets, too. It was sobering, but I have always loved command. Did I use it to the maximum to execute the war exactly like I wanted to? Absolutely.

The wing commanders liked it, too. I already controlled the planning, now I would also command the execution. Horner and I agreed that once the war started one of us would always be present at the RSAF Headquarters to deal with the unexpected.

The one thing neither he nor I could control was the weather. Two studies—one from Checkmate, and one from my own weather people—showed that unless history changed, I was going to lose one out of every four days to weather. When I came back I shared this with Horner on December 7.

"Well, you always have weather," he said.

I'd always briefed the timeline assuming good weather—but now I realized, and wrote in my diary, '*I never defined good weather . . . not to the CINC . . . Chairman . . . President . . . <u>I screwed up</u> . . . now . . . how to make sure they understand what I am certain they don't.*'

I thought we would execute in October, November or December, when the weather was good. After I got back from Washington, there was no doubt in my mind that the war would start around the middle of January. That changed the whole picture.

My big screw-up was that I did not force Schwarzkopf to understand that weather in January and February could slow Phases I to III of the campaign and affect the timing for Phase IV. Although I talked with him about the potential for weather to delay us, it didn't sink in right. His view was that nobody could be that precise in forecasting the weather. We would have to adjust to the weather as necessary. It sounded good— but his expectations remained too high and I failed to curb them.

After returning from Washington, I discussed my concerns about the impact of weather with Schwarzkopf. I reminded him of our 21 days for Phase I and II. Fourteen days before the ground war starts. That's a total of five weeks. After reviewing the best available historical data I have, if the weather pattern is just normal, not bad, but just *normal,* we're going to lose one out of every four days. So you've got to add eight or nine days onto that five weeks. I should have pushed to have a one-on-one meeting with him and explain this in private.

On December 10, Schwarzkopf and I made a visit to Cairo. The Egyptians had a substantial ground force committed to Operation Desert Storm and Schwarzkopf wanted to make sure the Egyptian leadership got the war plans briefing directly from him. He took me along to discuss air power if needed. In private, as we traveled, he joked about the kind of retirement he wanted: quiet, low-profile, doing just what he wanted to do. He wanted to be involved in the past, but not live in the past.

While on the plane, I took the opportunity to discuss JSTARS with him. I said, "Sir, the Air Force is not in favor of this. If I leave it up to them they won't do it and it's absolutely wrong to hold it back. I can't be associated with this request, but you've got to get JSTARS over here."

Schwarzkopf requested JSTARS, and JSTARS came—complete with a team of Ph.D.s to keep the system debugged and running. They'd all signed release forms so they could fly on the JSTARS when combat missions were flown even though they were civilians. Another wonderful example of Americans placing service before self.

Schwarzkopf was brilliant in Cairo. He took the Egyptians through the campaign, and discussed hot issues like Scuds and chemical and biological weapons. Schwarzkopf told them he was looking to them for leadership of the Arab corps and counting on them to keep the Saudis under control and on the move. In return, he promised the Egyptians would have close air support to the exact same degree as the U.S. divisions. He did a masterful job of describing everything without compromising anything.

The next day he called me over for a private meeting. Schwarzkopf wanted to make absolutely certain the close air support provided for the Egyptian corps would be as ample as for U.S. ground units.

"I've taken care of it," I assured him. "You can strike it from your mind."

As we walked down the hall toward his quarters I asked him, "How much time can we expect after Phase I starts before the ground forces will be ready to move?"

"Three weeks."

"I may need four to get the attrition I promised you due to the cruddy weather projections," I ventured again.

"You have it. The ground war does not start until I say we are ready. I will be ready when you tell me we have the Iraqi Army attrited 50 percent. If the powers that be don't like that, then you and I will watch this war on CNN in Tampa," Schwarzkopf said.

On December 14, I accompanied Representative Dave McCurdy on a visit to the F-117 unit at Taif. He asked me what my number-one problem was. "We are data rich and information poor," I told him.

I'd talked with Al Whitley about Ryan's pessimistic briefing at Langley. He was, not surprisingly, a little more disturbed by it than I'd been.

Now, in the small lounge for the F-117 pilots, I pinned a personal note on their message board: "The Pride of Our Nation Depends on You."

In my diary for that day I wrote *'I'm not sure if anyone shares this conviction with me . . . that's okay . . . it is my decision and I'm willing to live with it!!'* People had their doubts about the F-117 now, but I was certain that everyone would jump on the F-117 bandwagon well before the war was over.

This period of time also gave me a chance to fix another problem and move the F-15Es from their base at Thumrait, in Oman, up to Al Kharj, which was 700 miles closer to their targets.

"The Saudis will never let you do it," Horner said.

I asked Sudairy to come see me.

"I can't tolerate having my F-15E pilots fly 1,200 miles to their targets," I pleaded. "Please help me get them into Al Kharj."

"I will work on this for you," Sudairy said. "Please also tell General Horner to make this request to General Behery."

Low and behold, Sudairy got us permission to base the F-15Es at Al Kharj. Then Hal Hornburg moved the entire operation. The only thing located at Al Kharj when he started was the runway and the runway lights. Hornburg put 5,000 people there and his own wing, plus two more squadrons of F-16s, an F-16 Air Guard unit, C-130s and then tankers. He did it in less than a month.

With the rainy season coming, we tapped some of the funds contributed by Japan for the operation. We poured asphalt walkways between the tents. It made life much easier by keeping the wet sand out of the tents. By December 17, the F-15Es were in their new base and now just 540 nautical miles from Baghdad.

Hornburg was so proud of it he invited me to fly with them. I almost gave in to the offer but I could not spare the time. So I pimped him with, "Keep your focus on warfighting, not just building that pretty new base."

It was time for me to talk to my wing commanders as a group. They all came together for a meeting on December 17 around the table in the main conference room of the Black Hole. I spelled out what I expected from them. Top of my list was that I wanted each of them to fly a mission during the first 24 hours of the war. "Lead by example," I told them.

Point two was integrity. Unlike other episodes in our military history, I wasn't going to compromise on integrity. If they made a mistake, they had to tell me. I didn't want to hear about it on CNN or get a call from the intelligence community in Washington accusing us of doing something we hadn't admitted to.

Point three was that leaders don't lose people unnecessarily. You can argue it's a given that you're going to lose some number. I'd argue that if you take that approach, then you will wind up with a mindset that permits you to accept a loss rate that is too high. On the other hand, if you set a loss rate of zero, and do not willingly accept one loss unless you're convinced that everything was done to prevent it, then you are thinking correctly.

I summarized the campaign for them. This team had to work together. I wanted the F-15E commander to look in the eyes of the F-117 commander and the F-16 commanders and realize they all depended on each other to take out the targets they'd been assigned.

As I briefed each of the four phases, I told them this was a seamless campaign. Yes, we'd tried to insist that there was a strategic air campaign and that was a Holy Grail, and nothing else was going to happen until that was completed. Starting in November, I'd changed it slowly but surely because I didn't like the way that it was holding together. I wanted to have a seamless continuation of all phases in a way that there'd be no disruption and no noticeable starts and stops. I wanted it blended together as a theater campaign plan, just the way Schwarzkopf had portrayed it.

My final thought for them was: "Command and lead as if they are your own sons and daughters."

Bugs and Gas

While we'd been concerned about NBC targets since the beginning, the time from late October through late December was our best chance to refine what we knew and weigh the risks of different types of attacks on these crucial Phase I targets.

Saddam had already used chemical weapons both in the Iran-Iraq war and against the Kurds. An Air Force historian, Diane Putney, later concluded that from 1983 to 1988, the Iraqi Air Force had "launched over one hundred aircraft sorties to use chemical weapons at least ten times." Either their helicopters or fixed-wing aircraft could conduct chemical attacks.

"My nightmare is the ground force hung up in barriers, then a chemical attack. That's my first thought every morning and last thought every night," Schwarzkopf told his commanders in the November brief.

Destroying the NBC capability was a top objective but we had to find a way to do it with minimal risk. McConnell and Checkmate fed us whatever information they had through the fall. In early October I passed one of the latest updates to Horner. They told us there were six locations for refrigerated bunkers. We thought they held liquid, or more likely, freeze-dried agent. The Iraqis also had 40 custom-made aerosol generators that could spray out 40 liters per minute, wet or dry. Worse, they could move them around. Truck, boat, aircraft, whatever. I needed to know more about the size of these dispensers to truly understand the employment options.

By the time I made my trip back to Washington, it was crunch time. 'Bugs and gas. Everyone pointing at someone else,' I noted.

First, we had to identify the chemical and biological weapons storage areas, and then we had to take them out. The basic problem was we weren't sure what would happen when we bombed the bunkers. Nobody wanted to take responsibility for busting them open. Of course, nobody wanted to take responsibility if we didn't strike and the Iraqis actually used these loathsome weapons on our troops. Nobody even wanted to *discuss* that.

In mid-December, McConnell told me the discussion was heating up. It affected the Coalition allies, too. The Egyptian Minister of Defense had asked about it specifically during our Cairo visit. On December 10, the DIA gave a briefing on the situation. According to McConnell, Powell cut them off in the middle of the discussion. "I discussed that with Norm and we are bombing the storage bunkers so that all bugs will be killed. Everything is under control," he said.

That was B.S. I had no idea where he got that idea. Was he shooting from the hip again?

We had to force this issue now, not later, when selective recall would be in vogue. The idea that we could neutralize all the agent was B.S., as I told Horner. I didn't want them thinking that we really had the capacity to do that without some serious repercussions. We had to make sure that Powell and Schwarzkopf understood what we were planning and the associated risk. McConnell promised to forward me more DIA work in a few days.

For me, the bottom line was we were at war! The Iraqis, under Saddam's oppressive regime, were the ones who developed this stuff. We didn't put it there. They put it there. I didn't want to allow them even the thought of using it against the Coalition when the Iraqis started to lose the war and retreat. As far as I was concerned, there was no choice. It was just a matter of trying to plan and execute the strikes to have minimum impact on both their own people and our people—with an emphasis on our people.

Meanwhile we were preparing a briefing for Horner to give the Chairman and the Secretary of Defense. I urged Horner to make the weapons bunkers a prominent issue, but he refused.

We also were working on a plan to telegraph a message to Saddam about what we'd do if he used chemical and biological weapons. First, we were going to annihilate his hometown of Tikrit. Just rub it off the map, by bombing dams to release water and flood everything. We'd also take his oil production facilities out.

On December 18, I got the promised information from McConnell. Expert estimates of fallout casualties from our attacks varied enormously. One doomsday study suggested we'd kill a million people if we failed to vaporize the agent and the spores spread. McConnell had better news. Once the biological spores broke open, the sunlight would dissipate their strength. It was a mathematical relationship: they'd lose their potency, then be neutralized altogether in a matter of hours.

Schwarzkopf and I talked it over on December 19.

"Are we doing the right thing with the chemical/biological storage bunkers?" he asked.

"Yes, sir," I said. "Either we risk his people or our ground troops. That's an easy decision for me."

"I agree," Schwarzkopf said.

I explained to him that we were taking all reasonable precautions. We'd bust open the storage bunkers at sun-up. And only if the sun was shining, with no fog or clouds, and only if the wind speed was below five knots. The F-111s would use a GBU-24 to achieve the high heat we needed. The goal was to reach a temperature of 2,000 degrees within three-to-four seconds of the bunkers being broken open. That would vaporize the agent. If it took six or seven seconds, and the wind sent the spores adrift, the worst case appeared to be minimal.

"That doesn't mean we might not have fall-out. With biological weapons, nothing is 100 percent certain," I said. "But the impact will be minimal this way."

"What do you mean by minimal?"

"It is likely we will kill 500 to 1,000 people. In a worst-case scenario, we could kill 20,000 to 30,000 people."

"We both hope that's not true," Schwarzkopf said. "But it's a long way from a million."

"That's for sure," I said.

"Okay. But I've got to convince Powell," he told me. "His political concerns are driving his military judgment."

One political concern I knew about was the view of the British. In mid-December, they'd delivered a long memo outlining targets they were concerned about, from civilian electric power installations to the biological and chemical bunkers.

When you're planning a war, when you're executing a war, one of the most difficult things to do is to keep everything in proper perspective. Around you are the "naysayers" in five or six really contentious, potentially troublesome areas, and none of them are keeping perspective because as far as they are concerned, that one little thing is the most important thing on the face of the earth to them. You have to deal with all of this.

The British wanted to put in writing their concerns about how we attacked the biological and chemical storage areas and the potential for fallout—concerns that paralleled our calculations about the timing and type of weapons for the attack.

"On NBC, I have told my authorities that no commander can be expected to tell whether a missile, bomb or artillery round has a conventional, chemical or biological warhead and that therefore no constraints should be imposed on attacking weapons," Air Chief Marshal Hine wrote to Schwarzkopf.

"However, both you and we recognize that there is some environmental risk to Iraqi centers of population consequent upon the attack of NBC facilities, particularly the B and C storage tanks . . . Let me stress that our objective is to impose the minimum (if any) restrictions on the attack of NBC facilities; our purpose is merely to identify the risks then seek political clearance."

Hine closed the message offering any assistance Britain could provide.

Reading the message from the British was refreshing. They had it all in perspective. Rodgers Greenawalt added the message and accompanying paper to my memo file on December 21.

The issue got personal when we were all told to go get anthrax shots. A special room was set up for the general officers to receive their shots, one now, and one a few days later. I took my first shot and when I walked out, Horner was standing in the hall.

"Are you taking the shot?" I said.

"No."

"Why not?"

"Because not everybody's getting it."

"The medics told me everybody was getting it," I said.

"No," Horner said, "they're only giving them to selected people."

To me that was blatantly wrong. You either give them to everybody or you at least give them to the front line people that you think will be most exposed. I never took the other shot.

EVE OF BATTLE

We made it through Christmas Day without a surprise from Saddam, but it started out badly.

Since early December, the CIA had been suggesting Saddam might try "something" on Christmas Day. They had no idea what. First, there was a Scud alert. False alarm. Then satellites picked up a MiG-25 south of Baghdad lighting its afterburner. If Saddam tried a Christmas strike I thought it would be a sensationalist attack using chemical or biological weapons against troops or housing areas, where he would generate the most publicity. For an instant I thought, *was this MiG-25 it?*

All my impatience and frustration was sharpened by being without my family. On Christmas Eve, I talked to Vicki, Brad, Tanya and my mom. They were doing okay, considering. However, my major concern during Christmas was thinking about how many Desert Storm airmen, soldiers, marines and sailors would not be with their families *next* Christmas. Had we done everything possible in our planning to minimize losses? You can never be 100 percent sure until the war starts—then, there would be no second chances.

We made Christmas in the desert as cheerful as we could. Christmas lunch was served at Eskan Village, where everyone except the flag officers lived. *'May we always be mindful of the true meaning of this day,'* I wrote. *'We pray for the safe return of all those in this theater.'*

Several of the staff spending Christmas in theater signed a humorous Christmas card for me. "Hussein may be an Arab, but we should give him some fireworks for Christmas," wrote Callum Steele, one of the RAF liaison officers. "Is it true your hair was jet black before you assembled this bunch of slugs?" wrote John Kinser. I kept the card. After lunch, I insisted that the staff take the rest of the day off. I went back to my quarters to make sure they didn't feel they had to be in the office just because I was.

Now I was alone. I decided Christmas Day offered a great opportunity to sit quietly by myself and think. One of my greatest concerns was that I wasn't using enough time to think, and getting caught up in a self-generated activity trap.

Yet as soon as I tried to concentrate, personal thoughts intruded. This was only the second Christmas that my entire family had not been together in 25 years. Alone in Riyadh, all I could do was write about it. *'Family, family, family,'* I wrote. *'The foundations of one's beliefs, ambitions, and goals . . . ultimately one's success or failure—second only to God.'* Tanya, my daughter, sent me the most memorable Christmas gift I had ever received. Framed and matted, it said: "One of the greatest gifts I've ever had came from God . . . I call him Dad." I wrote at the time: *'any words I would use to describe my pride and thoughts would be inadequate.'* Still true.

Eventually, my mind cleared.

According to CNN, the war might start anytime between mid-January and mid-February. Schwarzkopf had privately indicated we should peak our readiness for war between the middle or the last part of January. Personally, I thought we were inside of four weeks and counting.

I reviewed the strategic plan from A to Z to see if I could spot a fundamental strategic mistake. The President's goals were:

- Iraq out of Kuwait
- NBC destroyed
- Neutralize the threat of Iraq's armed forces for five to 10 years
- Do this with a minimum loss of life

I took each goal and challenged myself: Have I honestly made every reasonable attempt to accomplish this and will I be successful?

Iraq out of Kuwait? I felt that the chances of that were 100 percent certain. Will I destroy the NBC? Air power was all we had to achieve this goal. We weren't sending divisions to the Baghdad nuclear research facility or the chemical plants at Habbaniyah. Unfortunately, I knew even at the time the answer to that question was totally dependent on how good the intelligence was. With good intelligence, we'd get 90 to 100 percent success. If they didn't know where the NBC was, or how much of it was left, it would be anybody's guess.

As for minimizing loss of life, I knew I was going to do that. That said, you always have a little bit of anxiety—you don't know what you don't know.

I then challenged myself to be critical of my own strategy for planning and executing the war.

• Minimum loss of life—the outcome of war is a given—we win!

• People win wars—so I reviewed the abilities of each commander and leader in my mind.

• Backbone would be stealth and precision, the F-117. I reminded myself not to overload them.

• Precision using F-15E, F-111 and A-6s must be maximized night after night.

• Aggressive and ruthless—timidity loses lives.

• Sequence and degree of destruction—must constantly review and update—the most fluid part of the strategic air campaign—Saddam's actions could dictate changes.

• NBC—I wished I could have higher confidence in our intelligence for these targets.

• Republican Guard—only force to support Saddam after the war—be ruthless with them!

• Iraq's leadership and communications—must ensure massive disruption maintained day after day.

• Baghdad and the entire country had to know they were at war—no exceptions.

I vowed I would dictate the pace—with zero tolerance for any business-as-usual attitudes. I would not tolerate the rollback advocates, for their attitude was akin to the brute-force school of war that I detested. However, I intended to take prudent risks only until ground forces crossed the border. Then there would be no limits—an American is an American—they are all precious. Mitchell's theory about using air power to the full was correct. I'll prove it, I pledged.

Neutralizing Iraq as a threat meant destroying critical military nodes, such as the Republican Guard, which I believed we could do. It also depended on eliminating much of Iraq's leadership, hopefully even Saddam himself. We had a list of desired MIAs—the Iraqi military leaders we hoped would be "missing in action" after the war:

- Saddam Hussein
- Lieutenant General Hussein Kamil Al-Majid (Minister of Industry, including NBC)
  - Ali Hassan (in Kuwait, and reputed to be running the torture there)
  - General Ramadan (Army Commander in Chief)
  - General Salim Shansha (Defense Minister)
  - Lieutenant General Ar-Rawi (Commander in Chief, Republican Guard)
  - Lieutenant General Al-Khazraji (Chief of Staff)
  - Lieutenant General Salah Mahmoud (Commander, III Corps)
  - Major General Mazakim (Iraqi Air Force Commander)

Truthfully, I always thought we'd have to get a little lucky on the senior leadership. They likely would be a threat again inside of 10 years, regardless of what we destroyed.

I fundamentally believed that the leadership of a country was the most important aspect of a country trying to go to war. The leaders are the things that make it tick. Now, some will argue if you take the Republican Guard away from Saddam Hussein, he's nothing. You take away weapons of mass destruction, then he's nothing. I did not accept these views. Despotic leaders have always found a means. You can even be a leader and have no capabilities. But, if you have capability, then your ability and willingness to use it is solely the discretion of the leader. Therefore the leader is the single most critical center of gravity for all Third World nations. The air campaign was riding on the F-117. That was my whole strategy from day one, and that's exactly how I would force it to go. The most important thing I did was decreeing that the F-117 was not vulnerable.

The second most important thing I did was set up a strategy to compensate for the lack of intelligence capabilities. My strategy was to have input from McConnell, input from the British, and input from the Kuwaiti resistance and the royal families of the region. And then try to lean on what I could gather from CENTCOM and CENTAF.

I spent quite a bit of time on Christmas Day reviewing how we got where we are, and what I thought was going to be the result of execution once it started.

What I was really trying to do was detect any fundamental strategic mistake. Make a minor tactical mistake and you're going to wind up losing people that you shouldn't have lost. That is bad, and it should not be tolerated in the profession of arms; but the disruption to the war is minimal.

It's that strategic mistake you have to guard against at all costs. Make a fundamental strategic mistake and you can lose a *thousand or more* people that you didn't anticipate losing. You can disrupt the campaign effort to the point where it takes you a week to get back on track. Those are the things that you really want to avoid at all costs.

There's only one person who can make sure that strategic mistakes don't happen. And that's the person in charge.

My first line of defense against a self-imposed mistake was to have Tolin, Lewis, Deptula, Rogers, and Baptiste focus on my priorities and my actions, not theirs. By keeping these five people thinking at the operational level, they would help ensure the President's objective really did get accomplished, and that we did not fall into an activity trap once the war got underway.

All of them were warfighters, all of them had been operators, all of them were very bright and they were a different combination of personalities, which was very important to me. Generals hear too much of their own words parroted back to them. I thought, *I've got to jar this crap loose or this organization will suffer.* The one thing I knew for sure about Tolin, Lewis, and Colonel "Joe Bob" Phillips from previous experience: they would never tell me what I wanted to hear. That was absolutely vital. I'm very hard-nosed. I don't accept fools very well. I don't accept mistakes very well. I have a lot of personal baggage, which I know about. Only an idiot doesn't fireproof himself against his own baggage and his own weaknesses.

Still, it's not everybody else's responsibility to make sure there's not a strategic mistake. It's the leader who is given the responsibility: that was me.

From time to time, I would try to find private time and just wrestle it out to see if strategically I was making a mistake. For example, if I'd been wrong about the F-117, just think of the consequences of that. It would have been catastrophic. It wasn't an easy decision. Everybody looks at it in hindsight and says, "Oh, no-brainer. Obvious thing to do." Why was it the obvious thing to do when several of the three- and four-stars in the

Air Force were calling me and telling me what a dumbshit I was for putting too much confidence in the F-117? I ignored their concerns; they would have the privilege of second-guessing me later. The issue was, if they were right and I was wrong, lives were going to be lost left and right. Instead of losing 39 airplanes, we'd lose 200. Instead of being a five- or-six-week war, we'd be there two or three months. Those are the things that I wrestled with.

One of the main concerns I had after reviewing the plan was that we were not putting enough sorties against the Republican Guard to disrupt them and attrit them sufficiently. Unlike most everybody else, I wanted the Republican Guard to move when we started the attack. I thought that if I could force any of the units to move, then I could just absolutely decimate them from the air. Nobody else wanted them to move. But I very much wanted them to move. Excess sorties were available, and I directed my staff to look at putting 50 to 100 more F-16 sorties against the Republican Guard.

After going through this exercise I felt confident—but not so confident that I wouldn't sit down a week later and go over some segment of the plan again.

I closed my long Christmas diary entries with the bottom line: *'Do not get distracted.'*

Lucky for me, though, I had a pleasant event scheduled. Flying. On December 27, I flew an F-15E from its new base at Al Kharj.

Just as I'd found in the simulator, the F-15E was terrific. There was no reason not to let them loose.

'Flying—how I love it!' I wrote in my diary that night.

Of course it got me in trouble. A few days after my sortie, Horner sent out a memorandum that began: "As you know, general officer flying receives a great deal of scrutiny at all levels." I was the only general officer flying, so I knew to whom the memo was directed to. Horner curtly reminded me that next time, I had to have his personal approval and that the rules were clear that all flying would be in a two-seat aircraft with an instructor pilot.

I was livid.

"If a commander in the Air Force can't fly, he shouldn't be commanding. How do you lead if you don't lead by example?" I asked Horner.

He wasn't buying. In fact, that was his way of setting the stage for not permitting me to fly during the war. I got my knuckles rapped and lost the battle—but it was worth it.

Organization

With the new year, I unveiled a new, formal organizational structure to shift the operation from drawing up plans to running a war.

I was dual-hatted as Director of Campaign Plans and Commander of the 14th Air Division in charge of all fighter units in theater. I also gave Tolin two hats to wear. First, he was the deputy 14th Air Division commander, and the chain of command went direct to the wing commanders and from them, to squadron commanders. This was standard Air Force organization at the time. Second, for planning, all major planning elements reported to Tolin, as shown, in Figure 4.

The campaign-planning task was non-standard, so I worked to clarify the organization so it could function efficiently in wartime. On the planning staff, in addition to Tolin, Bennett, Winstel and Robben, reporting directly to me were three individuals: my executive officer, Rodgers Greenawalt (assisted in administration by Staff Sgt. Heidi Pacheco); my special assistant, Rick Lewis; and my director for analysis, Tom Case.

The Campaign Planning team was divided into four major groups, with two people to run each, so we could cover both day and night:

• Guidance Apportionment and Targeting (GAT) Tolin/Osterloh
(Iraq planning and KTO planning came under the GAT)
• Air Tasking Order (ATO) Bennett/Feinstein
• Airborne Command Element (ACE) Winstel/Elliott
• Component Liaison (LNO) Robben/Pavloc

Central to it all were key individuals on my staff. Before Christmas, I'd made these notes about the roles they'd play:

• Lieutenant Colonel Rick Lewis—eyes and ears and loyal
• Colonel Tony Tolin—common sense and loyal—the right choice to be the Airborne Command Element the first night of the war
• Major John Kinser—loyal
• Jeff Feinstein—will get results
• Robben—line of communication to allies and services
• Major Buck Rogers—loyal, with a deep understanding of Phase I
• Lieutenant Colonel Sam Baptiste—can-do understanding of Phase III and IV
• Lieutenant Colonel Dave Deptula—will keep strategic planning on track come hell or high water

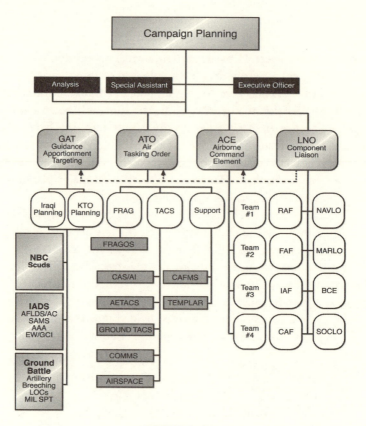

FIGURE 4

Lewis arrived on January 1; he wanted to come down a few days earlier but, in the end, I made him stay at Ramstein with his family until Christmas was over. As soon as Lewis showed up I sat down with him and went over Phases I, II, III, and IV. "Review every detail of the air campaign like you're going to fly each mission. Make sure it's seamless and that we have staying power," I told him. I estimated Phase I would last two or three weeks. Phases II and III would be conducted simultaneously, consuming two to three weeks total, and Phase IV, about one week.

"All of my people except Baptiste are too focused on Phase I," I told Lewis. "You and Tolin must balance it out quickly. You have two weeks before the war starts. Update me as required. Hourly. Daily. Whenever you decide. You must be my conscience. Review everything; remember not one life lost unnecessarily."

When Tolin arrived two days later, I had a similar talk with him. "You are my Deputy Air Division Commander and my de facto deputy for planning," I told Tolin. "You must keep the team pulling together." The air division chain of command—controlling all fighter units—ran direct from Horner to me to Tolin. I told Tolin about Deptula, Rogers, Baptiste, and Lewis and what I expected from each. Tolin's number one responsibility was to keep focused. This campaign was a marathon, not a dash. "We can hope and pray to stop sooner," I told Tolin, "but we sure are not going to bet on it."

I ended the conversation by telling him, "You have my full authority to make any decision, including sending people back to the States."

That same day, Deptula and Rogers got back from the Christmas leaves I'd imposed on them. "You are not leaving again until it's over," I told Dave and Buck. Deptula was now assigned to manage, along with Turk, the Iraqi planning cell under the GAT team, with Bob Eskridge as the point man for the Iraqi cell's operations. Baptiste and Sweeney supervised the KTO planning cell, using Oly Olson as point man. The KTO cell would ultimately handle over three-quarters of the air strikes. Separate dedicated teams focused on NBC and Scuds, the IADS, and the ground battle. Each of these teams had a double staff so some could focus on Iraqi targets while others concentrated on the KTO. Rogers would run the overall GAT team under Tolin and Osterloh's direction. The reorganization made it clear to everyone that Tolin was my deputy for planning and execution. Lewis became my special assistant with authority across the spectrum of my responsibilities.

'What a relief,' I wrote in my diary on January 3. 'For the first time since August I have the right people.' After the war, we'd have to overhaul the personnel system.

The newcomers weren't made welcome right away. Those who had been around on and off since August felt territorial, which was natural enough. Deptula a few times complained, "Tolin and Lewis just don't understand."

"No, the problem is they *do* understand," I said. "You and I have been too close to it to stand back and take an objective look at it."

Deptula was one of the brightest officers I'd ever known, and his contribution to the strategic air campaign could not be overstated. But like all of us, he had his biases and baggage. For example, Deptula frequently reminded me he did not think there would be a Phase IV—a ground war. I told him to think what he wanted, but we were planning for a Phase IV with the same focus and intensity that we had for Phase I. Deptula also was not as concerned as I was about Iraq's chemical and biological weapons. 'He is wrong,' I wrote that night. I wished we had a better understanding of the chemical and biological weapons we were dealing with.

These debates came to light as we all tried to anticipate Saddam's moves once war started. On January 5, Horner and I discussed whether Saddam would try to evacuate his front-line fighters, such as his MiG-29s, when he saw the war was going badly for him. Horner thought Saddam would send them to Jordan, and I agreed. Lewis contended that they'd be more likely to flee to Iran. I decided we needed to prepare for both, but to emphasize placing CAPs so as to catch the MiGs heading for Jordan. I figured a few of our young guys were about to become aces.

Pre-war Tension

The last ten days were the toughest. Waiting around to go to war made us all tense. I was frustrated, and worked it out by trying to tweak things.

First, the Black Hole was too open and noisy. I ordered carpenters to divide things up so there'd be a little bit of sanity. They made each targeting cell a separate little room: an Iraqi room, a KTO room, a Scud room, an area for working the Republican Guard, and a little office area, where I brought in a desk and a phone so I could occasionally have two minutes of quiet to think. Outside, I took one of the hallways and boarded it off to make an office for the liaisons and others.

The Saudis were not pleased when the 2-by-4s and plywood arrived in their headquarters. The Saudis often made our lives as difficult as possible on minor issues such as office space. The Black Hole construction project was a case in point. Fortunately, Sudairy calmed everyone down and sorted it out as he did on many other occasions.

I wasn't the only one feeling the tension. Powell worked out his prewar jitters by starting to question individual targets. He was still concerned about the collateral effects of attacking bioweapons bunkers. Fortunately, Schwarzkopf and Cheney held firm on the need to do so. Then, Powell called up Schwarzkopf and asked him to defend the choice of several specific leadership targets. I had a book with specific target numbers, as did Schwarzkopf and Powell. Powell wanted to know about targets one, four, six, seven, eight, nine, 11 and 13, I noted in my diary on January 5. The Chairman was also worried we were going to try to bomb a statue of Saddam in downtown Baghdad and attack Saddam's personal residence in Tikrit.

'Please not another Lyndon Baines Johnson!!!' I jotted down in exasperation. I made a mental note to remember the Saddam statue and his Tikrit dacha once the war started.

Other questions came from Army Brigadier General Creighton Abrams. He came to see me on January 5 because he wanted and needed help for VII Corps in dealing with Iraqi artillery. I was more than glad to help him. Had I been in his place, as head of artillery for VII Corps, I would have felt the exact same sense of urgency. Abrams' concern was that we had not put F-117s on the artillery, which if not taken out, could be devastating to VII Corps. However, the plan that Schwarzkopf wanted was a little bit different. We deliberately intended to wait before striking artillery. If we bombed it all in the first week, that would give the Iraqis another several weeks to move up replacements before the ground war was to begin. The strategy was to hold off on artillery pieces.

"I'll take them out before the ground war starts," I promised Abrams. "I guarantee I'm going to do that."

'We will not permit him to be hung out,' I wrote in my diary, *'The ground soldier must always be our most precious human life and protected at all costs.'* Abrams seemed satisfied that day, but soon after, his boss, Lieutenant General Fred Franks, Commander of VII Corps, asked me to come up and brief him and his commanders. This took place on January 8.

Unfortunately, the briefing backfired.

The thrust of my briefing was that we would provide whatever they needed at any cost. I provided details of our systematic approach to killing tanks, artillery and Iraqi troops. I needed a way to attack the Republican Guard and other Iraqi ground units continuously. For the record, shortly after Lewis arrived, I asked him to work with Baptiste and the KTO targeting cell to figure out a way to flow the sorties. Baptiste drew up a bomber stream curving over the Republican Guard. But the SAM and AAA threat and the need for continuous pressure dictated more freedom in tactics. Lewis' solution was to divide the Republican

Guard divisions up into 30-by-30-mile boxes. Flight leads could then approach from different angles to engage any target within their assigned box and drop ordnance regardless of weather. With the Republican Guard spread out as they were, we had enough boxes to enable a four-ship to attack every six minutes (although target ID delays later stretched the time to 15 minutes.)

Lewis suggested calling the squares "killboxes" or "kill zones" and the "killbox" name stuck. We paired it with the box grid already developed by the Saudi Air Force for air defense, and Baptiste briefed the concept to General McPeak during his visit on January 5.

With air power like this to bring to bear, we'd have a devastating impact on the Iraqi ground forces. I tried to assure VII Corps that the Phase III attacks would attrit Iraqi ground force units below 50 percent effectiveness, as Schwarzkopf directed. I wanted them to know they could count on that, so I spoke from the heart.

"If I have to lose every airplane in theater, I will do it to make sure that I attrit the Iraqis before the land war starts," I told them. I wanted them to see that I had the ability to kill tanks and that I was passionately committed to doing it.

But the Army commanders weren't buying. I came off too glib. Besides, they simply did not believe I would or could attrit those units. Nothing in their grasp of history and air power supported that. Perhaps I should not have been surprised at their skepticism, but I was. Only Army Lieutenant Colonel Joe Purvis later vouched that I was sincere in promising decisive support.[1]

I didn't know how badly it had gone at the time. In my notes later I wrote, *'Not sure brief was understood. Attempted to explain how important supporting ground troops was to Horner and I. Not enough questions. They have doubts. We will solve their concern once they see the support and results.'* Afterwards, I got to know a few of the generals, and they told me that they thought that I was making promises I couldn't keep. According to my briefing, they all might as well go home, because there wasn't any need for them, because I was going to single-handedly win the war. It was very unfortunate that the wrong message came across in that briefing and it came back to haunt us later.

Around this time I made a significant change to the plan. Finally, I

1. *Lucky War: Third Army in Desert Storm*, p. 182.

convinced Schwarzkopf that I needed to use more F-16s, F/A-18s and A-10s in the early phases. All fall I'd held off putting the A-10s into Phase I because Schwarzkopf wanted them held in reserve. He was concerned that if the A-10s flew too much, their losses might be high and they would not be available to support the ground campaign. I understood his reasoning. I just did not agree with it. He was the boss, so I left the A-10s out of the planning. It was not until early January that he gave me permission to go ahead and use all the air power that I wanted as long as I was sure that I'd have whatever was needed for the land campaign.

I added strikes by the F-16s from Al Kharj on SAMs in Kuwait. Navy F/A-18s were assigned to strike SAMs around Basra. I tasked more A-10s to hit early warning radar sites near the borders and ground control intercept sites. Other F-16s would now be sent against Republican Guard targets.

I also had clear guidance for fixed targets. I signed out this memo to all plans offices on January 12, 1991:

Targets and aimpoints will be selected so as to minimize collateral damage and limit the impact on the civilian population. All targets performing a military function or supporting a military function may be destroyed. Electric targets will be targeted to minimize recuperation time. At electric production/transformers stations the objective will be the transformer/switching yard and the control bldg. in these yards. Boilers and generators will not be aim points. The objective at POL targets is to destroy refined product storage. Distillation and other refining areas will only be an aimpoint for military related fuel production refineries.

"NOTE," I added. "Exceptions to the above targeting require my personal approval—BCG."

Careful as we were with our secrets, we got a scare when Air Marshal Sir Patrick Hine flew back to London to brief British Foreign Minister John Majors. One of his aides took along a briefcase with a laptop computer containing war plans. The briefcase and laptop were stolen out of the aide's unmarked, official car while it was parked. Although I did not know exactly what the laptop contained, the most significant information was probably the location of Coalition forces such as aircraft beddowns. We thought the targeting data was generic, not specific. '*I am concerned,*' I noted.

As it turned out, we got very lucky. Three weeks later, the computer was returned by mail to the British Ministry of Defence. In it was a message: "Sir, I am a common thief but I am also patriotic and I love my Queen and country. Whoever lost this should be bloody hung. Yours, Andrew."[2]

The final week before the war saw a flurry of diplomatic activity. On January 10, Secretary of State James Baker went to Geneva to meet with Iraqi Foreign Minister Tariq Aziz and offer one last chance for peace. Nothing was achieved, and I confided in my diary, *'the outlook for preventing war is bleak.'* Just in case we had any doubts, the Iraqis ran a major air defense exercise on the morning of January 11. Everyone handled the tension well. We got word around that time that they were still trying to practice launching Mirage F-1s equipped with a tank to spray chemical/biological weapons agent.

I was starting to think we had dotted every "i" and crossed every "t".

Then on January 11, Lewis walked in and asked, "Do you know what your number one problem is?"

"Why don't you tell me, along with a solution?"

"CAFMS is not going to provide you what you need to manage the execution planning. You'll be using stubby pencils to track this campaign."

Lewis was right as usual. The Computer Aided Force Management System (CAFMS) was never going to make it. In fact, CAFMS had hiccuped and failed when we stressed it in exercises. With 60 to 70 targets and 600 to 1,000 sorties every 24 hours, it was possible to track the results by hand. But with 320-plus targets and 2,400 sorties per 24 hours—tilt! We would be saturated. At this late date, I could only Band-Aid the problem and try to control the bleeding. It was the 11th of January and I knew we were starting in five days. So I wasn't about to try an untested new system or upgrade; the risk was too high that it would not be accurate. I decided I would just try to get a few extra people and brute-force our way through it. In fact, let history reflect, it became almost unmanageable toward the end of the campaign; but it never became a showstopper.

Visits

My number-one priority the last few days before January 17 was to talk to my aircrews. Over 600 airplanes and 1,400 aircrew members were under my command in the fighter units of the 14th Air Division. On New

2. Sean C. Kelly. "RAF officer demoted over theft of war-plans computer." *Air Force Times,* June 29, 1991.

Year's Day, I'd telephoned each of the wing commanders and told them to be ready to discuss their number-one concern with me when I visited. The point of these trips was simple: get the professional adrenaline pumping. *'Hellfire and brimstone. . . . what I expect, why, and the consequences. Failure is not an option,'* I wrote in my diary.

They were about to put their lives on the line. Some of them were not going to be there when it was over. It's part of the commander's responsibility to help the aircrews get the right mindset. You owe it to everyone to help mentally and emotionally prepare them for war. That's as important as planning, training, and all the other things that you do. Adrenaline helps. You just have to make sure they peak at the right time.

"Your Role in Offensive Air Campaign" was the title of the briefing I took to the wings. In Vietnam, nobody cared or bothered to try to fit it all together for us. In that war, I was responsible for eight F-4 fighters with 12 front- and back-seaters—pilots and weapons officers—not a position to have a very broad overview of the Vietnam war, but broad enough for me to realize that we never had a clue, at the unit level, what our overall effort was trying to accomplish. We became almost mechanical. Without even realizing it, we distanced ourselves psychologically. It stymied initiative. You didn't feel responsibility as an individual for the total success of the war.

No one cared enough about us in Vietnam to explain how we fit into the overall scheme of things. I wanted to make sure that we didn't repeat that mistake. My aircrews deserved to know the total plan—its strengths and weaknesses—where they fit, what happened if they failed, and the anticipated synergistic impact of their successes.

I spoke to each unit individually, starting on January 10 and 11, with the 388th TFW, 363rd TFW and 4th TFW. The F-16Cs at Al Minhad were working hard to be ready—under Mike Navarro and his outstanding deputy, Cash Jascazak, they'd make it. Ray Huot's number-one concern at Al Dhafra was more waiting—I agreed, his pilots were almost too ready, and I directed Ray to back off and wind down the torque on the screw slightly for three or four days. The 4th TFW at Al Kharj, with Hal Hornburg in charge, were definitely ready. Hornburg's number-one concern was his span of control, with 48 F-15Es from Seymour Johnson, 24 F-15Cs from Bitburg and 24 F-16s of the Syracuse and MacIntyre Guard units, his span of control was being tested. I had total trust and confidence in Hal—I knew he would be ready.

On January 12, it was on to the 1st TFW at Dhahran, which had been my wing three years earlier. Now it was ably commanded by Boomer McBroom. His 48 F-15Cs were focused and ready, concerned only about being shot down by nervous Saudi air defense batteries while returning to base. I promised I'd work with Prince Turki, the Saudi commander of the eastern region and a member of the royal family, to make sure the Saudi batteries held their fire unless they had his personal clearance to shoot.

At the 354th TFW at King Fahd Air Base, Colonel Sandy Sharpe, too, was really only worried about more delays before his 72 A-10s and OA-10s got into action. Colonel Dave Sawyer at the 23rd TFW, another A/OA-10 wing sharing the ramp at King Fahd, had no concerns, and to me his pilots looked professional, eager, and ready. At Doha, in Qatar, Mike Nelson's top concern was being at the end of our logistics supply line with his 24 F-16Cs.

On January 14, I made visits to the 33rd TFW at Tabuk and the 48th TFW at Taif. Rick Parsons at Tabuk reported his number-one concern was crew fatigue, so I directed he talk with the flight surgeon, and gave my approval for him to use go no-go pills as needed. These were stimulants and sleeping pills concocted by the flight surgeons to rev up and ramp down the pilots when flying six- to eight-hour missions day after day.

Parsons' 24 F-15C pilots were the best air-to-air unit. He'd hand-picked one squadron's worth from among the three squadrons in his wing at Eglin and brought them to the desert. They were the cream of the crop—and within days their wartime kills proved it. (The 33rd wing would tally up 16 air-to-air kills, the highest of any unit in Operation Desert Storm.)

Tom Lennon at Tabuk had 64 F-111Fs, a longer-range fighter-bomber with the all-important precision. Tom had a reputation as a tough taskmaster, and aquired an unprintable nickname that symbolized it. However, I could see that his pilots and weapons systems officers were professional and peaked. These guys were ready to fight, now!

For all these pilots and aircrew under my command, I had a few important things I wanted to tell them, from the heart.

"Bravery is controlling fear and apprehension. Stupidity is the absence of fear and apprehension. Don't get the two confused."

"Make sure your take-offs and landings stay equal."

However, my main point of emphasis was, "There's not a damn thing in Iraq worth you dying for until the first American or allied soldier crosses the border."

I really meant that. Many of the fighter pilots quoted that later. I wanted Desert Storm to be fought that way. If they backed off on occasion and it meant that I had to retarget something, then that was not a big deal to me because I knew that we were going to be successful. I didn't want to lose lives that we didn't have to lose.

To the wing commanders, I said, "You are in command. Keep your people number one in your thought process. The first two or three days will be tough; there will be more SAMs and AAA than any fighter pilot's ever seen. Stay focused. Integrity will not be compromised. Mistakes will be made. Keep me informed. Expect no second chances. Lead by example."

The reason that integrity was so paramount in my thought process was the debacle we'd gone through in Vietnam (and Panama, with the F-117) by not reporting things accurately, and trying to put the best face on events. I would not tolerate that for one instant and there would be no second chances.

When I got back to Riyadh I took my notes from these talks to the wings and taped them to the top of my desk, where I would have them in plain view day after day during the war.

There was one unit I did not visit: the F-117s at Khamis Mushayt.

"You don't need to give your number-one unit in the theater a pep talk," I said when I telephoned Al Whitley. His number-one concern was he wanted six more F-117s to augment his force and help with maintenance flow, critical for the stealth materials of the aircraft. I personally called Bob Russ, told him what I needed and indicated Horner did not support my idea. "I'll work it for you," Russ said. Then I directed Whitley to remind his unit of what I'd written on their message board a few weeks earlier in December: "The Pride of Our Nation Depends on You."

Back to Riyadh

The visit to the wings indicated they were ready. I was filled with a combination of pride and emotion. But, back in Riyadh, I had to tend to a few more critical tasks.

One was blocking out a warfighting schedule so my key personnel and I would fit in work and sleep cycles with the right overlap and time for meetings and discussions. I staggered my schedule around the times when Horner would be active to make sure one of us would always be available; and I drew out out a schedule to make additionally sure that either Tolin, Lewis or myself would always be present in the Black Hole. From 1600 to 1800 each day, the three of us, plus Deptula, would be there together, clearing a solid block of time for key decisions as the war progressed.

As hard as this might be to believe, I intentionally waited as long as I could to put together the work schedule. If I'd put it together in December, I'd have been short some of my key players; Lewis wasn't there yet, and neither was Tolin. Also, while I'd had much of the staff around for months, I was re-evaluating people all the time. Some people keep increasing in value in your eyes, while some people plateau and level out and some people come down. That was another reason I wanted to wait. This way, I knew who was at their peak and who would be minding the store.

With the schedule in place and my reorganization of the campaign plans staff, I felt we were as ready to go as those pilots spread out across Saudi Arabia and the region. But there was one more extremely sensitive matter.

On January 15, I called McConnell and asked him specifically, "Is there a presidential directive on the war?"

"Yes," McConnell acknowledged.

"Let's discuss it," I said. "Make a memorandum for the record on this, because I don't want anybody second-guessing me after the war."

National Security Directives are the top-secret presidential guidance issued before any use of military force. Most generals would not necessarily know that one existed but my time in Washington had taught me I'd better ask, because there most certainly would be formal guidance, even if it was locked up in a safe.

Saddam and his nuclear, biological and chemical weapons resources were the most highly sensitive issues of the war—and I knew in my gut it was the type of issue that caused people to suddenly develop selective recall after the war. I had to know exactly what the president had authorized us to do, and I wanted McConnell and me to discuss it for the record, although for now, it would not see the light of day. As McConnell discussed the critical points of the NSD for me, it was clear that the directive authorized taking out chemical weapons, biological weapons, and suspected nuclear sites. If Saddam used chemical or biological weapons or conducted any type of terrorist attack, we could respond. In other words, if Saddam used chemical or biological weapons or initiated a terrorist attack, such as mass killing, or destroying Kuwaiti oilfields, then Saddam himself was a target by definition.

Not a Pretty Sight

Schwarzkopf then came to visit *us*. It was his first visit to the Black Hole, and it was not one I'd soon forget.

I had told him he needed to come over and show his face, now that the war was about to start. Schwarzkopf, Horner, and I gathered in one of the walled-off areas of the Black Hole. Deptula, in his flight suit, stood in front of the huge map of Iraq and Kuwait with Schwarzkopf standing next to him. Deptula talked through our plans for the first 24 hours: leadership, NBC targets, integrated command and control systems, and so on. It all went smoothly until Schwarzkopf asked, "Where are the B-52 strikes on the Republican Guard?" He didn't see them on the chart. "You promised me they were going to be attacked from day one. All the time. I won't have this," he said in a very loud voice.

I had never told him anything approaching that. It was always the strategic air campaign first, centered on the President's objectives, which were leadership, NBC, then military objectives, with an emphasis on the Republican Guard. What I promised Schwarzkopf was that once we started attacking the Republican Guard, I would basically attack them every three hours, the equivalent of a B-52 over them every hour. I had always indicated B-52s would be used at night and fighters during the day.

I said to him, "I never told you I was starting the B-52s right up front on the Republican Guard. In fact, that's not the right way to do it."

Schwarzkopf said, "That's what I want done."

"Well, then how many B-52s are you willing to lose in order to do this?" I asked.

"Don't be smart with me."

"I'm just being honest with you," I countered.

Horner stepped in and said, "Let's discuss this when we get up to my office."

"We're going to discuss it right now," Schwarzkopf said. "I said I wanted this done this way, and this is the way it's going to be done."

"Well, we can do that. The chances of losing airplanes are significantly higher. And if that's what we want to do, we can go ahead and do it. But it's not the right thing to do," I said.

"It is the right thing to do. Because that's what I want done. I'm directing you to do that."

I said, "Then we'll do it. I'll make the changes."

The staff in the Black Hole looked devastated. They thought they had this fantastic plan and for the CINC to be upset at that late stage was a little unsettling.

After his explosion, Schwarzkopf, Horner, and I went into Horner's office. We sat down and Schwarzkopf was in a totally different frame of mind. He looked over at me and said, "I told the SecDef and the President."

Suddenly, I understood why this was an explosion issue.

Schwarzkopf had not remembered that I had said I was going to start the B-52 attacks on the Republican Guard on Day Two. We'd be hitting some of their fixed targets sooner with the precision fighters. Earlier, I'd explained it to him this way: think of a B-52 dropping 108 bombs on a Republican Guard unit every 60 minutes, 24 hours a day, seven days a week, until the war is over. That's the best way to describe the intensity.

My mistake. It was just a way to describe what the B-52s could do. But I hadn't made it clear for him and that's what hurt. When he was talking to the President on the telephone, he told him "I'm going to drop 108 bombs on the Republican Guard every hour from the time this war starts." That was why it blew all his circuit breakers, because he knew instantly when Dave was reviewing the first 24 hours with him that this was not what he'd told the President.

His explosion that night was totally my fault. Not the CINC's fault. Now, do I believe that he and Horner and I should have gone off to the side and sorted this out, rather than have a nuclear explosion in front of a lot of junior officers? Absolutely. It was not his finest hour. But I inadvertantly caused that situation.

The end result was just as I promised. I increased our attacks on the Republican Guard during the first 24 hours. It turned out to be three B-52 strikes against the Tawakalna, a mechanized infantry division arrayed in killboxes AE6 and AF6, just inside Iraq on the northwestern border with Kuwait. Like most of the Republican Guard units, the Tawakalna was back from the conscript front lines on the Saudi border and ready to move as a second-echelon reserve.[3]

3. Department of the Air Force, Gulf War Air Power Survey, (Washington, DC: US Government Printing Office, 1993), Volume V, p. 463 for RG div locations by killbox.

Tactically, it was premature. My strategy was to wait until later to attack the Republican Guard, when the attacks might pressure them to move, making it easier to destroy them. But, you can only have one CINC during a war.

On the eve of war, however, the most important thing was keeping that trusting relationship with Schwarzkopf. I reflected on how during World War II, Eisenhower and Spaatz did not always agree, and often Spaatz gave in to what Eisenhower wanted. I could have the best ideas on the face of the earth, and if Schwarzkopf hadn't believed in them, and believed in me, they would never have seen the light of day. I had to keep his trust. Still it bothered me—not least for the effect on my Black Hole staff. The CINC's outburst revealed a side of him I had never witnessed before. '... *really bad ... voice very high ... junior officers everywhere,*' I scribbled down in my notes. '*Tension and pressure affect people differently ... he should be slowly rising to the top and taking the high road, instilling confidence.*'

Schwarzkopf would regroup, I was sure, but it left an everlasting scar.

Eve of Battle

Soon after, the warning order alerting us to an imminent operation came through in a telephone call from Schwarzkopf on January 15, 1991, at 1803 hours local time. Execution would follow in the next 18 to 20 hours. Barring a last-minute change, this was it.

'*War is never the desired option,*' I wrote down in a memorandum for the record. '*However, I don't know that the President has any other option.*'

I called some of my staff and wing commanders to pass on the warning order: Boomer, Tom, Jerry, Al, Ray, Dave, Sandy, Hal, Rick and Mike. All were positive; they were reserved, and somber, but ready.

So was I. At this time, I started a new diary. On the inside front cover I copied down a verse that had given me strength and comfort in Vietnam.

> *Where there is Faith, there is Love*
> *Where there is Love, there is Peace*
> *Where there is Peace, there is God*
> *Where there is God, there is no Need.*

I added '*En Shalah*'—Arabic for "God's Will."
On page one of that new diary book I wrote:

"Glosson's Rules for War Execution"
Care more than others think is wise
Risk more than others think is safe
Expect more than others think is possible
                                                    —Buster

Looking back at this diary, it strikes me that sometimes the truth shows in a peculiar way. I notice at the end of what I wrote is a prayer. I said: *I pray for the strength and wisdom to be aggressive, determined, but caring.* That's me. That's what I really wanted to do. I wanted to be more ruthless and more aggressive, and I wanted to be willing to take risks, but I wanted it to be prudent risk. I cared about the aircrews. Every fighter pilot who is in that airplane at night going north is the most important thing on the face of the earth to his wife and his children, his mother and his father.

Anytime a commander doesn't force himself to take enough time to think about that, that commander is going to make wrong decisions. You don't have to dwell on it, just think about it. Now if you dwell on it, you're equally likely to make the wrong decisions.

Finding the balance is the tough part. This is the way I look at it: You always make sure that you do everything that you possibly can to enhance or increase the probability of that pilot returning. Ultimately, you have to ask yourself, is this mission important enough that there is a 20-percent chance I'm going to lose two airplanes and the crews? What if there's a 50-percent chance I'm going to lose two airplanes? You have to ask yourself, is there any other way to do this? Is there another sequence to follow to reach the same objective? Maybe it will take a little longer, but is there another way to do it?

Don't default to brute force. Every commander should look at battle from the perspective of what is the best way to do this? How can you meet the needs of the nation, and with minimum loss of life? It doesn't matter whether that person with his or her life on the line is a marine, an airman, sailor or soldier. It doesn't matter to me whether they are wearing one stripe or four stars. It matters only that it's a human life.

I was obsessed with that. Coalition airmen in the Gulf had such superior training and technology we had no excuse for not finding the way to do the job with minimum loss of life. I don't think I ever let it get to the point where it caused me to take actions that were not in the best interest of the nation.

War Rhythm

January 16, 1991, was the eve of battle. *'Now is execution time,'* I wrote in my new diary. We'd have to live with the good decisions and the bad ones—I prayed the latter were few and far between.

I took a moment by myself to write down my thoughts on the men who'd dominate the pace of the war. Secretary of Defense Cheney— *'strong and decisive, he'd be the glue that held the political and military effort together.'* His leadership had already forced us generals to think through each step, in depth, and I believed our nation was fortunate to have him.

Advising Cheney, of course, would be Powell.

Of the CINC, I wrote down *'massive man . . . massive heart . . . volcanic temper.'* Discounting a few hiccups, like the previous day's outburst, there was no question that Schwarzkopf had us—the entire Coalition— ready to fight and win. What more could a nation ask?

Of Horner, I wrote: *'warrior mind . . . very savvy . . . super relationship with the CINC.'* The impact of that could not be overstated. Horner understood war from A to Z and he had molded CENTAF with his hands and mind. *'The results would speak for themselves. Thousands of lives will be saved as the result of his leadership!'* I finished.

Later that day I had a host of small things to do, but the big thoughts kept intruding. Schwarzkopf wasn't content with targeting the Tawakalna Division, the fix I'd given him on the Republican Guard issue, and now wanted the Medina and Hammurabi targeted instead! In a word, *dumb.* The solution was we did a little against all three.

Horner and I discussed the intricate plan to notify the king just one hour prior to the strikes. Horner said that General Behery had told him that the king must be the first person notified, but the king didn't want to be notified until one hour before H-hour.

This was a problem. How could the Royal Saudi Air Force make their take-off time with such short notice? I looked around for Sudairy.

"Look," I said, "You're the one who told me that you want your people airborne when this war starts. Do you want them airborne or not?"

"Yes," Sudairy said.

"Well here's what Horner just told me. You're briefed on the plan. Your crews need advance notice. Now how would you like for me to solve this?"

"You tell me what time you want them to be airborne, and I will have them airborne."

"Don't you think it's going to look a little strange to those fighter pilots down there when all of our fighter pilots are going to their airplanes at an odd hour of the night and it's obvious that the tension is very high?" I asked him.

"Just let me handle it."

So I put the sequence for the Saudis on a piece of paper and handed it to Sudairy.

"You get them airborne," I told him. And he did.

Shortly after noon, the CENTAF execution order was released. Its code name was the mascot for my alma mater North Carolina State: WOLFPACK. H-Hour would be 0300 on January 17.

Sudairy stopped by, and I promised to meet him later in the RSAF ops center at 2:30 in the morning. "Make sure CNN is working," I told him. He looked puzzled as he left.

I called McConnell, who said everyone at the Pentagon was tense but confident.

"Stay in touch," he told me as we hung up. As if I had a choice. Mike was our lifeline!

Gerry Riley came by to tell me the weather was fine now, but was probably going to go bad around noon on the 19th. He was almost in tears, so badly did he want the weather to be perfect for the campaign.

By four o'clock, low fog was settling in around Baghdad. The Black Hole was quiet and tense. I found another few minutes to scribble in my diary. I knew the air campaign would be a success — *'The only question is, what will be the price?'* I wrote. *'I can only hope and pray that I have made the correct decisions.'* I was confident, but like my wing commanders, not without my concerns. I prayed for accuracy on the biological and chemical weapons bunkers. I was truly leaning on the F-117s. We'd hit about 110 top strategic targets in the first day's segment, and 52 of those were assigned to the F-117s.

Finally I talked with my son, Brad. I will never forget his final words, "I pray for you every night. You have no idea how much you are missed. I love you. I'll keep tabs on Mom and Tanya." A moment of pride for a father! I wanted so badly to tell him we were about to go to war. But I couldn't. Over the telephone the risk was too high. *Lives at risk,* I sternly reminded myself. Instead, I did about the only thing left to do, especially for a general on the eve of battle, trying to instill confidence in everyone.

I got a haircut.

Back at my office, I cancelled the tactical deception plan to fake out the Iraqis by broadcasting that we'd had an F-117 crash. The AWACS that was part of the plan had a sudden abort; now, it was just too high risk to continue. McPeak called, lending support and telling me the Secretary of Defense wanted "no more Panamas" where the Air Force had initially covered over the F-117 missing the target. I told him I'd already discussed this forcefully and directly with my aircrews. *'Don't need anyone to remind me about integrity,'* I noted down.

There were more calls to Washington, and I reviewed the last-minute notification schedule with Horner.

Next I talked to Vicki. She was trying to be strong but I could tell she was worried. *'I love and miss her so much!'* I wrote.

Then I was back to my diary again.

'Sad thought of War (loss of lives) . . . relieved that it will soon be over . . . Nations must not be allowed to ignore a sovereign nation's rights and basic human rights—as Lincoln said, "Everyone must accept history."'

Lastly, I called my mom in North Carolina. She was nervous, and had a right to be, supporting her son through two wars. She was not the first mother with that experience and she wouldn't be the last, I knew. Still, I prayed for her comfort.

Around nine o'clock I vowed to go and get four hours of sleep, which would put me back in the office before H-Hour at 0300. I at least wanted some quiet time to finish a few tasks. I called Colonel Jack McGuiness at the U.S. Embassy in the UAE and told him to notify Sheikh Mohammed in the UAE that we were about to launch so that he wouldn't be surprised. Then I lay down on the bed and tried to sleep, but I could not relax.

Well before midnight, I realized my mind just wouldn't stop. I showered, dressed, and went back where I belonged.

H-HOUR

'God, I pray for your guiding hand on the stick with every fighter pilot that I'm sending into harm's way—keep each one safe and comfort their families. I pray for the strength and wisdom to be aggressive, determined but caring.'

War is similar to opening the door to a dark room. Uncertainty abounds.

I took out the creased 3-by-5 notecards I'd used when I talked to the wings. Now I read them over myself. *'Not one target worth dying for unless Allied lives are on the line.'*

With one minute to go, all was calm. *'Everything's on track, the tension is rising,'* I jotted down. The attitude was very professional, very focused.

I went back over to the Black Hole. Lewis was standing just inside the door waiting for me. He abruptly said, "I'm worried about the TACC (Tactical Air Control Center) dealing with the unexpected."

"Not an original thought," I shot back. "So am I."

We walked to the TACC. Horner came in, and I directed Lewis, Deptula and Rogers to stay in the TACC until H + 3 and answer any questions from Horner, Olsen or Corder and come to me right away with any glitches.

Horner and I sat together in the TACC at H-Hour. It seemed surreal to a certain extent. We were by ourselves, looking at the screens in the half-dark of the room, not really talking. CNN announced the attack was underway and ran film of barrage firing in Baghdad.

Soon we started getting reports of MiGs airborne at Tallil and taxiing at Al-Taqqadum. The Iraqis were waking up. The thing that gave me the greatest comfort was that I had put Tolin on the AWACS as the airborne commander for the first 12 hours. He'd respond when he needed to—decide whether to reroute a package if support aircraft did not link up, for example. Tolin would make all the instantaneous decisions, which is why I was so comfortable because we had planned it together and now that execution was taking place, I had my deputy aloft as the airborne commander.

A report came in from Al Kharj: one F-15E had aborted before take-off, and the three other F-15Es in the package had taken "sympathetic aborts."

I called Al Kharj immediately. The vice wing commander answered the hotline. "What is this sympathetic abort stuff?" I demanded. "This is not an exercise at Nellis. We're at war."

I left no doubt in his mind that whoever made that decision shouldn't be making any more decisions. I wanted Hornburg to rectify the situation at the speed of light and I was sure he would when he found out about those sympathetic aborts.

Next I had another promise to keep. I had promised Sudairy that he wouldn't be stuck in the loneliness of the Saudi ops center by himself as the war started.

I walked down and put my arm around him and we talked.

The first thing Sudairy asked was, "Why is CNN announcing what we're doing?"

"Look, don't worry about that; it's okay," I replied. "The news coverage will not hurt our efforts; it will help us." The Middle East—the whole world, really—was about to learn from watching their televisions exactly what happens when a nation-state steps over the line. Sudairy and I then went over some of the RSAF missions in detail.

Back at the TACC, the massive campaign we'd orchestrated began to unfold. Twenty-one minutes prior to H-Hour, one Air Force MH-53 Pave Low led three Army AH-64 Apaches to attack an early-warning radar site on the border. Another team of two Pave Lows and six Apaches hit a second radar site 12 miles away. The helicopter attack opened a five-to-eight-mile corridor for the F-15Es and EF-111s to attack stationary Scud sites at H-2 and H-3 in western Iraq.

We told the helicopter aircrews to stay below 200 feet. As it turned out, they stayed below 100 feet. The fast-movers—the F-15Es and EF-111s—were restricted to a minimum altitude of 300 feet until north of the helicopter area.

The 18 F-15Es and 10 helicopters were less than 150 feet apart in some cases, with the F-15Es headed to the target and the helicopters coming out. The F-15Es could see the helicopters on their LANTIRN night vision systems, and the helicopters saw the F-15Es through their night vision goggles. The airmanship, determination, and courage demonstrated by both the helicopter and fighter crews were very impressive. Passing in the dark of night less than 300 feet apart with a 600 mph closure speed will flutter the strongest heart.

If the helicopter mission had failed, the probability was high that the Iraqi early-warning radars would have detected the F-15Es 15 or 20 minutes before they attacked their Scud targets. With that much warning, the Iraqis may have launched Scuds from fixed sites toward Israel on the very first night of the war.

Already threading their way through Iraq were the first six F-117s. Their job was to collapse the major pillars of the Iraqi command and control for air defenses: the Integrated Operations Center at Nukhayb and at Al-Taqqadum, the sector operations center at H-3 airfield, the Baghdad Telecom center, and the North Taji military research complex— a suspected nuclear site. The third F-117 on my list had the target we were all watching for: the Al Karakh telephone and international exchange building, or as we all called it, the AT&T building. As soon as the F-117 hit it, CNN's live feed from Baghdad went off the air. At the TACC our television tuned to CNN showed blue-gray snow and static. The TACC erupted into a cheer. The war was underway.

The first hour went so well that it bothered me. You could feel the tension sliding out of the room and that could cost us if we had to react fast.

I knew the fighter pilots out there in the dark skies were not guilty of this stupidity. They were seeing more anti-aircraft fire and SAMs than they'd ever seen in their lives.

To keep the staff on the knife's edge I started asking questions.

"Why don't we know what's happening here?"

"We've got an F-111F that diverted, tell me why."

"We have an F-117 that hasn't checked in. Where is he?"

Questions made people stay tuned in to what was going on—and a lot was going on. More F-117s hit integrated and sector operations centers, the Baghdad air defense headquarters and another target at Taji. F-15Es let loose on suspected Scud launch sites at Iraq's western-most airfields, H-2 and H-3. TLAMs from Navy ships in the Gulf worked over many targets in and around Baghdad including Saddam's presidential palace and the Ba'ath Party headquarters. F-111s equipped with laser-guided bombs (LGB) attacked control centers at other airfields and a chemical weapons storage site at Mosul. Navy A-6s, also ready with laser-guided bombs, took on the hangars, runway, and ramps at Shaibah airfield in the south.

The remaining hours of darkness brought more waves of F-117 attacks on airfields, leadership sites, biological weapons bunkers, and command and control. F-16s and A-10s pounded SAM sites and ground forces and later on, as Schwarzkopf directed, three B-52s pounded two of the Republican Guard divisions.

Through it all, F-15s and F-14s swept the sky and pooled to protect high-value assets such as the EA-6Bs. The Iraqis got 55 fighters up that night. Seven Iraqi fighters fell to the Air Force and Navy that day—not including one Iraqi fighter that flew into the ground after being outmaneuvered by an EF-111 electronic jammer.

'All we know at this point is our losses have been zero but our success or failure is unknown until BDA . . . why . . . doesn't everyone understand . . . I should have worked this point harder during planning,' I put in my notes. Another 20-20 hindsight thought.

The first call I made back to Washington was to Admiral McConnell. "Washington's very upbeat," McConnell said. I didn't need to hear that. I was concerned about people over there being *too* upbeat too soon. It was the first night of the war for goodness' sake. I asked him what the overheads were showing on the special operations forces and also if he had any indication of where Saddam was. He didn't.

And then to make my night totally complete, I turned on the radio and heard one of the AM radio networks announce 'the Iraqi Air Force and Republican Guard are destroyed.' This was 6 or 7 o'clock in the morning! It was only three hours after the war had started!

Schwarzkopf called. "Absolutely great!" he said as I scribbled down notes. "Our plan is working. Keep it on track. If you need my help on anything, let me know. Really a super start."

I was pleased but not about to show it. Besides, I had some concerns.

"You know," I said to him, "before we started, people were talking who did not know what was planned, now people are talking and they don't know what's happened."

He and I agreed we needed a high-quality news leak to balance it out, so I released some material to the *New York Times*. I did not want the American people to think it was all over on night one.

Sand-on-sand

On the whole, it was a triumphant night for the F-117s. But just before noon, the first major operational issue reared its head. Al Whitley from the F-117 wing called. "The sand-on-sand problem we talked about is now real," said Whitley.

Before Christmas we'd pondered over whether the F-117s would be able to get good, precise hits on the bunkers. Whitley was concerned because the contrast was extremely difficult. "Dirt on dirt," said Bob Eskridge, one of the F-117 wing representatives on my staff. They thought that we'd only have about a 50-percent success rate the first night out on the bunkers. For another opinion, I'd asked Tolin about it, since he was a former commander of the F-117s wing. "They're probably right," he said.

Sure enough, Whitley's pilots from the first missions came back, showed the mission tapes of their targeting images and told him during the debriefs that the sand was giving them problems. Several of the first night's targets for the F-117 were bunkers with three to five feet of sand over the top of them. The F-117 targeting system used forward-looking infrared to generate a picture of the target area, which was why they had to be below the clouds to hit accurately, since clouds broke up the infrared sensors. The pilot used the infrared picture to accurately place his laser-designator right on the spot where he wanted the bomb to impact. With buildings, the edges and angles created a sharp, clear image. But the sand-covered bunkers were tricky to pick out. With the desert background, you don't have enough readily apparent discrimination for a precision weapon. In other words, unless you happen to get a temperature delta or some other way to discriminate, you're down to the old routine of looking for shadows, and that's a "hope and a pray" way of placing precision weapons.

A quick assessment of missions indicated it was a combination of problems: fusing, more sand than we expected, less contrast. And it was a serious issue because the sand-covered bunkers included bunkers we suspected might have biological or chemical weapons in them.

"Thanks for the update," I told Whitley. "You've got to do whatever is necessary to improve immediately."

After talking to Whitley I decided not to say anything to anyone else. In my notes I wrote, *'I'll wait and see how long it takes the system to pass the bad news up.'* That was at 11:40 in the morning. Within a few hours, Deptula and Eskridge came to me and admitted the F-117 Battle Damage Assessment (BDA) of the bunkers looked bad. As Whitley had warned, only one chemical/biological bunker was breached. We'd tried to target eight bunkers and got one. In addition to the contrast problem, the fusing was wrong. Someone's brain had momentarily disengaged. Never select an instantaneous fuse setting when you're dropping on sand, unless you want to dig a foxhole. The bombs should have had a few milliseconds' delay to penetrate the sand layer and get to the bunkers.

Next I discovered Deptula had moved strikes off some of the biological and chemical sites without my knowledge. In other words, he'd decided not to strike two or three chemical and biological weapons storage sites so we could put those sorties on some other target and ensure more parallel warfare. I directed him in no uncertain terms that all target changes concerning nuclear, biological and chemical weapons had to have my personal approval. I was being a bit ruthless, but he was too bright for a mistake that basic.

We also had dramatic feedback on the issue of F-117s and EF-111s. Before the war, the planners from the F-117 wing came to me and asked for jamming. I thought it would backfire, but I did not want to dictate their tactics to them. "I'm going to put the EF-111 exactly where you want it and everybody's going to see barrage fire like they've never seen in their life," I'd warned them in exasperation. "The EF-111s are going to tip everybody off. Now you're going to be subject to losing an airplane because somebody's convinced you back on the other side of the Atlantic that you can get shot down. I'm telling you that won't happen."

Well, we lucked out. Of the two EF-111s that were supposed to jam, one of them aborted. The first three F-117s went in unaided. Nobody saw a shot.

But the other EF-111 did show up. This EF-111 started jamming, and the next F-117 pilot saw the fireworks display of his life.

"The F-117 pilots aren't interested in any more EF-111s," Tolin told me the next day. He'd talked to several pilots in the wing. "They said the barrage fire was unbelievable," Tolin told me.

1900 Staff Meeting

At 1900 we were scheduled to meet with Schwarzkopf to review Day One and plans for the upcoming night. The 1900 staff meeting became a nightly routine and the setting for some of the most significant discussions and decisions of the air war. Deptula, Lewis and I started pulling together the first night's results. I put Lewis in charge of building my briefing to review each night's activities. *'Lewis is the only person objective enough to work this problem daily,'* I jotted down. *'Must keep this straightforward and easy to track: what did we plan; what did we do; what are we planning.'*

The first day was about what we expected, save for the good news that the losses were unbelievably low so far. On the negative side, the Iraqis had evacuated the Ministry of Information and the Ministry of Defense, which we'd bombed. I didn't see any sense in blowing up a building just to get rid of it. I told him about the sand problems with the F-117 strikes on the chemical/biological bunkers. Most of all, we wanted to stress that this was not a one-day war. Schwarzkopf certainly appreciated that. At the meeting, he was very low-key, and stressed the long-term.

"It will not be over until we occupy Kuwait," Schwarzkopf said. He reiterated how he wanted to focus on the Republican Guard and talked over the status of other strategic targets. I was glad the meeting went well but I left with a feeling that there was not enough tough scrutiny. Overall, I wrote in my notes, *'it was almost a "love-in."'*

As soon as I got back from the meeting I called McConnell to debrief him. This, too, became a nightly ritual. From McConnell, I learned we'd had no luck against Saddam so far.

Then, there was confirmed bad news. The missing Navy F/A-18 was down southwest of Baghdad. The first reports indicated we'd lost it to a SAM.

And my friend Tom Kortz had been shot down in an F-15E. As a flight surgeon, Tom was a doctor who'd also been through pilot training and qualified to fly the F-15E. He always wanted to fly, and be a doctor both, so we let him. It was a heart-rending loss. He was the best flight surgeon I'd ever known. He'd been my flight surgeon at Moody Air Force Base in Georgia, and everybody agreed that he was a potential Surgeon General of the Air Force one day.

I had already told Hornburg that I was going to ground Tom after three flights. He'd died on the first one. I hated the way it happened. Tom's F-15E was the sixth one in bombing an oil refinery target southeast of Basra. That should never have happened. We were never 100-percent sure because there was heavy AAA in the area, but we thought it was a heat-seeking missile that hit him. *'God, comfort his family and give them strength,'* I wrote in my diary.

The Iraqi Air Defense System

Despite the losses, our first night's success was overwhelming. More than a thousand sorties flown. That first night more than met all our expectations; it was a success beyond anything imagined by commanders in previous wars. The major target was the Iraqi command and control system, constructed largely by the French and to a lesser extent, the Swedes.

The Ericsson Company in France was the brain behind much of their technology. Ericsson's executives were very helpful in making sure we understood the capacities of the systems they'd installed. For example, the system was not unlimited. It could be saturated, and when saturated, it shunted into a memory mode once it had upwards of 100 targets being tracked at one time. With Ericsson's assistance, we used all of the limitations of the Iraqi system to our advantages. If you could put one of the integrated operations centers or sector operations centers into a memory mode, or force it to hand off to another one, then that was to your advantage, because it progressively degraded the system. Our plan was to saturate certain sectors intentionally.

There are still things I can't divulge. Let me just say, with the help of Ericsson, the Thompson Company, and the Navy's analysts at Dahlgren, Virginia, we knew so much about the Iraqi Air Defense System (IADS), we could have built it ourselves. For all practical purposes, there was nothing we didn't understand about the command and control of their IADS. I'd say we knew more about Iraq's system than we did the Warsaw Pact's, even though we had studied the Warsaw Pact air defenses for many more years. There's no substitute for sitting down with the engineer that built something and listening to him explain its strengths and weaknesses from A to Z.

Of course, there was one area that was not perfect, and that was the physical structure of the facilities. It turned out we had a hard time at first getting the bombs to penetrate the structure of the operations centers. Later, we determined this was because the Iraqis had layered sand, gravel, and steel on top the facilities. Mixed materials played havoc with weapons effects. It was actually better for us to drop the bomb near the edge, rather than directly in the center, in order to penetrate the mixed densities. That final piece of information came to us only after the war was underway.

Larry Henry worked the IADS plan, and had it in place by October. Thanks to him, the electronic warfare assault had prevented the Iraqis from disrupting the first night's attacks. That had permitted us to be very successful in taking out the integrated air defenses and Iraq's ability to strike back in a coordinated fashion with surface-to-air missiles. It was not by accident. Henry thought it all out. His scheme of drones and massive, simultaneous HARM launches pulled a great psychological trick on the Iraqi air defenders.

Basically, we were limited in the ability to find and hit Iraqi radar sites. The HARM missile did a great job when it was in range to lock onto emitting radar. The problem was finding and locating the radars. The F-4Gs had a special system that allowed them to hunt down SAMs and triangulate to the location of the radar based on its emissions. The Navy's F/A-18s lacked this system, so their tactics were different. They launched a barrage of pre-emptive HARMs in areas where intelligence believed radars might be active. The Navy's HARMs in the air would lock onto any radar that came alive while the strike package passed, essentially clearing a corridor, via brute force.

We did not have enough F-4Gs to find all the radar sites in Iraq. But I wanted the Iraqis to think that we did.

The only thing to do was to create a situation where it gave the impression that they were more lethal than they were.

Thinking out loud, I said wishfully, "If only we could have them think that every time they turn on a radar, they've got about 30 seconds to live."

"We may be able to pull that off if we use the F-18s," Henry suggested.

We quickly named our effort Poobah's Party, using Henry's nickname of Poobah. Henry ran the drones ahead first, getting everybody in Iraq to turn on their radars. Henry coordinated it so that when the barrage launch came they'd have the maximum number of radars up emitting signals for the free-fired HARMs to lock on and hit.

"We'll strike so many radar vans and radar control nodes that they're going to be paranoid and they won't turn their radars on. They're going to start ballistically firing missiles," he said.

That's exactly what happened. We'd never have enough HARM

shooters to pin down every radar site in Iraq. Instead, the onslaught on night one took out enough Iraqi radars and had enough direct hits that it looked like we were omnipotent. We had sixty-some airplanes in a period of less than 30 minutes launching HARMs.

To the Iraqis, Poobah's Party looked like we had a very lethal way of dealing with any surface-to-air threat they might throw at us. They were afraid to turn on their radars. Actually, the image of that first night was far in excess of what we really had. However, that worked beautifully for us and it contributed massively throughout the rest of the war. The Iraqis never recovered, psychologically speaking. That's why they launched so many SAMs ballistic, because they didn't want to run the risk of having the radar on.

The other portions of the strategic air campaign were finely tuned to accomplish their purposes. I believed the majority of everything important to Saddam could be taken away from him with the strategic attacks in Phase I of the war. My philosophy was I want there to be a purpose for everything that we're doing, every bomb we drop.

Now, there are some cases where you have to send political messages to the leadership and to the people, for psychological reasons. I bombed things Saddam was proud of, including his nuclear, biological and chemical weapons research sites and apparatus.

I bombed police stations, intelligence facilities, and places where I knew the Iraqi regime tortured people. Anytime potential dissidents were arrested, the Ba'ath Party and its henchmen would use a certain list of buildings. I wanted to destroy things that were associated with Saddam's fake mystique, the aura he tried to keep up in front of his people, linking himself to the lineage of the ancient ruler Nebuchadnezzar. I wanted Saddam to feel the pressure.

Day Two

No one could have flown as many sorties as we flew, almost flawlessly, without letting it go to their heads a little bit. I leaned over the other way, being critical.

First on my list was the ATO.

"This ATO is taking so much time that we are going to wind up having to act like the Navy and take every third day off if we don't watch what we're doing," Lewis said.

It was just taking too long to build an ATO people could execute properly, and part of it was because of unexpected problems with the computer itself. The program that we finally used worked fine when it was being used in a more leisurely way, but when you're trying to get things laid out under the stress of being at war, those things have a tendency not to work quite as well as you expect. If it was a minor problem for us now, it would be a big problem within a few days. I directed Lewis to find the problem and correct it.

From talking to wing commanders and others, I also sensed we had a tanker problem brewing. One-hundred-sixty tankers were airborne the first night.[1]

We also had air control problems. As one of the wing commanders told me, it was only by the grace of the good Lord that we didn't run a few airplanes into each other on the first night. On January 18, Tolin was back from his 12-hour shift as airborne commander. He debriefed me on his concerns: lack of the overall 'big picture' in the TACC was one.

"They don't really understand what we're doing," Tolin said. "They just take the ATO and they execute it. They don't understand how it all fits together. It's like they're operating in a vacuum."

Without a grasp of the operational intent, the senior officer in the TACC could approve changes on the fly, but by changing a target here or there, the whole purpose of the night's attacks could drift away. "It's absolutely essential that we put somebody up there as the Airborne Command Element (ACE) that has an understanding of what we're trying to accomplish during the whole 24 hours, so that when they make changes or decisions, they know the impact of what's happening," Tolin said.

Since my hour of pretend sleep the night before, I hadn't even thought of sleep again. From the night of January 16 until the morning of January 19, I didn't sleep at all. I reminded Horner that either he or I had to be available to the TACC all the time. He would be out of the TACC from 2300 until 0600. I'd leave after he arrived, about 0700, and sleep until 1300. Horner established a staff meeting at 0700. I told him there was no way I could be there according to our agreed-on sleep schedule.

"No problem, don't worry about it," Horner said charitably. "Just let one of your guys be there." Deptula or Buck Rogers usually covered that meeting for me.

Iraq launched Scuds at Israel on night two of the war. It was a tough

1. James P. Coyne, *Air Power in the Gulf.* (Arlington, VA.; Air Force Association, 1992.)

night for Israel. Six or more Scuds fired off and three hit in population areas, injuring seven Israelis. A seventh Scud headed for Dhahran where the Army's Patriot missile batteries brought it down. Fortunately the Scuds were armed with conventional warheads, not poison gas. In response, Israel launched dozens of attack jets before dawn, but miraculously, they stayed in Israeli airspace.[2]

The Scud alert spotlighted a problem I'd already sensed: I needed more flexibility. The ACE and TACC had failed to keep F-15Es on quick alert on the tanker tracks as word of the Scud launches came in. They permitted airborne F-15Es return to base at Al Kharj when we had intended that they stay on the tanker; if they'd been there, they could have responded to a Scud alert and gone out to destroy the launchers.

Responding to targets of opportunity was one of my main concerns about the war. It was at the root of my apprehensions about the TACC. If we got a good lead on a Scud launcher or if the Iraqi ground forces pulled a stunt or if McConnell had a lead on Saddam's whereabouts, I had to be able to get a strike aircraft on it right away and it had to be precision. What I wanted was six to eight airplanes, either F-15-Es or F-111s, already on alert, pre-loaded, with full frag orders—call signs, etc.—so that I could get them airborne within an hour and send them wherever I wanted. If nothing else, the random nature of the Scud launches was going to demand flexible attack. Tolin and I talked it over and decided to task the F-111s as my flexible force.

Lewis also brought me several of his concerns, as I'd told him to do.

"I have a lot of balls in the air," I told him. "Your job is to make sure I don't drop one of them."

By the second day, in Lewis' opinion, at least four of the big issues we were juggling were threatening to crash down right on my head. The first was the TACC, which I already knew about.

"Look, I know that, but I can't just totally get rid of them, so we've got to figure out how to take critical things away from them and move the responsibility to the Black Hole so it won't get screwed up," I said.

Next Lewis said, "Boss, the number-one problem we've got that has the highest potential of going wrong tomorrow is the ATO for the tankers. It's out of control."

Lewis was the quiet, soft-spoken type and he didn't make state-

2. *It Doesn't Take a Hero*, p. 417.

ments like that unless they were accurate so I knew that now this was my number-one problem.

Lewis had more bad news. The weather had been fine on night one, but he looked up a long-range forecast, and it was bad. With the weather fronts coming across, there was no way that we were going to be able to execute days two, three, and four in the way we'd planned.

"This is a potential disaster," Lewis said. "We have got to start rethinking the plan, especially our priorities."

All of our precision targeting platforms—F-117, F-111, A-6, a few F-15Es—relied on infrared imaging for laser guidance and the clouds were going to blot it out. Here we sat with a minutely choreographed plan built around the F-117. The weather forecast meant we'd have numerous weather cancellations or F-117s bringing back weapons if there were clouds over the target area. We could not just wait it out. We would sequence our strike aircraft with the storm fronts: fly in ahead of them, between them, or behind them. Like it or not, we were going to be forced to change the plan and coordinate it with the weather.

Finally, I had to get a firmer grip on the process of changes. "No plan survives contact with the enemy," Patton had said. Sure enough, we had changes rippling through the whole air plan. A target would not be struck for multiple reasons, because an airplane aborted for maintenance, for weather or a refueling that got screwed up. Deptula and Baptiste monitored that and they would just unilaterally decide to take airplanes off another target and move them over to hit the first target. Lewis gave me a heads up that they were making some changes to the targeting and asked if I was aware of it.

Targeting changes were yet one more twist in the execution and as a commander, I had to watch them closely. TACC staff was used to making changes in execution at their discretion. I solved it by getting Horner to mandate that there'd be no change sheets by anybody unless I initialed the change. It was unheard of for the TACC to have to get approval to make a change. Normally, a planner does not sign off on execution changes. But this time, I owned all the fighters, as well as the planning. I wanted to make sure that all the small changes did not add up to a different air war than we meant to prosecute.

Horner backed me up. "Look, you planned the thing," he said to me, "so you have a better understanding of what you're trying to accomplish and how things are going. You can't have other people making changes to what might be the critical cog of a particular night's efforts without you knowing about it, because you know the impact of moving this and not doing that, and nobody else does."

It fit in with his philosophy, as he explained later. "I did not want them to become so enthralled with preplanning that they were unable to react when the war started," Horner said a short while later. He wanted us to be proficient at action and reaction, and leave room to spot and capitalize on the enemy's mistakes. He called it "chaos war."[3]

Chaos

How right he was. We did have chaos. At times it seemed no one could follow basic guidance, even direct and clear orders. For example, I directed McBroom and Hornburg to set up a Combat Air Patrol of F-15Cs over Baghdad. I told them to keep one CAP over Baghdad and the other circling nearby so Baghdad would be covered at all times.

I had two reasons for this. First, the tactics: Baghdad was just a short distance to the Iranian border and I did not want Saddam to escape in an aircraft; second, I just wanted to show Saddam Hussein and all of Baghdad that we were in total control. Not partial control, total control. I wanted to deliver the statement, *We're right overhead of your capital, your major city, and there isn't a thing you can do about it. If we decide that we want to come down and land, we'll do that too.* It was a little bit of a psychological game.

Unbeknownst to me, Corder as the CENTAF/DO had put out a message directing the F-15Cs to stand off at a distance, instead of circling Baghdad. I called McBroom and Hornburg and made sure they understood: "Circle Baghdad unless I direct otherwise."

Word soon came in of a massive screw-up and tragically, the loss of two aircraft. I'd sent 48 F-16s to the Baghdad nuclear research site. F-117s had already hit the target, but the F-16s were going in to level it. This was one target that needed destruction, not effects. The mission put the F-16s up closer to the center of Baghdad than anybody else ever flew, except for the F-117s. I knew that. But I believed that we'd timed and sequenced the package with ample SEAD support.

I called Nelson over in Doha. "What happened?"

"A refueling problem. The F-4Gs were late, so I split the package 24

3. GWAPS I, Part 2, p. 208.

south and 12 north. Air-to-air and SEAD went with south package," he added.

I was furious. "I had 24 going south, 24 going north. The 24 going north were in the most high-threat area and yet you send the SEAD with the south package so the 12 went north alone and we're surprised they lost two to SAMs?"

"Did I not tell you there was no target in Iraq worth dying for right now? Why didn't you just abort 6 or 12 aircraft?" I asked.

"We screwed up," he said.

"That is an understatement. That kind of bullshit will not happen again," I thundered. I was so angry I just handed the telephone to Tolin in mid-conversation without another word. I was livid. The thought process of how that decision was made was absolutely mind-boggling to me.

Nor were the results worth it. The F-16s were bombing from 20,000 feet and to make it even harder, the Iraqis had smoke generators obscuring the target area. The Iraqis had a berm around the reactor area, and of the 36 F-16s attacking, we later counted only seven bombs that fell within the berm, and none hit the target.

When the ACE for that day landed, boy did I ever rip into him. He'd let it happen, at least tacitly. "Why do you think you're up there?" I said to him. "That's the kind of decision you're supposed to be making. You just sent the whole 36 airplanes on and forgot about it." It was a disgrace.

Television

To the outside world, the air campaign so far looked like a resounding success—for the Navy. They suddenly released so much footage of their carrier deck operations that it looked like the Navy fliers were the only ones at war.

A carrier launch is great TV. Glowing afterburners, huge roar, the whole thing over in two seconds. In reality, they were only flying about 10 percent of the sorties, but on television, they were getting 99 percent of the coverage, because the networks had no other combat video to run.

It was insane. Of course, we did not have cameras filming at all the Saudi bases. I released bombing footage from the precision strikes of the F-117s and F-111s, just to make sure the playing field stayed level.

These gun-camera video frames were the first pictures of their kind, and the public loved them, even in black and white, with no sound, just an image no one could fail to grasp: precision bombs driving straight into the targets. That became the classic image of the Gulf War.

Back in the United States, one person watching her television very closely was my mom. She was doing all right, considering, but I wanted to encourage her not to worry, so I found time to call her on January 19. She was very distressed because she'd been watching TV and all she was seeing were all these bombs going off. I knew she was just picturing her son sitting in the middle of that, plus seeing the Scuds hit in Israel and Riyadh.

Mom, in her southern way, always said, "If it's worth doing, it's worth doing right." I always tried to make her feel good like everybody does with his own mother. So when I called her I said cheerfully, "Mom, remember when you told me if it's worth doing, it's worth doing correctly? I just want to tell you that's exactly what I'm doing so you don't have to worry about anything."

"I'm praying for you, son," was her response.

She saw right through it. She knew I was just putting the best face on everything.

Mom's prayers were needed, because by six o'clock that evening, nothing seemed to be going right. All the predictions about trouble were coming true. We were supposed to send out the Day Three ATO, with strikes to start after midnight, but by eight o'clock, less than half of it had been generated. Corder sent it out to the wings anyway. Lack of tanker availability caused many strike packages to cancel.

Execution was threatening to overwhelm us and turn the brisk, forceful campaign into a labyrinth. The best defense was a good offense: make changes. For weather alone, we made 29 changes on Day Two, 47 on Day Three, then 109 on Day Four and an astronomical 395 changes on Day Five as the weather fronts got a chokehold. Changes of all types—from weather to maintenance to target changes and other cancellations, started at 68 on Day Two then soared to 449 on Day Three, 813 on Day Four and 975 on Day Five before settling to a more typical 552 on Day Six.[4] The only other days with over 900 changes were during the ground war.

Although I didn't have the numbers at the time, it was clear to me that our ability to pull off changes when needed was key to the operational art.

The ATO process was like sludge. As Lewis had warned, the computers and software of the day just weren't up to it. The Computer Assisted Force Management System Software even as babied by Cosby was stressed to the limit and then some. At least most Air Force units had

4. GWAPS Vol. I part 2 pp. 216–18.

CAFMS terminals. The Navy did not, and there was no place to install them on the carriers. So the ATO went out to the Navy by the COD—the C-2 Greyhound aircraft that ran all carrier on-board delivery.

The number of sorties we were flying stressed the staff as well as the computers. They'd never experienced anything like that. It was just overwhelming. Ultimately, it took us almost two and a half weeks to get to a point where the ATO went out at a time that was acceptable to me: between 1500 and 1700. For the first two weeks, the ATO would be published somewhere between 1800 and 2100.[5]

Ralph Waldo Emerson said, "The future belongs to those who prepare for it." I copied that down in my diary after Day One. I used that quote a lot. I wanted to make sure that everybody understood that our success going forward was going to be the result of what they were doing to *make* it a success. It wasn't going to just happen on its own. I didn't want them thinking it would all unfold through some mythical act or run on its own perpetual motion.

I started firing the Emerson quote around in the Black Hole because I knew that if I used a quote, it would make more of a sobering impact on some people than it would if I just was ranting and raving about glitches. Emerson's quote was also a reminder to myself that success on Day One had nothing to do with success tomorrow. We had very early warning of potential problems: the ATO process, tankers, Deptula's targeting. If we sat back and waited, catastrophe would strike us. I wanted everyone else to have that thought process in mind.

I started making another diary entry every day, to remind myself. Every time I would write down the new date in my notes, I'd write down on the side: '*SAVING LIVES.*' That way, I had to be honest with myself and ask, "Are you still trying to do that to the maximum extent that you're capable of?" I knew that I solely could control the number of lives that were lost more than any other one person on the face of the earth during this war. Even more than Schwarzkopf. I knew that. And I took that responsibility very seriously.

Staff Meeting Night Two

Few of these brewing issues surfaced at Schwarzkopf's second wartime evening meeting.

5. GWAPS Vol. I part 2 p. 223.

The typical meeting format was a weather briefing, intelligence briefing and then me. I'd give a run-down on the air war, and then Yeosock discussed the ground planning. Over time, more and more people filtered into the meetings, until Schwarzkopf had his executive assistant, Colonel B. B. Bell, cut the staff meeting to the absolute minimum. After that, some briefers would come in just for their portion of the meeting and then leave. My format was that I'd always show him what we had done, using the slides Lewis generated. Lewis generally came with me to the meetings. Then I would either show videotape, or perhaps an acetate vu-graph with a picture to give Schwarzkopf an overall feel for an upcoming target or previous strike. I'd give him a little bit of the logic as to why we were attacking particular targets.

For example, I might say, "the Ba'ath Party is now operating primarily from Tikrit and they have moved their operations out of Baghdad, so therefore I'm going to take out these three facilities up in Tikrit. I'm going to take out the bridges and try to isolate Tikrit as much as I can because that may get Saddam to do something stupid, and expose himself." Schwarzkopf's support was total; he never questioned me on any of that, until much later in the war.

On this night, I told him privately after the meeting that from what McConnell was saying, Powell and Cheney, especially, were very concerned about the Scud attacks on Israel.

"It's a distraction, not militarily significant," Schwarzkopf said dismissively.

I could not believe that came out of his mouth. Of all the things he said during the entire war, the only thing I thought was intellectually not up to his standard was that statement. By definition, if it's politically significant, it's going to become militarily significant, especially when the Secretary of Defense is telling you this could blow the Palestinian-Israeli-Arab mess all to shambles. It's got to be important militarily by definition. I was sure we'd be forced to deal with the Scuds and soon.

Despite two good days, the war still held many uncertainties. Schwarzkopf announced there would be a press conference soon and he wanted either Horner or me there with him. When I heard this, I jotted down, 'We may be reading too many of our own press clippings' and I underlined it. We were being too euphoric over two days of things going like we planned. Here we were, a superpower fighting a Third-World dictatorship and one that was not able to muster a sane strategic attack when they were fighting another Third-World dictatorship in Iran. And here we're celebrating because we're doing so well? We should have been absolutely appalled if we hadn't been doing unbelievably well.

That same evening, Sudairy pulled me aside.

"Is the RSAF carrying its share of the load?" he asked. The real issue, I sensed, was whether the Saudi pilots were taking their turn at striking the difficult targets. As he said to me later, "American blood is not going to be the only blood shed in this war."

For me, that flew in the face of saving lives, whether they were Saudi lives or American lives. I told Sudairy in no uncertain terms that I could not compromise on that principle.

"I'm planning and executing this war in a way that had the highest probability for the minimum loss of life and that includes Saudi lives," I said.

But it was a sore spot for Sudairy and eventually, he went to Horner to get approval for the Saudis to strike tougher targets. "You know what this is about," I said to Horner. "All Sudairy's concerned about is they show that the Saudis are going to tough targets just like everybody else. I'm not sending our conventional airplanes to tough targets where they get shot down, and I'm sure not going to send the Saudis."

"You need to let Sudairy make the decision for the Saudis, not you," Horner replied.

So Sudairy and I reviewed upcoming tactical attack plans. He looked it over carefully and made a selection.

"I'd rather for the Royal Saudi Air Force to hit this target," Sudairy said, pointing to the list. I looked and sure enough, it was high threat. The target was also in close proximity to a mosque and Sudairy played that card with flourish.

"In case we have a stray bomb, I want it to be a Saudi bomb, not an American bomb," he said. What possible response did I have to that? Nothing. Sudairy was very intelligent and clever. Of course, the only reason he wanted the RSAF to go there was because it was high threat. It had nothing to do with the mosque, but he pretended it did and he presented it in a way that I couldn't refute it. I was certain he wanted to get a Saudi airplane shot down so they could say they lost somebody, too.

Low-Altitude Tactics

While Sudairy wanted tougher targets, I had another ally taking a pasting. The British GR-1 Tornado carried a special submunition, the JP 233, that was highly effective at keeping runways closed. But it had to be dropped from extremely low altitude. The RAF—cool as ever—did it, but as I noted on the 19th, they were losing too many aircraft. Theirs was one of the toughest missions going.

I needed to give them more help with the anti-aircraft guns and SAMs, and that meant moving them up to medium altitude, where our initial attacks had all but bought us a sanctuary. *'One more day,'* I noted in my diary, *'and I'll move them to medium altitude.'*

The RAF commander, Bill Wrattan, was getting pressure because Whitehall believed in the low-altitude tactics. "I'll move them if you tell me to," he said, "but I have to let them think I'm fighting the issue." Wrattan was a super guy, very bright, absolutely top drawer, and he got the promotions after Desert Storm to prove it, eventually becoming the commander of RAF Strike Command.

The USAF had its own problems with the low-altitude Mafia, as did the Navy. We'd all trained for low-altitude tactics for a European war. It was gospel doctrine to most of our units. But in Iraq, it flat out did not work, and with the success we'd had against the Iraqi IADS, we'd carved out air superiority at medium altitude. Nothing would ever eliminate all their hand-held SAMs and AAA. They'd been buying those systems from the USSR with oil money for years and if you flew right at them they were deadly. Nothing could get rid of all the anti-aircraft guns and missiles that worked at low altitude. That was the real threat now, because for the most part, the Iraqis weren't going to turn the SAMs on after their experience on night one. Therefore, if I let the aircraft fly at low altitude, they were heading straight into the threat. That would be the equivalent of being brain-dead.

The B-52s had the same problem. After one got shot up, I directed them all to move up.

Brigadier General Pat Caruana couldn't believe I was going to do it. General Jack Chain, commander of SAC, trained his B-52 crews and told them they'd fly the war at low altitude because that's where they were going to survive. "Chain is livid," Caruana told me.

"That's fine," I said.

But Chain was a CINC, and a four-star, so I immediately called Schwarzkopf to warn him

"You might get a call from CINCSAC," I said.

"Buster, it is your decision, not his," said Schwarzkopf. "Do I need to do anything?"

"No," I added hastily. "I just did not want you to get a telephone call out of the blue."

Schwarzkopf said, "Let's see, no low altitude for B-52s. Correct?"

"Correct."

"Got it."

I never knew if Chain called him or not, but I appreciated his support as always.

I didn't want to dictate tactics from headquarters. But this was a bigger issue. It was time to junk low-altitude tactics, and for most of the aircrews who'd tried it, I didn't need to tell them twice. In peacetime it would have taken years of exercises and analysis but in wartime they learned that lesson in a couple of days.

The nation over which I had absolutely no control was Israel. McConnell gave me a heads up on January 19 that Israel might not stay on the sidelines. *'The type of attack is a real concern,'* I noted, which was a discrete way of saying that we had indications the Israelis were loading their unconventional weapons. It was an open secret at the time that the Israelis did indeed possess nuclear weapons. Few doubted their resolve to use them, if pushed to it.

Israel joining in the attack was a problem so serious I could hardly contemplate it. We had to find a way to hold them back. Powell and Schwarzkopf were going to run through the options, McConnell said.

Milk and Cookies

Once planning and execution were back in a smooth flow, I intended to fly a sortie myself. Then, just like in December, Horner issued an edict: No General Officer Flying. He'd already talked to Schwarzkopf about it.

"You've got to be joking," I said to Horner. "How can you not have general officers flying? I'm a division commander. Are the Army generals going to stay back on this side of the border when the division goes across?" My heart was set on flying at least a few missions.

"I can replace you as a division commander, but I can't replace you as the planner and your involvement in day-to-day execution," Horner said.

"I don't agree with this," I retorted. "Did Schwarzkopf talk you into this?

"No."

"Well, given the opportunity, I'm going to complain."

"You do whatever you want to do, but you're not going to fly," Horner said calmly.

First chance I had, I got Schwarzkopf in private and started to explain to him that in the Air Force, we expected our combat leaders to fly. He listened to my petition for a moment.

"Come have a cup of milk and some cookies with me," Schwarzkopf said. We walked down the hall and sat down. His aide brought out a glass of milk and some cookies. I took one.

"Let me ask you a question," Schwarzkopf said. "If you were in my place, and I were in your place, would you let me fly?"

Direct hit. I was sunk.

I said ruefully, "Sir, why is it that you always have a way of asking the tough questions?"

"Because I don't think this needs to be a very long discussion."

I had to smile. Schwarzkopf was 100-percent right. His whole point was, I can replace the division commander on the ground, I can replace anybody else, but I don't have a replacement for you. And that's what he basically was saying to me.

"Thank you for the cookies and milk," I said. "Have a good evening."

Schwarzkopf took Horner with him to the press conference on January 19. It went well. Schwarzkopf could be a little lighthearted sometimes, as when he showed gun-camera film of the lead vehicle just making it out in front of an exploding bomb that wiped out the rest of the convoy. "Here's the luckiest guy in Iraq," he said to the reporters.

At the CINC's meeting on Day Three, the pressure and tensions were apparent.

During my segment of the briefing, I broached the weather problem. "You can't control the weather," Schwarzkopf said dismissively. Afterwards I wrote, 'The CINC's starting to forget that he promised me 21 days minimum, total number depending on weather days.'

What I really needed was 21 effective days of good bombing—however long it took on the calendar. I was beginning to realize that Schwarzkopf had never completely bought into that. The number 21 was fixed in his mind; a constant around which he'd be phasing the crossing movements of VII and XVIII Corps to get into position for their attack. Allowing him to think like that was a major mistake on my part. Now I was paying the price. This was Day Three and I might have only 18 days left. With the obstacles we'd run into, I was going to be nowhere near where I wanted to be.

That was as much my fault as it was the CINC's. We kept talking about it, and he'd make a light comment, as he did on January 19, saying something like, "Well, you and I can't control the weather."

Sudairy was certainly not taking anything lightly. I'd never seen him laugh, or smile much, in all my dealings with him. He was a very serious man. Sudairy came to me later that night with a very serious question, even more so than I realized at the time.

"How long do you think the war will last?" Sudairy asked.

"About a month, followed by a very short land war. This'll be over by early March, God willing," I assured him.

He paused and looked at me. "I am worried we won't complete what we have started," Sudairy said.

TIME AND EFFECTS

"We might only have 14 days," I grumbled to Tolin and Deptula on January 22. "We could all be relaxing on the beach in two weeks!"

That was the last thing I wanted. From Day One, I believed we had a limited time to eliminate what we could of Saddam's arsenal and power structure. We didn't know how long the Coalition would hold together, how long the air war would really last, or when the ground war might start.

Despite our months of planning, the campaign was going to succeed or fail depending on how well we executed it—and that meant reacting to Scuds, to a dysfunctional ATO process, to tussles over effects-based targeting, to the weather, and to the pressure from Schwarzkopf and above to get ready to launch the ground war.

Scuds

Perhaps the greatest test of our ability to react came with the Scuds. The intelligence community told us the Scud launchers were at fixed sites like H-2 and H-3. We destroyed those sites. Then all of a sudden, Scuds started flying. Nobody could figure out what was going on. It was news to us that the Iraqis had honed this mobile capability, and now we were going to have to hunt them down. This meant extreme vigilance and quick reaction from the TACC if intelligence got a lead or satellites picked up signs of a launch.

Lewis, as usual, broke the bad news.

"The TACC is just going through the motions on Scuds," he said. "They're not serious." Privately, I rued what the CINC had said about Scuds being a distraction, not a serious threat.

On January 20, McConnell called me with a good lead on Scud launch sites. He'd picked out at least seven distinct sites: Qasr Amij, Wadi Amij, Wadi Al Japaiyah, Wadi Al Ratqa, plus the airfields at H-2 and H-3 (the usual suspects), As Salman North, and Qurna. McConnell believed that these were sites where the Iraqis were pre-positioning. Some of the Scud launches might come from these sites, while other mobile launchers would move a short distance before they launched.

I directed the TACC to use McConnell's coordinates. The TACC had several options for directing aircraft to the potential Scud sites. Each day, a specified number of aircraft took off with instructions to check in with JSTARS or AWACS after they were airborne. Their whole mission was to be responsive to targets found by JSTARS or AWACS, or relayed by the airborne control team, usually aboard the AWACS. We also sent F-15Es and A-10s to tanker tracks where we could frag them off the tanker— contact the tanker, change the targets, and have the tanker crew pass the information to the pilots as they refueled. For the Scud hunt, the only ones that could be diverted while airborne were the F-15Es and A-10s on the western tanker. That was near where most of the Scud launches could be. We'd tell them to anticipate Scud hunting as their mission, and then they could get their exact coordinates when they came off the tanker. Occasionally we directed that block of aircraft elsewhere if there were no lucrative leads on the Scuds. However, there was a routine block of airplanes in every ATO designated for Scud hunting.

After I left that morning for a few hours' sleep, CENTCOM received a batch of coordinates from the Israelis via the Joint Staff in Washington. The orders were to attack. CENTCOM passed them on to the TACC. Instead of following McConnell's fresh coordinates as I directed, the TACC vectored between 12 and 24 aircraft to the new coordinates supplied by the Israelis. When I came back early that afternoon, I found out they had not attacked McConnell's prime sites, gleaned through the might of all our intelligence capability, but had gone off chasing the Israeli coordinates—some of which were sites we'd already hit—and with no success. It was unbelievably dumb.

Horner complained to Schwarzkopf.

"Sir, this is insane. We can't have a bunch of Israelis who have no idea of our overall campaign plan telling us where to put bombs. We're throwing bombs into dunes. We're starting to endanger pilots' lives." Schwarzkopf backed him up and turned off the Israeli link.[1]

There was no cure-all answer for the Scuds. Lewis and Tolin and I were wrestling with how best to take on the Scuds. Later, when Joe Bob Phillips arrived with his team from Nellis, he helped us, too. We believed the greatest chance for success was to use A-10s during the day and F-15Es at night, and attack the launchers. But it was tough. The presence of the SA-9 and abundant AAA increased the difficulty for our aircraft. Of course, the overall problem was that we simply did not know the location of the launchers. McConnell had his people and formidable assets working hard to get a better intelligence picture, but not much had come through yet.

My objective was for the intelligence community to be able to tell us *where* they were hiding the launchers, so we could destroy them. It wasn't until the war was halfway over that they found out that the Iraqis were hiding the launcher vehicles in roadside culverts. That's why they could get them out and shoot them so quickly before we detected them. Looking back, I have a hard time understanding why we didn't pick that up on our own. With as many airplanes as we had filling the skies over Iraq you would have thought somebody would have seen something. But no one did, and so it wasn't until we put the Special Forces in there that we started understanding where they were actually hiding the launchers. It was a sophisticated operation. Their communication system was a tough nut to crack. They weren't up on the radios chattering away. Their communications went through fiber optic cables, which were often strung underneath bridges, we learned later. The Scud units also used dispatch runners to deliver launch messages.

Maybe the single greatest threat from the Scuds was that they'd draw Israel into the war.

McConnell forewarned me that the Chairman might push for a "what if" drill on possible Israeli military action. Schwarzkopf and I discussed it. "What are we going to do if Israel tries to come into the air war?" Schwarzkopf asked me.

"You have three choices," I said. "One, you can do nothing. But when you do nothing, it means we can't fly while the Israelis are flying. Two, we

---

1. *It Doesn't Take a Hero*, p. 418.

can prohibit them from doing that. We can tell them, if they cross the border, we're going to shoot them down, and we can do that."

Schwarzkopf stared at me. "Well, that is definitely not an option," he said.

"The third thing," I continued, "is we can get the SecDef to really weigh in on them and agree to hit targets they believe have to be struck, but in return, they'll just have to stay on the sidelines."

I paused. "Those are the only three choices. We don't have any more choices. This is not one of those things where you can study it for a week, and come up with eight different options," I concluded.

Schwarzkopf picked up the phone and called the Chairman.

"I've looked at the Israeli issue, and we only have two choices," he said to Powell, and he whipped them out.

Eventually the decision was made for Wolfowitz to go to Tel Aviv to talk with the Israelis. At the CINC's meeting on January 22, I recommended an intensive push against the Scuds. Diverting sorties to the Scud hunt effort was jerking us around. Also, after our earlier conversation, I thought it would help Cheney and Bush's position with Israel if we just took the next three days and said, okay, we are going to focus on Scuds and do nothing but obliterate everything that's west of Highway 10.

I showed Schwarzkopf the maps of the area. "Whatever's out there, we're going to level it," I told him. "We'll make it nothing but sand."

"Buster, do you consider that to be the real focus of the war?" he asked.

"Of course not," I replied. "There are a lot of things that are not the real focus of the war that we have to deal with."

"I don't want to draw attention off the real focus of the war," he said dismissively. "It's just something we have to deal with, and we'll continue to deal with it in a piecemeal fashion."

I was surprised but I quickly realized I'd made a tactical error. This was the only time I ever presented a new idea to Schwarzkopf in public. Never before, and never again. I always talked to him in private, told him what I wanted to do. And then he would announce his decision at the staff meeting. Had I handled the proposal for an intensive Scud push privately, I think the results could have been a lot different. I blamed myself for a lack of sensitivity.

Overall, Schwarzkopf still wasn't concerned about the Scuds. "An irritant," he called them. How he ever got on the kick that the Scuds were not militarily significant is beyond me. He was much brighter than that. The Scuds did matter. Had we gone out and just decimated everything out there, the Israelis would have been appeased. It would have lifted a burden off of the President and the Secretary of Defense, who were continuously being bombarded by Israeli demands that they be allowed to strike back. It also would have freed up a lot more airplanes in subsequent weeks to go against the Republican Guard—and I mean probably another 30 airplanes a day, and that was militarily significant, no question.

But it didn't happen. We soon ended up diverting tremendous resources to the Scud hunt. We almost had to build a mini-campaign within the campaign.

ATO Problems

The Scud situation was just one of the many whirlwinds threatening to rip apart our carefully plotted planning and execution process. By January 21, when I came in after a "night" of sleep from dawn 'til noon, Lewis was waiting with his grim report.

"The ATO is a disaster," he said. The biggest problem, I learned, was that tanker allocation threatened to stop the war cold. It was a miracle we didn't lose airplanes.

Getting the ATO out every day was a mammoth task. Tolin's GAT team kept a handle on the master attack planning—barely—but the ATO itself was a much larger, more detailed document. It specified everything from radio frequencies to tanker areas and take-off times; all the huge array of necessary details for an air war involving more than a thousand aircraft a day. On top of that, we were dealing with front-end changes. The ATO was going out too late in the evening to start execution by 0300. Again, Lewis bailed me out, talked me into slipping the start to 0500 so that the F-117s and other night flyers would not be adversely affected. Day sorties were easy to plan and execute in comparison.

Scuds came from Saddam and the weather from higher authority, but the ATO and tanker problems were *my* fault. Before the war, I was looking at the general flow of things, but I never went that extra step and said to the staff, "Okay I'm going to take two hours and you're going to flow me through each track—show me what's happening." I did not put my best and brightest on air refueling during the planning phases.

To fix it, I grabbed Lewis, and told him that he didn't have any other responsibility in life other than getting that straightened out.

"Solve it," I told him. "And I don't care if you don't sleep until you do."

In two days or so, he had it straightened out. Part one of our solution was to set up dedicated tracks for the A-10s and the F-15Es, something that I had previously directed but which had not occurred. Anytime planes needed fuel, day or night, they went to one of their tracks and took on what they needed. With these thirsty assets out of the way, the refueling slots for all the other aircraft could be planned in a manageable fashion without jackknifing the whole rest of the ATO—unless I had changes. For that, he set up a 25-tanker reserve—25 out of 290 tankers employed daily on average. All the strikes had been planned in such a tight timeframe that when changes occurred, the tanker plan had no room to accommodate them. Lewis' reserve made fresh tankers available for the TACC to execute as needed. It gave us the flexibility we had to have, whatever the reason: scrambling A-10s, changes by me, whatever. Those 25 tankers a day and the dedicated A-10 and F-15E tracks stabilized the whole execution process.

However, this had been a major mistake. Horner always teased me about the Black Hole being my "talent pool." It was, but it should have been twice as big a pool. Before the war, I knew I needed to enlarge the staff and I had—with Tolin, and Lewis, for example, whom I was working to death—yet how could I have missed the fact that I needed even more people? I needed 10 more fast burners to help Tolin, Lewis, Deptula Rogers, and Baptiste—simply to get through the work cycle review.

If you want everybody to have eight hours on, eight hours off, well then that means three people a day, for one job, right? I rationalized that if I was on duty, or Tolin or Profitt was on duty, that a combination of the three of us covered the leadership and I did not have to worry about anything. That's how I'd blocked it out on January 12.

For planning, putting together upcoming ATOs, I rationalized, my little schedule was sequenced such that Deptula would start off the daily planning, then Rogers and Baptiste would finish it up. Bob Eskridge would also be available to help with the daily planning.

That was all well and fine for a three-day war. After a time, it started to take a toll. You need twice that many people. You wind up working 12 or 16 hours. If you don't force yourself to leave and sleep at least three or four hours, you become less effective. And you don't think as well.

The fix was that we got more people and moved them different places within CENTAF, but that never really solved the problem because they weren't the quality of people that I could have gotten had I done it earlier. It plagued me the whole time.

Some of the ATO problem was self-generated because key people were being stretched too thin. I talked with Deptula, but a week later, it became apparent that he had to focus on planning, not execution, or our overall strategy was going to suffer.

One afternoon, I really upset him by accusing him of having an Army mind. "You want to do a plan," I explained to him. "And then if the weather stops it, you want to go ahead and recycle that plan two days from now and not be disrupted from what you're doing tomorrow. That's bullshit. There's no flexibility involved in that. That's diametrically opposed to what we say air power is all about." *'Directed Tolin to totally remove Deptula from execution . . . I must help!'* I noted after our talk. I was overloading him—he was only one man and there are only 24 hours in a day. Like it or not, I had to stop overworking him to the point of exhaustion. He never complained, but the best never do. Not until January 26 was I able to write *'ATO process starting to work.'*

This conversation left me in a reflective mood, and in my notes, I continued on. *'Very few have the opportunity to be in a leadership position where the task-at-hand is a perfect fit . . . I hate war with every fiber in my body . . . but, warfighting is almost second nature, intuitive to a degree . . . I am thankful God has given me this insight at day's end. It will result in unbelievable low casualties both air and ground . . . I pray for your guiding hand, to always use it wisely.'*

That was not meant to sound arrogant, although it probably does now. Not many people have a chance to be in charge of something that was really a perfect fit.

Warfighting is planning and strategies and execution and outguessing the enemy or trying to guess what he will do. My reading of history was either you have that insight or you don't.

I thought that I had that intuition for war, but I never knew for certain until Desert Storm. Commanding the 414th Fighter Weapons Squadron at Nellis gave me an inkling of it. On the tactical level, that taught me a lot about what to expect, how people react, how force packages behave and so forth. From a warfighting standpoint, that assignment was the most useful assignment of my entire career, without a doubt. But like I said, I didn't know for sure until Desert Storm. Now, as a commander, I had to trust my intuition even when it made me unpopular.

Desperate Moves

On January 22, McConnell warned me of the possibility that Iraq could use its remaining aircraft to launch a massed attack on Israel or Saudi Arabia. He had information from the CIA, and his staff analyzed and believed they saw indicators that Iraq was gearing up to make a one-day last stand, maybe dumping chemicals or biological weapons on Israel or Saudi Arabia, perhaps by crude methods.

I listened carefully to his warning, but I wasn't sure how much stock McConnell himself placed in the analysis. We talked so frequently that I felt I could always tell when McConnell really believed something versus when he was giving me raw data that his people brought to him. This sounded like raw data.

Fundamentally, I didn't believe they had the capacity to pull it off. Maybe a few of those F-1s that had charged the border last fall could try it. I was sure we could stop them if they did. However, there was always a chance they could get one airplane through loaded with chemicals or biological spores and, if nothing else, crash it. Even as cocky as I am about our fighter pilots, I realized that only one aircraft had to get through, and we'd have a disaster on our hands. We had to take the threat seriously for that reason.

I told only Tolin, Deptula and Lewis about what McConnell had said. I didn't want the Black Hole to overreact, so I gave them explicit guidance:

"Focus for the next few days on the air-to-ground bases where they could actually do this," I told them. They picked out four or five bases where there were hangar facilities, air-to-ground fighters and weapons storage bunkers—all the ingredients needed for such an attack, if the Iraqis were planning one.

We bombed shelters at those airfields like there was no tomorrow. While working them over, we learned a key lesson. The F-117s and F-111s figured out how to penetrate even the vaunted Czech-made hardened aircraft shelters. Raids at Balad SE and Al Assad airfields demonstrated their effectiveness. We kept sending the F-117s and F-111s back to totally eliminate the shelters and any other threats on the airfield—including two we hadn't expected.

On January 23, the day after McConnell's warning to me, we caught a potential Iraqi kamikaze aircraft out in the open. A Badger/Blinder air-to-ground fighter was spotted out in the open at Al-Taqqadum. Mc-Connell thought it was a potential kamikaze because he'd discerned that the Iraqis were trying to modify the Badger to be able to deliver chemical weapons. They'd already been trying to jerry-rig drop tanks for chemical weapons on the MiG-21s. So, with McConnell's tip, we caught the Badger out in the open and bombed it.

My one regret during this shelter campaign was that I didn't put CAPs out to catch more aircraft. When we bombed the shelters, the Iraqis were likely to launch for survival. All air forces practiced that tactic. I should have done what I did on the first night: Put up CAPs, assign F-15Cs to the particular airfield having its shelters attacked, and issue orders saying if anything comes off the ground, kill it. You don't have to get any approval. You don't have to verify what it is. Just kill it. We certainly would have shot down more airplanes.

Later that same day, McConnell had an amazing story to tell me about another attack of Iraqi aircraft on a runway—this time, by F-117s. Two F-117s assigned to strike shelters on the airfield at Al-Assad spotted a pair of MiG-29s on the ramp, with their engines running, readying for take off. If the F-117s bombed aircraft shelters but missed the MiG-29s, it would be one scary trip home for the F-117 pilots. So the F-117s bombed the MiGs! A satellite overhead snapped the image of the MiG-29s burning on the ramp at just the right moment. McConnell had one fine picture to send to me.

McConnell was indispensable. He had absolutely the clearest intelligence picture of what was going on with the war. Without him, the fog of war would be off the scale, I thought.

We were unguarded in our conversations with each other. McConnell also filled me in on how the President was taking everything in stride, while Cheney worked the Israeli problem very hard. The only nervous person was the Chairman of the Joint Chiefs of Staff, according to Mc-Connell's report.

"The CINC and Chairman do not appear to have a smooth relationship from the Washington end," he commented

"Not from Riyadh either," I said.

The Republican Guard

Soon after our success with the airfields, Schwarzkopf telephoned me. Usually, most of my interaction with him was during or after his evening staff meetings, but periodically, there was something that couldn't wait.

"Buster, put more focus on the Republican Guard," he instructed.

"That's premature," I protested.

The Republican Guard was a critical target, but they were also sitting ducks. We could attrit them at will after we finished off NBC targets and the like.

But Schwarzkopf would not be completely swayed. Iraq was coming apart like a cheap watch. Schwarzkopf sensed he'd better start thinking about a land campaign, because it might come sooner rather than later. This time, I cajoled him into agreeing to just put a few extra F-111 sorties over the Guards for now. (We did it, and I forgot to brief Horner, who gave me the evil eye when it came up at the staff meeting that night. Fortunately, Horner never let things like that ruffle him, and this was no exception.)

My point was we had time. *'Time is on our side,'* I put down in my notes. *'We dictate the conditions of this war, not Saddam.'*

Phase I had unique objectives that could not be accomplished any other way.

A case in point of key strategic targets that we'd only get a chance to attack with air power was the "baby formula plant." McConnell told me that according to his analysis, less than 25 percent of the total space was being used for the manufacture of civilian end products such as baby formula. The rest of it was being used for something else, something we strongly believed was associated with chemical weapons production. The plant was actually camouflaged.

Also high on my list of remaining priorities in Phase I was the Rashid Hotel in Baghdad. McConnell confirmed late on January 23 that the hotel was being used as a command, control and communications center. The Iraqis had it all set up on the bottom two floors and in a bunker in the basement area.

Iraq's communications backbone was a network from Saddam's presidential palace, to the Ministry of Defense to the Ba'ath Party headquarters to the Ministry of Intelligence and then to one other node, the Rashid Hotel. The five nodes permitted all elements of the organization to stay in contact with each other. The network carried communications of the highest level—transmissions from the political and military inner circle around Saddam. We'd taken out the other four nodes, but the Rashid Hotel site was still operational.

The problem was that most of the journalists left in Baghdad now inhabited the Rashid Hotel. That's when we came up with the idea of announcing to the world that we were going to bomb it. Our announcement would give the journalists there plenty of time to pack up and leave.

Horner and I briefed the idea to Schwarzkopf privately on January 23 after the staff meeting. Major General Burt Moore, CENTCOM's J2, violently disagreed, as did Major General Jack Leide, CENTCOM's J3. However, Schwarzkopf agreed to discuss the idea with Powell.

"Believe me," Schwarzkopf said after their discussion, "there's no way we're ever going to get Powell to agree to that."

Whatever the obstacles, I felt I owed it to Schwarzkopf to give him not-so-subtle reminders occasionally. After the staff meeting on January 23, I said to the CINC, "Give me the last name of the person that dictates all the conditions for this war."

"Schwarzkopf," he said, going along with me.

"No doubt in my mind," I said. "One thing for sure, it's not Hussein."

Effects

Another self-inflicted problem in the strategic campaign, was our attempt to overuse effects-based targeting to achieve our objectives. The F-117s, F-111s and F-15Es allowed me to work the strategic campaign based on the effects I wanted. I had more options than probably any other air commander ever had. But I soon found that "effects" meant different things to different people; I had to watch my planners closely to make sure the ATO was laying in the effects and the destruction levels I wanted.

Targeting for effects ran a risk of not hitting some targets hard enough. In essence, we were using our superior knowledge of the targets, the new precision of the F-117s and others, to say, *I think I can disable that target with fewer bombs,* and without turning all of it to rubble. Since we weren't trying to do a scorched-earth policy in Iraq, the greater awareness and precision fit hand-in-glove with the President's objectives, which were about creating certain conditions, not bombing Iraq back to the Stone Age.

In some cases, the campaign objectives dictated hitting targets hard. We went after the NBC targets, the sector operations centers, and others as hard as we needed to in order to destroy them. So it was a balance. Obviously, your choices are not always 100-percent accurate.

Controlling the strategic campaign took a lot of focused effort. I'm sure that the F-117 wing getting whip lashed at the other end of the process thought I micromanaged every sortie. There was a certain amount of truth to that, because I only had 42 F-117s.

I gave Deptula a lot of latitude in planning the sorties for the F-117s, F-15Es and the F-111s. I basically told Deptula what I wanted, and he then would put the ATO together, and as he was finishing it in the morning, I'd go get some sleep. When I came in a few hours later, early in the afternoon, if it wasn't the way I wanted it, I'd change it. I knew that was very frustrating for him but it was a reality he learned to live with.

Of course, I also changed the ATO because of weather. We had a limited amount of time. Waiting out the worst weather Iraq had experienced in 15 years was not an option. Did I review and approve every target that struck every day by the F-117s? Yes, in theory. No, in practice.

I'd instruct Deptula, "Take out the following things in Baghdad tomorrow." Later in the day, I would always ask the question, "Are you striking all the things I said to strike?"

If Deptula said yes, then we'd go over all the details together in a give-and-take discussion. I'd ask, "How many F-117s are you putting on each target, and how many bombs?" If Dave erred, it tended to be in the direction of not putting enough warheads on a target. It was just a fact of life. So, if he said, "I'm putting one bomb on that target or two bombs," I might come back and say, "No, I want four bombs on it."

"Well, I can't strike all the targets if I put four on this one."

"Yes you can," I'd tell him. "Go pull them off of something I didn't tell you to strike and put them here." But if Deptula's numbers were satisfactory to me, I wouldn't routinely review what the other F-117s were doing.

It would not be a misrepresentation to say I came close to micromanaging the F-117s. In fact, in order of priority I micromanaged the F-117s to a degree, then the F-111s and next the F-15Es. I really didn't micromanage much below that, except on special occasions. I might want the Tornados or the F-16s to do something special, or several times, the B-52s. I also will admit Schwarzkopf helped me micromanage the B-52s on occasion, especially as it related to attacking the different Iraqi divisions.

So, to that extent, yes, I micromanaged the ATO. For anyone who thought it took 72 hours to make ATO changes, I was living proof it could be done much faster—closer to 72 minutes, in a few memorable cases. Realistically, up to an hour or two prior to the aircrew stepping out of the squadron operations center to man their aircraft, I could call up and give them changes, whether they liked it or not. Of course, the hundreds of sorties checking in with AWACS or ABCCC every day and night could get new targets in minutes.

Now, if only I could have micromanaged the supply of intelligence.

The kind of war I wanted to run demanded fresh intelligence on a much larger scale, and the intelligence channels just weren't set up to handle it. During previous wars, the intelligence officers decided key issues like the number of weapons to be put on a particular target. They might have help from a few weapons officers in the squadron or wing, but it was their show.

I gave the authority to decide on the number of weapons to drop on a target to Deptula for strategic targets (about 15 percent of the sorties) and to the weapons officers at the wing for all other targets. I made this decision because the intelligence officers had no capacity to understand how I wanted to balance effects and destruction.

I did not want to sit and wait for intelligence to inform me that the campaign had totally decimated the defense industry or totally decimated the Ba'ath Party facilities or totally decimated the power grid or the telephone system. I wanted to simultaneously take everything down in a way that it would create chaos and confusion. Because the more I could do that, then the quicker I could have the Iraqis on the defensive.

These first attacks were deliberately broad, reaching all across Iraq. I did not want pockets of Saddam's military or political henchmen to be sitting out there thinking they hadn't been selected yet, and going about as if everything was normal.

When you are attacking with that mindset, you don't need somebody from intelligence to tell you that you need to put a dozen 2,000-pound bombs on one target to make sure it is 100-percent destroyed, with extra insurance for weather problems, weapon guidance problems, aircrew errors, on and on and on. Left to their own devices, that's exactly what the intelligence officers might do. It wasn't their fault as individuals. It was a result of incorrect training on the part of the Air Force, something we needed to work on after the war.

I wanted our effort to be one big mass effect, or as near to that as I could, so in my mind I kept calculating, almost intuitively, how we could spread the effects of the bombing around to produce the most impact. When standard procedures would recommend three airplanes and six bombs for a target, I might put only two airplanes and two bombs against it. Sheer destruction was not my criterion, not at all.

A war had never been fought quite this way. Were we 100 percent or were we perfect in doing that? No.

Sometimes we would make a mistake and we'd have to go back and hit a target again. The reverse also happened. Even with our determination not to use too many bombs on a target, occasionally we wasted bombs.

Restrike decisions were a big variable determining how fast we'd finish off the strategic targets, or letting us move our best assets onto other target sets. I needed prompt bomb damage assessments so I'd know what effect the night's attacks had on the targets. If they weren't hit as needed, they had to go back on the Master Attack Plan list.

This was all so new—and for me, so intuitive—that I did not expect most of the Black Hole and TACC and other CENTAF staff to understand what we were doing. Deptula and Buck Rogers understood, and so did Lewis and Tolin, 100 percent. I didn't really care whether anybody else totally understood or not, because one of the four of them had to sign off on everything that was done. But for most others, they'd been steeped in the tactics of completely destroying a target. Their hearts were in the right place and their work ethic was second-to-none; but I knew what their limitations were. There's no reason to spend a lot of time trying to explain something to a group of people who are not going to understand what you just explained. I made sure that the key decision makers and the key planners understood, and they'd keep the rest of the team moving in the right direction.

As much as I relied on him, the fact was that Deptula could in some cases be too effects oriented. He would try to stretch the impact too far. However, I'm sure that much of that stretching was a result of the enormous pressure I was putting on him to deliver results.

The nuclear sites, and chemical and biological plants and weapons storage bunkers were a case in point. This was no time for "effects" designed to let the Iraqis know we were onto them. We had to totally destroy these weapons capabilities. I didn't want the Iraqis to be able to go into those facilities and move things out that weren't destroyed.

Salman Pak, a weapons laboratory and factory, was one of those targets I wanted turned into rubble. I wanted to make sure there was nothing there for them to put on trucks and take out. We planned a strike with six F-117s. The weather precluded the second wave going in, so instead of plastering it with twelve bombs, only three of them hit.

The next morning, after the partial strike, McConnell called me to say that they were loading things up in trucks and carting them out of Salman Pak before we could attack it again the next night.

Just intuitively I knew that would happen. I had discussed this exact issue with Tolin several times. I told him to make sure we did not permit "effects bombing" to tip our hand to Saddam—giving him an opportunity to move critical assets.

The effects-based targeting approach was new as a method for structuring the early phase of the war. It's incorrect to say it's the first time effects bombing or attack or planning had taken place. What is correct is this: In previous conflicts, total destruction was a desired approach. Effects were only resorted to when there were limited munitions available, and so therefore you had to cut corners. Think of the Battle of the Coral Sea. The Navy threw everything they had at the Japanese, which wasn't much; they wanted to destroy that task force coming down toward New Guinea. The Navy only hit one small Japanese carrier, but it was enough to convince the admiral in charge of the Japanese task force to turn around. No doubt the Navy would rather have destroyed every vessel if they could have but they couldn't, and they got the effect they wanted anyway that day.

In the Gulf War, there was no such thing as limited munitions or limited air power. We had anything and everything we needed by the time we got ready to do it, and so I had a choice about how to defeat Iraq.

But your effects are only as good as your intelligence. For example, Baghdad had one major telephone exchange and two or three other backups. We called the main one the AT&T building (which AT&T did not appreciate when it got to the press). What we did not know was that the Iraqis had very masterfully gone through and duplicated the system. For example, Floor 3 was responsible for all domestic internal operations. Floor 4 handled international calls. Floor 5 cleverly duplicated Floor 3 in every respect; it was identical. So if Floor 5 got burned out, they would not lose a thing; they could switch to Floor 3. Floor 6 duplicated international switching on Floor 4. Floor 7 and 9, another twin pair, were responsible for other switching and phone support that was within the Middle East region.

Without knowing all this, we dropped two GBU-27s from an F-117. The first bomb had a delay fuse on it so it penetrated through the building, while the second one followed up. I thought that was ample for anything. But we miscalculated—and the lower, duplicate floors survived. So I had to go back and schedule another F-117 to put two bombs down closer to the ground to knock out those floors.

If we'd put four bombs on it to start with, we'd have probably come close to taking the building down and it would have been all over with. Was that a mistake? Yes, you could say that was a mistake. Because if I had to do it again, would I do it differently? Yes. I would use four bombs and take the building down. No matter how good intelligence is, they can't know everything. War will never be perfect because humans wage war. Overall, effects bombing was remarkably successful and consistent with our objectives. Destroying Iraq was never our goal—not at all. We had to eliminate certain strategic capabilities to gain air superiority, take out weapons of mass destruction as directed by the President, make the Iraqis feel the heat, and attrit the field army so the ground war would be as short as possible with minimal casualties. Those were all *effects,* and in many cases, blindly destroying targets would just take too much time and hold us back.

Here was the overall impact I wanted to deliver to Schwarzkopf. After Day One there was no doubt in Iraq that everybody was at war, not just that field army in Kuwait. Ideally, it gets to the point where you've disrupted the military apparatus and cut the field army off. The only supplies they'll have is whatever was pre-positioned and whatever they can get their hands on. Then, when you start attacking that field army, they have nowhere to go. They can't resist for long. To me, that's the logical way to bring about victory the quickest way with the minimum loss of life and with a minimum expenditure of resources on your part.

Billy Mitchell foresaw it all. You can't do anything without air superiority. If they control the skies, they're going to shoot down a lot of those stealth airplanes, just by accident. You have got to have the control of the skies and once you have that, stealth technology and precision weapons can force a nation-state into submission or make ground action little more than a police action. The real challenge from Day Two onward was trying to drive through our operational philosophy for the rest of the campaign. It had to constantly be evaluated. The rest of the campaign would be what we made it. We had scripted the first three days, but that was all. We tweaked the balance of effects versus destruction so that we wouldn't seduce ourselves with our own rhetoric, as I used to call it, and end up thinking we were having more impact than we were.

Pop-Up Targets for F-117s

A large part of our success over the next few weeks was riding on our ability to make rapid changes and adjustments. I wanted the wing commanders to take the lead, helping to match aircraft and targets, working through their representatives in the Black Hole. Also, I wanted them to ad lib if necessary. They understood the overall picture and why I needed them to be flexible.

For the most part, that happened with no problem. Ironically the one group that I had the most problem with was the F-117 wing.

The F-117s had been on their own for a long time. They trained to fly silver-bullet missions, not the day-in, day-out flying schedule they now had for Desert Storm. The heart of the problem was their highly regimented mission planning. The F-117s all flew a carefully constructed profile, keeping their signature at its lowest as they entered a threat zone. They needed up-to-date intelligence for the route. On a map, the result was a spaghetti weave routing them around some threats and putting the best foot forward, so to speak. No one else was going into threats that dense, and magnificent though it was, stealth was essentially passive. The F-117s could not outmaneuver a missile or kick in the afterburner. Mission planning was their life. After the work was done, they'd rehearse the tough part in a simulator and adjust the path if need be, then load it into the aircraft's computer. It took a lot of time.

It all came to a head when I wanted to quickly retarget F-117 missions. Nobody guaranteed them when they started flying F-117s that they'd be able to do a rehearsal on every mission they ever flew. There was a pop-up on a terrorist training camp that was identified just south of Baghdad, in the vicinity east of Salman Pak. The information came to me at seven o'clock in the evening. The camp was active and I wanted to bomb it that night. I looked over which aircraft might be in that area. The F-117s were scheduled to take off about eleven o'clock that night and bomb somewhere around one in the morning.

Tolin called the wing planner at Khamis Mushayt. He requested coordinates for the final turn point on a mission scheduled to attack an air-field near Baghdad. It happened to be a dam on the river, which worked out beautifully.

"Based on your F-117 experience, how difficult will this be for them to go to the new coordinates?" I asked Tolin.

"Sir, it should be a no-brainer for a fighter pilot," Tolin said.

Then I personally called the wing planner Tolin had spoken to, because Whitley was in crew rest, sleeping before his next mission.

"What I want you to do is go to that same dam, then I want you to fly up the river to the first bridge you come to and then take this heading and bomb the training camp at these coordinates." I gave him the coordinates and more instructions. "Drop one bomb on each pass. Tolin will discuss the mission with you after you have it drawn out on your map. This is a must-hit target," I said.

Minutes later, I got a call back from Whitley's deputy for operations, the wing planner's superior.

"We can't do this," the deputy started to say.

"Wait a minute. Explain to me why you can't do this," I interjected.

"We can't get it in the computer to change the route."

"I didn't tell you to change a thing," I said. "Leave the computer set up the way it is, go to the dam, and then go manual override, go to the next bridge, turn to a heading of 037 and drop so many seconds out. Here's the picture you are going to see. Tolin has already sent you the imagery. If the pilot doesn't see that picture on his run, he won't drop."

They had been pampered. I called Whitley, woke him up out of crew rest and said, "This is no longer a request. This is a direct order. Now if you don't have any pilots who can pull this off, then you strap your own butt in that airplane and go do it yourself, but I want it done."

Whitley was a leader and a fighter through and through. He was embarrassed by his deputy's whining. Whitley's final comment was, "Sir, don't worry about it, I'll make it happen."

Later that night, they hit the target and everything was fine. You can't be driven by the way we do things in peacetime, especially when it ties you to a decision loop that makes what you are doing useless by the time you do it—as it might have with that active terrorist training camp. There is no substitute for flexibility and timely application of air power. When we set up structures that inhibit flexibility, it's self-defeating. It's absolutely absurd. There has always been and always will be a large part of the Air Force that believes everything has to be planned and scripted. I'm not one of them.

After a couple of these episodes, I put Tolin in charge of passing changes to the F-117s. "Do not let me ask the F-117s to do something that's not within reasonableness in your opinion," I said to Tolin.

The irony of it was, never once did Tolin say, "that's unreasonable, we can't do it." After he started passing along the changes, never again did I hear any back-talk about anything that I asked them to do. One time, later in the war, they coped with target changes 40 minutes before the pilots stepped out to their waiting jets. It wasn't pretty, but they got the job done.

The F-117 crews adapted well. It was a straightjacket they'd created themselves, and now they were free of it. The F-117s were the single most important element to the air war and without them, goodness only knows how many lives we'd have lost and what price we would have paid.

RSAF Loss

It was around this time that the RSAF lost an F-5, shot down while attacking one of the Iraqi airfields. It was in the south, and the F-5 was lost due to anti-aircraft fire.

Sudairy came to me.

"I don't need to review the targets anymore, unless you want my input," he said. He was satisfied. His only issue had been making sure the RSAF went into a high threat area. Now Saudi blood had been spilled in this war. God bless him. He was a good man, a warrior and a leader. His heart was in the right place. He wanted to make sure his people carried their weight.

The discussion with Sudairy reminded me how his visits had become an important part of the war. Sudairy and I hit it off very well. He was not a very talkative person. When he did speak, he used that formal, beautiful language of someone educated to speak the King's English.

I spent quite a bit of time with Sudairy. We were always very truthful with each other. During one meeting, he went out of his way to make sure I did not take everything the Saudis said at face value. As Sudairy acknowledged, hedging the truth was socially permissible, as long as the ends they are trying to accomplish are noble. In his culture, a bit of hedging was not inappropriate; it's just a way of life. It was difficult for me to become comfortable with that.

However, Sudairy was not like that in his relationship with me. He liked my directness. I told him exactly what to expect. In return, he started to give me access to a significant source of information: the Kuwaiti Resistance. Sudairy's tips would make for some of the most heart-stopping moments of the war.

EIGHT DAYS OF HELL

'Weather has made this eight days of hell!' That's how I started off my new diary page on January 24. On the theater campaign calendar it was Day Eight. *'It is very difficult to execute a strategy with any consistency . . . we are effectively at Day Four,'* I continued. Bad weather had essentially cut in half the time I needed to carry out the strategic air campaign. *'A few more days and I will need to pare down strategic objectives,'* I worried. *'Time at day's end is on Saddam's side . . . if we delay and delay we have two months max, probably less.'* Ramadan was in March and I was sure we'd be out of time long before then.

Taking two or three days out to wait for better weather would give the Iraqis too much latitude, and I wasn't willing to accept that. Some would say that I fought the weather too much. You have only two choices. You either try to compensate, or you just cancel everything and wait for another day. I wasn't about to do the latter, because when you wait it out, you give the enemy a chance to move things around; you've also tipped your hand in certain directions. Unless they are brain-dead, your enemy will figure out where you're headed.

In fact, I accepted a higher level of risk for losses if I was making changes for weather—higher than I would on a normal day-to-day basis. The F-117s took the brunt of it again. The F-117s needed clear weather for targeting—or they needed to be below the cloud deck to use their infrared systems. The best place for the F-117 was at medium altitudes. Better for survivability, better for weapons release, and no problem at all in good desert weather, which I didn't have. Holding them back would have pulled the guts out of the attack plans. Once again, I didn't go along with their desire to restrict their altitudes. I put the F-117s over downtown Baghdad at some altitudes that had never been considered.

One night in particular, I ran two F-117s in under a cloud deck that was at 5,000 feet. I brought them in right over downtown Baghdad, sent them to two different targets. I directed them ahead of time to drop both bombs at once. "I want you to come in from the north," I said. We'd never done that before—customarily their attack heading was to come in from the south, east and west. Approaching from the north ought to throw the Iraqis off but the tactic was admittedly very high risk. Yet they made it work.

That same day I noted another problem. *'F-117s are slightly dirty . . . need to be prudent,'* the notes continued. Flying took a toll on the complex coatings that helped make the F-117s stealthy. The old rule of thumb was that two-thirds of signature reduction came from shape, and one-third from coatings. Normal wear and tear on the skin of an aluminum jet didn't affect its performance in combat very much but a bad patch on the F-117 might bump up its signature. I needed to make sure the F-117s got time for maintenance to put them back in pristine condition.

When you go into war, there are some people who believe you push the button and put a fighting force on autopilot. Nothing could be further from the truth. That's an infantile way of thinking. If you want to brute-force everything, you might do that. Autopilot won't work if you are going to do it correctly, with minimum loss of life, and meet the objectives as expeditiously as possible.

I was willing to drop down and task fewer sorties when the wing told me they needed a little down time to resolve signature problems. I didn't want to lose any F-117s at any cost, especially since I was the one that had decreed that they would not be shot down when almost everybody else was a naysayer. Several senior Air Force generals continued to weigh in to say that I was going to be an embarrassment to the Air Force because of my hardheaded attitude. I felt like telling them where they could all go. Their opinions were based on a lack of knowledge, or on fear. They wanted to be able to say, "I told you so." I was going to do it the way I wanted it done because I was convinced the F-117s gave us the highest probability of success with the minimum loss of life. History has the last say on this issue: no F-117 was lost or even hit by enemy fire.

So when they needed to pull jets for maintenance, we lowered the tasking rate for a couple of days to let them do some touch-up. We did that periodically throughout the campaign.

Up North

Then, I sent the F-117s far north, to attack 21 bioweapons bunkers at Mosul—and I sent the tankers along with them.

To strike that deep, the F-117s had to have fuel sooner than normal. The tankers would have to go above 33 degrees north.

Corder was adamantly against the idea, but Horner approved it. *'Horner has more courage in his little finger than most men have in their entire body,'* I had scrawled down on January 23, as we were planning the attack.

We couldn't fight this war with a peacetime mentality. I felt the risk of sending a tanker into Iraq was acceptable to hit the biological weapons bunkers.

The plan was for the tanker to drag the F-117s into Iraq and set up one last pre-strike refueling. If the track was placed in an area where we had no SAM indications, then I believed the risk was acceptable. I was only concerned with a tanker getting shot down with a SAM. I knew I could put F-15Cs up and keep that one Iraqi fighter pilot from becoming his country's hero. The F-117s would make their long flight to Mosul and back, then join up with a tanker again near the border.

The mission took place on January 24 and McConnell had his resources focused to find out what the Iraqis did. Twenty-seven minutes after the tankers turned south, the Iraqis opened up with barrage firing of anti-aircraft guns and SAMs over Baghdad that went on for seven minutes.

"The Iraqis convinced themselves the F-117s must be overhead Baghdad by then, so they just started barrage firing," McConnell told me. That's how bad the Iraqis were. The F-117s hadn't flown anywhere close to Baghdad. I called Whitley to pass on the story.

The attack on Mosul showed again how indispensable the F-117s were. There was no other aircraft that could have successfully completed that mission. While we had three dozen F-117s in theater, there were 20 more back in the U.S.—that was the whole inventory—so I wanted more over here, not because of maintenance, but so I could hit more targets. I had a very difficult time getting that request approved, but, with Russ' help, I was finally permitted to deploy six additional F-117s into theater, bringing the 37th TFW's total to 42 F-117s.

I watched the F-117s very closely. McConnell told me around this time that the Iraqi "Tall King," USSR-built, low-frequency, early-warning radars sometimes got the general location of F-117s in flight. This wasn't a problem since they used the SA-2 sites as turn points on their routes. The low-frequency radars had great range but didn't produce usable tracking information, so we usually ignored it. Still, I didn't want the F-117s to become complacent or predictable, so I talked it over with Tolin and Whitley. We decided that when intelligence found a Tall King radar, we'd blow it away. After we destroyed two, the Iraqis seldom used them.

Later that day, the Saudis saved us from a massive screw-up with AWACS. Two Iraqi Mirage F-1 pilots cleverly dropped in behind a strike package that was coming south out of Baghdad after a mission. The Iraqi F-1s dropped down to 200 feet and kicked it up to Mach 1.3. They fell in behind the strike package so they could sneak up behind them and shoot one of them down. AWACS did not figure it out and declare the F-1s hostile until they were over the coastline and in Saudi airspace. I'd always told the squadrons there weren't 10 decent pilots in the Iraqi Air Force who could qualify to be in an American fighter squadron—but these must have been two of them. In fact, we'd observed that some of the better Iraqi pilots were in the older systems like the F-1.

Once the AWACS figured out what was going on, the nearest interceptor was a Saudi F-15C. AWACS vectored him over and after a brief but agonizing interval, the Saudi pilot bagged both of the intruding F-1s.

The AWACS wasn't paying enough attention that day. They didn't need chewing out; once they realized they'd come close to losing an airplane, they became their own best critics. They'd be hard enough on themselves. If anything, they were going to be overdoing it from now on. However, after this incident, we put a British fighter CAP in the area to back up the Saudi CAP, just in case.

We were still attacking selected airfields to eliminate last-ditch moves, but we had to remain aware of the threat. When my brain trust put F-111s on the list to strike the shelters at Balad, I said no. This was just too risky for the F-111s and I didn't want them going back up there. Balad had the most sophisticated combination of SAMs, AAA and radar-guided guns of any base in Iraq. This was a natural job for the F-117s.

It seemed like we were moving quickly through the NBC targets. Intelligence was reporting we had destroyed a lot of things that, it turned out later, hadn't really been destroyed; and there were a lot of other targets left unscathed that we should have been destroying. But I didn't know that yet. So, with the added priorities, I carved out precision assets for a shelter campaign and a bridge campaign, too.

When I briefed Schwarzkopf on the start of the shelters and bridges effort, he also decided this was a good time to start dropping leaflets on Iraq's front-line troops. We'd discussed the basic plan in December. B-52s would disperse pamphlets over the front lines, with a pointed message: "If you don't surrender, we're going to bomb you tomorrow." The B-52s would bomb them, and then drop pamphlets again, and bomb again. I thought the tactic would be reasonably effective on the non-Republican Guard units, since I always felt they were ragtag and likely to desert anyway. Timing was the only question. I'd planned to wait until we were within a week or so of the ground campaign. *'Now we will both see if it gets results,'* I noted during the staff meeting. Schwarzkopf and I would see if our December idea was as good as we had convinced ourselves it would be. We both had our egos stroked, because the leaflets were very effective.

Typical Day

On my way back from Schwarzkopf's meeting, I reflected on the past 10 days. Just like I'd thought when I woke up that morning, weather and intelligence were whipping us around in ways I hadn't expected. I wrote, *'Weather and limited intel BDA have provided "Fog of War" with a new meaning . . . We Must Keep Our Focus and Intensity . . . With God's Help.'*

Truth was, I hoped my own focus wasn't starting to slip. In the diary I sketched out a typical day:

• 1200–1400: Black Hole for update of past 6 hours with Tolin, Deptula, Lewis, Baptiste. First call to McConnell. I always called him to see if what he told me would agree with what I'd hear from the staff, or if he had any other urgent information.

• 1400: Previous night BDA and intel update (Tolin, Deptula, Baptiste, Lewis, Holliday, Eskridge). Holliday was an intelligence expert, a really good kid.

• 1500: TACC with Lewis to discuss upcoming CINC meeting. We'd discuss what I wanted to tell the CINC as Rick prepared the charts.

• 1600: Office. Telephone calls to Wing CCs. I'd call a couple of the wing commanders, depending on what they had done the previous day, or if there was a specific issue I wanted to discuss with them.

• 1700: Review next 24 hours and direct changes; very hands-on, maybe excessive (Tolin, Lewis, Deptula, Baptiste)

• 1800: Review CINC meeting charts (Lewis)

• 1900: CINC Meeting (Horner and Lewis)

• 2030: Debrief CINC Meeting (Profitt, Tolin, Deptula, Rogers, Baptiste, Lewis)

• 2200: Telephone calls to Wing Commanders. I'd make more calls regarding upcoming tasking and other issues.

• 2300: TACC (Discussions with Horner)

• 2400: Last minute ATO changes for next day—Rogers and Baptiste

• 0200: TACC . Around 2 AM I'd start paying a lot more attention to the TACC because Horner wasn't there by then, he was off on his sleep timeslot. This was an active time: most of the strikes took place between 8 PM and midnight, and between midnight and 4 AM.

• 0300: Office—reflect, plan, personal letters or telephone calls. I'd go up to the office and maybe write a personal letter, put more notes in my diary.

• 0500–0630: Black Hole to give Rogers direction for Tolin and Deptula. Deptula came in somewhere between five and six; then Horner arrived before his morning staff meeting, and we would have a short update discussion before I headed off to bed myself.

• 0700: Sleep

I could see that my typical day didn't leave enough time to *think*. That's how you make mistakes. Everybody just starts becoming complacent unknowingly, and all of a sudden, nobody's doing any thinking outside the box. You become predictable. Bad things happen to you when you start not having a time to reflect and think, especially during a war.

After this, I scheduled in a "think" period, right after we returned from the CINC's meeting and I debriefed everybody. Around 2030 or 2100, I would go to my small office upstairs. I didn't necessarily have to be by myself, but I didn't want very many people around. Sometimes Tolin or Lewis joined me for a little brainstorming. These think periods normally lasted about an hour to an hour and a half. A commander must have private time to think or the activity trap will eat him alive.

Desperation

Saddam started to make desperate moves. On January 25, satellites picked up a massive oil slick forming along the Kuwaiti coast. The slick was 20 times bigger than the spill from the Exxon Valdez tanker accident in Alaska a few years before. No wonder, because the Iraqis had simply opened the pipeline running from Kuwait's Ahmadi Crude Oil Storage Terminal to the Sea Island terminal, a tanker filling station eight miles off shore, and let the black gold run out into the Gulf.

Fortunately, the pumping station for this mess was on land, in Kuwait.

I called Lennon.

"Get two F-111s ready for immediate launch," I ordered, and told him about the oil slick.

"Let's use the GBU-15s we just got in," he suggested. With their precision targeting, the F-111s could blow up the pumping station and shut off the oil flow. We were ready to go.

Unfortunately, it turned out I didn't have authority to blow up a piece of the Kuwaiti oil works. We needed approval from Washington first. Powell wanted the blessing of the Kuwaitis. A day went by, and Powell and the Kuwaitis were still conferring. Oil continued to flow. It was crazy. Absolutely crazy.

The decision should have been Schwarzkopf's. He had the authority to bomb any other war-related target in Kuwait. Why was this an exception? Why didn't we just shut it off? This was the biggest environmental disaster in the region. After the war, one estimate calculated that almost 10 million barrels of oil had surged into the Gulf—making Exxon Valdez's 262,000 barrels paltry in comparison.[1]

'The chairman caused the CINC to be indecisive on this issue—the CINC was frustrated beyond belief.'

Another day dragged on. *'We continue to watch impotently,'* I noted on January 26. *'The flow could be stopped with one or two LGBs . . . we should have stopped the flow within three or four hours . . .'*

Instead we permitted it to become a political decision. I could not stand the delay any longer, so I pressed the CINC.

"It's not my decision," he confided.

1. *Crusade*, p. 185.

I couldn't understand it and don't to this day. McConnell indicated that Powell wanted to make sure both the Emir of Kuwait and King Fahd of Saudi Arabia agreed we could blow up the pumping station.

Sudairy was perplexed, too.

"Saddam is ruthless beyond belief," Sudairy said. "He will make the Saudis suffer to the maximum extent possible."

Finally, on January 27, I was cleared to direct two F-111s from Taif to bomb the pumping stations. The oil flow was reduced to a trickle within one hour of receiving clearance for the mission.

Releasing oil was not all the Iraqis did. The same day they opened the manifolds; an attack of 25 to 30 Scuds was launched against Israel.

On the shelter campaign, the F-117s found a lucrative target at Al Qawyarah Airfield. Satellites indicated that 30 to 40 aircraft were at the field with engines running when the F-117s attacked.

Still, I felt the control of Phase I slipping out of my hands. Bad weather, Scuds, shelters, restriking targets—it was starting to lose its synergy. *'Directed Tolin to take firm control of changes,'* I entered in my notes. The TACC was acting more and more like a black box, ignoring weather, oblivious to our priorities. It affected the whole sequence of the attacks.

I went to Horner to complain.

"You command the fighters. You direct the changes you need," Horner said. That's when I got really heavy-handed. I told my wing commanders not to take any directions from the TACC, unless I approved it. I cracked the whip with my own staff, too. To Tolin and Lewis, I said, "You are in charge of execution—stay out of planning." To Deptula and Baptiste, I said, "You do planning—stay out of execution." It was the only way to stay focused on our strategy.

Why Rush?

Schwarzkopf's staff meeting on January 26 confirmed my worst fears about the telescoping of the strategic campaign. On that day, I noted the weather was now two or three times worse than the most pessimistic predictions. In fact, it was on the way to being the worst weather recorded in the theater at that time of year in over 14 years.

However, both Schwarzkopf and Vice Admiral Stan Arthur, the Joint Force Maritime Component Commander (JFMCC), suggested it was time for the air campaign to begin to move to Phase III.

'Why do we need to rush? The ground war won't last more than a week!' I scribbled in frustration during the meeting.

This was a huge philosophical difference.

Arthur was a good man, but focused on the tactical. The Navy mind-set of the time was sequential: start at the coast and fight your way in. According to that logic, the IADS were down, and he saw no reason to hold up Phase III.

Schwarzkopf at some level saw the strategic campaign as step one in a sequence. He wanted to make sure we had done everything we could before the first soldier crossed the line.

I just didn't think we had to be in a hurry to get there since we were behind on strategic targets. "This is Day Ten," I told them, "and we've actually accomplished what we planned to accomplish in the first five days."

On the surface, Schwarzkopf was seeing such success that he thought it satisfied his purposes. According to intelligence, the number of locations of chemical and biological weapons, storage sites and so forth, was relatively small. We'd attacked all of them, or were in the process of attacking them, by that time. It's a common tendency when you're comfortable with where things appear to be going to want to go ahead and make sure that you are preparing for the next stage and the next step.

I remained uncomfortable, and things only got worse. By January 28, I noted that we should have flown 300-plus sorties into Baghdad by then, when in fact we'd flown less than 100. Only the F-117, F-111 and LAN-TIRN-equipped F-15E were truly effective against targets in Iraq. All the other fighters were playing in the minor leagues. Even the target set threw us curves. McConnell told me that day that the biological weapons bunkers had a firewall in them, meaning they'd need two attacks each instead of one to destroy them.

Mission results from Whitley and Lennon for Days One to Ten confirmed my fears. We'd scheduled 814 precision missions for the two wings and had flown 665, but of those missions flown, a high percentage was non-effective for weather or other reasons. For example, the F-117s would get to the target area and not be able to drop due to weather, which had happened to 13 out of 27 missions on Day Seven. On Day Three, we'd scheduled 22 F-117 missions, flown only 19 due to weather, but even then, 10 of those pilots found their targets cloud-covered.

Unit	Scheduled	Flown	Non-eff Wx	Non-eff other	Total Non-eff
37 TFW F-117	286	278	64 (23%)	45 (16%)	109 (39%)
48 TFW F-111	528	387	84 (22%)	149 (38%)	233 (60%)

Despite our success, it was an open question whether we'd truly accomplish all the objectives we'd laid out for Phase I.

Scuds Again

I also had to face the fact that we still weren't doing well against the Scuds. McConnell and I talked it over on January 26.

"How are they giving launch orders?" I wanted to know. It was difficult for me to understand why we didn't have more information. I wanted McConnell to be able to tell me how Saddam was giving the launch orders for the Scuds. If you can't destroy all the Scuds, then maybe you can stop the communications, I thought. They're not going to launch anything unless they're told to, so how was Saddam giving the orders? Were they sending them messages? By car, or what? We seemed totally inept at figuring that out.

I was also pushing all our contacts with the royal families in the Gulf states and the Kuwaiti resistance to see what they could tell me. About a week later, I had a telephone conversation with Sheikh Mohammed of the UAE.

"Why are you leaving the fiber cable operational?" he asked. "My man tells me that all of the communications both east and west, the fiber optic cables, are still intact." Mohammed also told me the fiber optic cables ran under the bridges in Baghdad. I don't know how he knew it, but he did. I asked McConnell to start checking around, and sure enough, my friend was right.

We took out the normal communications over time. We never touched their military fiber optic network, as far as I know. We could only stop communications to Iraqi units that were not in close proximity to one of the terminals. At that point, they'd just call one person, he'd get in a car, drive off and tell five different Scud launch units when to launch. That's very difficult to deal with unless intelligence can get inside the decision cycle by knowing where the communications are. If not, you're always chasing.

Around January 26, I directed increased bombing of the culverts where we thought the Scud launchers might be. We tasked F-111s and F-117s to hit them at night, but this wasn't the right mission for them. What we really needed were A-10s up there doing road reconnaissance.

McConnell and I also talked about Israel that night. He told me Cheney and Powell were still worried. Everyone was working to keep the tensions down.

Wolfowitz (who'd lived in Israel as a teenager) ended up making another trip back to Israel, with Baker's deputy, Lawrence Eagleburger. On the second visit, President Bush offered Patriot batteries in exchange for Israel dropping its petition for an "air corridor" across Saudi Arabia to attack Scud sites.[2]

Honestly, for all the bright people we put on it, we only had limited success against Scuds throughout the war. We never got inside that decision cycle. Never.

Fatigue

On January 26, I took a look at the faces around me after 10 days of war. Tolin, Lewis, Deptula, Rogers and Baptiste were all starting to show wear and tear. I made a note in my diary: *'forced sleep . . . no other choice!'* Adjusting my own schedule for more time to think wasn't going to help if my key people were drooping from fatigue.

Frustration was high, too. Occasionally, you just have to step back and have a low-key chat with your key guys, and tell them, "Look, we're not going to let this beat us down because we're going to win this, it's just a matter of how long it takes us."

I could tell they were fatigued because they weren't coming up with new ideas. I would always ask myself, "How many new ideas have I heard from the guys today?" Or, I'd ask them, "What do you think of doing something a little different," and see what they said.

That was the telltale sign. When the four of them were rested, I was inundated with really new thoughts. Some were very good, maybe some not so good, but the sparks flew. You could tell that they were thinking and not just working.

Their constant, critical reasoning was essential. If you don't think that way, you then have a plan that you're executing too blindly. You have to stay focused on the plan but you've also got to massage it as you go along

2. *Crusade*, pp. 130–32.

and take advantage of actions that the enemy makes, or does not make. There's no way anybody can put a plan together that anticipates every action or non-action of the enemy. You try to drive him into doing things you want him to do, and taking the actions you would like him to take, so you have your next step already planned, but that is not necessarily how it plays out.

Your inner circle has to think about that constantly, because you rely on them. Fatigue cuts into that. When a person starts to go through the motions of putting the ATO together and preparing a briefing, look out. You're about to make a tremendous mistake—and in time of war a tremendous mistake costs lives.

That's why it's so critical to keep everybody sharp and alert. So I forced them all to be away from the office for a minimum of 12 hours at a stretch for three or four days in a row. Just forced them to do it.

Fatigue and frustration were taking a toll on us all.

Schwarzkopf's 1900 staff meeting on the evening of January 27 was anything but low-key. I could understand why Schwarzkopf was upset. The Scuds were turning into a big distraction, with the final outcome unknown. But on this night, he was keyed up. He lamented about the Secretary of Defense worrying about Israel, and not showing enough concern for U.S. forces under Scud attack. That indicated to me that the CINC was fatigued, too, because no one was more concerned about our soldiers than Cheney.

Sudairy was also hot under the collar. "Why are we worrying about these Scuds?" he asked me. I tried to explain, but I'm sure I failed to get through.

Obviously, you wouldn't expect a Saudi general officer to have much empathy for how many people might get killed in Israel when his own country was at war with another Arab state. It was asking too much. I tried my best to explain to Sudairy that no matter how successful we were with the Coalition against Saddam, we needed desperately for Israel to stay out.

Sudairy understood that as a person and as a military officer. He didn't understand it as a Saudi.

I tried a different tactic.

"Look," I said to him, "if we don't do anything, and just let them fire on Israel, at some point in time he's going to turn around and start firing them all here at you."

Now Sudairy was interested. "Those launchers have got to be destroyed," I continued. "If we don't destroy the launchers now, when they're firing on Israel, they are going to wind up firing on Riyadh. I'm sure you don't want that."

Sudairy could work with that. The Coalition was trying to destroy the Scud launchers firing on Israel to keep them from firing on Riyadh. Quite right.

The fact was, the Scuds were a good move on Saddam's part. He did several things that were politically and militarily very significant and very astute on his part. However, compared to the number of things he did that were absolutely dumb as a brick, I have to assume he stumbled into the better moves. With the Scuds, I think Saddam had probably thought it out. He schemed that if there was any way he could get Israel into this conflict, it would be through the Scud attacks. Then Saddam would really win big time. Syria and Egypt would object; he already had Jordan out of the fight. With Israel embroiled, the Saudis would start getting cold feet about Coalition operations as long as Saddam didn't threaten to attack the Kingdom directly. There's not an Arab alive that's in a senior position in the Middle East that doesn't know how to play the Israeli card. Doubtless Saddam had thought of that.

Planes to Iran

As soon as I got to the Black Hole on January 28 I learned we'd almost lost a B-52 out at Al Qaim. The Iraqis fired four SA-3s and one SA-2.

I called Profitt and said to him, "Glenn, the Al Qaim A B-52 problem looks like somebody has gone brain dead." I was very surprised and I was very upset, and I let him know it in no uncertain terms.

Al Qaim had been bombed so relentlessly that in all honesty, I had convinced myself that the threat had almost completely dissipated. In all fairness to Glenn, he'd cleared lanes for our strike aircraft. He'd been looking at every aircraft's ingress and egress routes to make sure they were free of SAMs.

What happened with the B-52 was that we diverted it after it was airborne. Profitt didn't know that the B-52 was going to this area.

"I'd have screamed to the high heavens if I'd known that," he told me.

Part of me understood, but this was still unacceptable. Any time you are in a war, if a nation has SA-9s that are mobile and to a certain extent, SA-6s, then you are always going to have to be cognizant of those things.

That's why you need SEAD. It's never going to be pure. But SA-2s and SA-3s, give me a break. I wanted them all destroyed.

"Airplanes are going to go wherever I want them to in the entire country of Iraq," I told him. "I want to own it. We either have air supremacy or we don't. Air supremacy means you can fly anywhere you want to. Air superiority means you can fly as long as you have F-15C protection. That is not my objective. I want air supremacy where I don't have to make sure somebody is safe. I want to be able to send a B-52 right over the middle of Baghdad if I want to!"

That made the point. "Now," I continued, "I know we'll never get to that level until all the AAA and everything else is used up, which won't happen and I know that, so I'm not being unrealistic. But I don't want SAMs flying through the sky at airplanes because we failed to take them out when you knew they were there."

After this, Profitt and I went to personal micromanagement of the SAMs.

"You ought to have nothing but sand out there by this time," I said to Profitt. Then I directed him to develop a chart and show me every SAM site and next to it, the date on which every SAM site had been destroyed.

Next, I told Deptula that until further notice, I wanted one of the F-117 bombs on every airplane that went near a SAM that he thought had not been destroyed to be put on that SAM site to destroy it. That turned up the heat on everybody, and they started to pay more attention to it. Fortunately, this was about the last time that we had a significant issue with SAMs.

The next issue that rasied its head was based on unwelcome news from intelligence.

"Have they briefed you on the firewall inside the bunkers?" McConnell asked.

"No," I said.

It turned out that the bunkers had a double-wall construction.

"How do you know this?" I asked him.

"Because a couple that you busted open, we could see the firewall," he said. "So you've got to bust it open and then put another one on it after you bust it open," McConnell explained.

Here Schwarzkopf was thinking about the ground war and I'm just being told by intelligence that we have to bust open the firewalls in the biological weapons bunkers.

The day was capped off with another surprise from Saddam. Since we'd begun attacking the hardened aircraft shelters with intensity, the Iraqi Air Force wasn't doing much flying. *'No Iraqi fighter activity today,'* I noticed on January 26.

Then on January 28, thirty or more Iraqi MiG-29s and other fighters bugged out and headed to Iran. We were surprised. Iran was supposed to be their mortal enemy. Lewis would have won the office betting pool if there'd been one. Everyone except Lewis thought they'd go to Jordan, so there wasn't a CAP around to catch them when they headed to Iran.

Having the Iraqi Air Force run out of the stadium was an irritant, but not militarily significant to the war. For a time after that, Boomer McBroom and Hornburg kept F-15 CAPS east of Baghdad to the maximum extent possible. They got three fighters on February 7. I wanted to shoot down as many MiGs as I could if more tried to escape, but I didn't want to make it such a priority that it interfered with everything else.

As for the Iranians, they promised to keep the jets safe. *'Ten to one they don't return,'* I scrawled in my diary.

Attack at Khafji

Saddam's next move was another act of desperation: trying to start a ground fight early, before air devastated his forces. It happened on the evening of January 29, near a Saudi border town called Ras Al Khafji.

Sudairy and I had just been mulling over how to focus on tracking down Saddam.

"He must not remain," Sudairy said again. I explained that we needed more help from him if we were ever to pinpoint Saddam's location in advance with enough time to kill him.

After the meeting with Sudairy, a cryptic note came up from the TACC. I quickly made this diary entry: *'Iraq invades Saudi . . . 50 tanks at 2830 North and 4740 East. 30 tanks and vehicles at 2830 North and 4800 East.'* Two units were on the move.

I rushed down to the TACC. I could not believe my eyes. It looked like business as usual in there. The TACC had no sense of urgency.

"What's happening?" I asked.

"We've got a few tanks moving towards Khafji," someone answered.

"Are you diverting aircraft over to JSTARS?"

"We've got an A-10 going to take a look at it."

"This could be a major thing," I said forcefully. "You've got to get enough air power up there to stop this."

I called Horner to tell him that we needed him in the TACC. "You

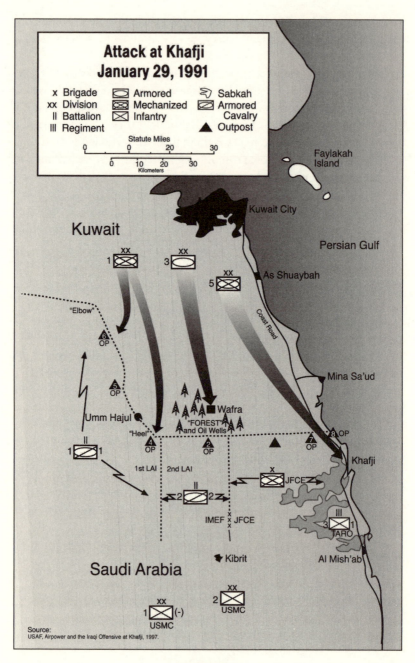

**Attack at Khafji
January 29, 1991**

x Brigade
xx Division
II Battalion
III Regiment

Armored
Mechanized
Infantry

Sabkah
Armored
Cavalry
Outpost

Statute Miles
0   0   20   30

0   10   20   30
Kilometers

Faylakah
Island

Kuwait City

Kuwait

Persian Gulf

1 xx

3 xx

5 xx   As Shuaybah

"Elbow"

Coast Road

6 OP

Mina Sa'ud

5 OP

Umm Hajul

Wafra

"FOREST"
and Oil Wells

8 OP

"Heel"   4 OP   2 OP   7 OP

Khafji

1 II 1

1st LAI   2nd LAI   x

X   JFCE

2 II 2

2   2

IMEF   JFCE

III
3   1
TARO

Kibrit

Al Mish'ab

Saudi Arabia

1 xx (-)
USMC

2 xx
USMC

Source:
USAF, Airpower and the Iraqi Offensive at Khafji, 1997.

FIGURE 5

need to get down here now. We have a real problem and no action is being taken," I told him.

My instinct was that the Iraqis were probing, and I was afraid I knew why. Khafji itself was empty. All the Saudi civilian residents had been evacuated weeks ago because the town sat right on the border. However, we'd been trying to do some pretty aggressive things to the Iraqi telephone system and there was a Khafji connection to all of that. I remembered we had a special four-man team around Khafji that had been there a few days at least. Part of Iraq and Kuwait's system ran through northern Saudi Arabia and one link was at Khafji, so it had access no other place had. My first impulse was, could the Iraqis have somehow figured it out and gone into the town brute force to put a stop to it?

But that wasn't it. We didn't know it at the time, but the Iraqi attack was the brainchild of Iraqi III Corps Commander, General Mahmoud, from our unofficial "most wanted" list. Iraq's III Corps was still an intact force in late January and Mahmoud had initiative. He had met with Saddam and some other senior military leaders around January 25. As forces from Iraq's III Corps began preparations, JSTARS sensors detected and recorded the increased activity, but we didn't know what to make of it. Later, looking over the tapes, the pieces fell in place. Earth-moving equipment dug berms and reinforced artillery positions on January 26 and 27. Armored vehicles from the 3rd Armored Division moved into position on January 28.

Iraq's 5th Mechanized Division—veterans of the Iran-Iraq war—started the attack by advancing three battalion-sized elements toward Khafji as shown in Figure 5. On the 5th Mech's right, the Iraqi 3rd Armored Division was to follow and reinforce with company-sized units attached to the 5th Mech. First Mechanized Division, part of Iraq's IV Corps, was further along to the right, west-northwest of the coast road, to provide a protective screen. The Tawakalna and Medina Republican Guard divisions to the north were on alert for a possible follow-up attack down the Wadi into the Egyptian and Syrian sectors.

We saw the attack in the TACC because of JSTARS. JSTARS flew about 10 hours each night, rotating the only two aircraft in existence at that time. Its sensor software was still in the test phase. Even so, its moving target indicator mode generated an excellent picture of Iraqi movement along major and minor lines of communication. We were fortunate that JSTARS got a look over in the Khafji areas. For most of the first two weeks, JSTARS was tasked mainly to look to the west to support VII Corps and to the north to assist with Scud hunting. Only 40 percent of its time was spent monitoring the KTO.

At about 2130 local time, JSTARS fanned its sensors over the southern part of Kuwait. The moving target indicators spotted signs of an attack. To the west, Marine outposts along the border made the first contact with the advancing Iraqi forces. Forward outposts and fire control teams returned fire and fell back as planned to hold the line on the ground while Marine forward air controllers directed air strikes against the Iraqis.

Lead elements of the Iraqi forces entered Khafji about 2300. The town had been evacuated earlier because of its vulnerable position. The Navy also detected and stopped about 15 Iraqi patrol boats joining in the attack.

Horner walked into the TACC shortly after this initial contact. I stayed with him there for about an hour. When he arrived, Horner ordered the single JSTARS aircraft flying that night to swing back to the KTO, and concentrate its arc of coverage over the border area near Khafji. For the rest of the night JSTARS applied 40 minutes of coverage every hour to Khafji and 20 minutes to the western sector of the U.S. VII Corps. This retasking was just in time. At 0200 on January 30, the JSTARS sensors began to detect more movement as the 5th Mechanized entered Khafji and elements of the 3rd Armored advanced through the adjacent Wafra forest. To the west, the Iraqi 1st Mechanized Division probed across the border.

Horner directed the attack from the TACC. Using the communications relay of AWACS and ABCCC, Horner rushed in every F-16 that was airborne, plus A-10s and some of the F/A-18s. During this time period, the killbox system could direct a four-ship through each box every eight minutes in daylight and every 15 minutes at night. We had strikes going into the killbox area for other targets in Kuwait. The TACC diverted sorties from fixed to mobile targets. These were sorties pre-planned on the ATO for alternate targets in the KTO, but they were diverted in real time. Horner just rolled them all in there to stop the advance. The A-10s, AC-130 gunships, and Marine AV-8s had excess sortie generation capability and were surged to stop the incursion and provide close air support.

As we had always thought, pilots found the Iraqi armored vehicles were easier to identify and target once they were on the move. "It was basically a free-fire zone north of a certain latitude," one of the gunship crewmen later commented. Pilots reported that target identification was initially difficult "until the Iraqis were really on the highway moving, and then they were very easy to see." A-6s joined in with Rockeye. Near Al Wafra, one A-10 pilot described the sight of a column of vehicles on the road as like "something you're taught from A-10 school." Using his Maverick missile, the pilot recalled, "I picked out a vehicle in the middle since there was a vehicle burning on either end of the column."

Another A-10 pilot, Captain Rob Givens, later recalled with some amazement, "I, myself, one captain in one airplane, was engaging up to a battalion-size of armor on the ground," and "keeping these guys pinned for a little bit." AC-130 gunships waiting on alert were scrambled after a hasty briefing. As lead elements of the 5th Mechanized with some support from the 3rd Armored reached Khafji, one gunship caught the column and stopped many of them from entering the town.

We drew back the Coalition ground forces in the area so the aircraft would have full sweep to work over any vehicles. In the process, the Marine teams got stranded in Khafji itself, along with our "telephone linemen." They courageously stayed put and spent the better part of the next two days hiding from patrolling Iraqis and helping call in air strikes.

Radio Baghdad's publicity machine swung into action, calling Khafji "the omen of the thundering storm that will blow on the Arabian Desert" and claimed they were teaching the Coalition aggressors a lesson.

They were. Khafji was hot evidence that if Iraq's forces moved, we could pin them and kill them.

The swiftness with which we took care of it and the overwhelming air attacks absolutely blew apart that 5th Mech Division. It showed how vulnerable they were. By early morning we knew air power had contained whatever was up. Air attacks on the columns had been so effective that the objective of the Iraqi attack remained unclear to the Coalition. "So few Iraqis made it across the border," Horner later recalled, "that it appeared to be some sort of minor action."

'A-10 and Marine ground elements stopped Iraq attack on Ra's al Khafji relatively quick,' I entered in my diary. 'However, 4 tanks slipped into Khafji ... we must destroy, with Saudis leading and without collateral damage.' Actually, it was more than four tanks. By the morning of January 30, a few hundred Iraqi troops occupied the town of Khafji. Having

the Saudis take the lead was the correct decision, militarily and politically; Khafji was their town and it was in their military sector.

Prince Ben Sultan al-Saud Khalid begged Schwarzkopf to send in the
B-52s. Schwarzkopf later had to write a formal letter to King Fahd ex-
plaining why he would not level Khafji—destroy it to save it.

Instead, Schwarzkopf decided to use the Saudis, Qataris and Egyptian
forces along with U.S. Marines and air power to run the Iraqis out of
Khafji. To increase the margin of safety, he ordered a phased redeploy-
ment in the Marines' sector that put a buffer of about 20 kilometers of
territory between Coalition forces and the Iraqis. As long as air could
reach deep to stop the offensive, the ground forces in MARCENT sector
and the Egyptian sector would not have to be reinforced, and Schwarzkopf would not have to reposition ARCENT forces.

Mahmoud knew he was in trouble and contacted Baghdad for permission to withdraw, but was told to continue the attack.[3] Recapturing
Khafji itself and stopping any Iraqi attempts to reinforce the town were
the top priorities. Marines moved into place south of Al Wafra to hold
the sector. Attack helicopters, artillery and fixed-wing air joined the
close-in battle around Khafji. Cobra helicopters with TOW missiles cy-
cled throughout the day to attack targets like Iraqi armored personnel
carriers (APC) at close range inside the town of Khafji. Throughout the
day, fixed-wing sorties scheduled on the ATO checked in with the Marine
forward air controllers to seek out targets. An OV-10 spotted an Iraqi
tank column moving south toward the town and passed the location to
several airborne F/A-18s. Pilots later told forward the air controller, Marine Corps Major Jim Braden, that as soon as the first Iraqi vehicles got
hit, they stopped moving, and became a much easier target for the aircrews.

Beyond that, I sensed that Khafji was very significant because of what
we learned about the Iraqis. *'Maybe the largest ground action of the war,'*
my notes continued. *'Lessons: Iraqi ground forces as weak as I have been
saying . . . not a viable fighting force . . . ground campaign will be a "police
action" if we don't become impatient!'*

With the offensive now about 24 hours old, Saudi and Qatari forces
gathered to retake Khafji on January 30. Mahmoud's only chance was to
attempt to send more elements of the 5th Mechanized and 3rd Armored

3. *The Generals' War*, p. 283.

down to reinforce. However, Mahmoud's "second battle" of Khafji never took place. Soon after midnight, JSTARS detected a 15-mile-long armored column moving on the coastal road south toward Khafji. Air controllers directed airborne assets to nip at the Iraqi III Corps' attempts to recommence operations. About 0200 local time on January 31, JSTARS recorded an air attack in progress on a column of vehicles. Lead vehicles swerved off the road and into the desert as the attack began. Multiple JSTARS tracks of the primary and secondary Iraqi lines of communication across Kuwait confirmed that air attacks had disrupted vehicle traffic throughout the area. Instead of advancing toward the Coalition, Iraq's forces were being stopped, rerouted, delayed and destroyed. Iraq's forces were unable to continue organized maneuver and the offensive unraveled by the morning of January 31.

It was the first time air power had been this successful at night against moving armor. A vivid U-2 reconnaissance picture the next morning showed a formation of Iraqi tanks on fire across the desert, each with a plume of smoke still rising.

"From Iraq's standpoint, the Battle of Khafji was a debacle," Schwarzkopf later wrote in his memoirs. "The 5th Mechanized Division, which had been rated one of their finest armored units, just a notch below the Republican Guard, was almost entirely destroyed—we monitored Iraqi reports afterward that indicated that only 20 percent of that division made it back."[4]

A captured Iraqi soldier from the 5th Mechanized Division remarked that his brigade underwent more damage in 30 minutes of air attacks at Khafji than it had in eight years of the Iran-Iraq War. We'd destroyed enough vehicles in time to stifle the Iraqi III Corps' effort to regain the initiative.

The final counting that went on later showed some pretty impressive statistics. The 1st Mechanized, 3rd Armored and 5th Mechanized divisions were located in five killboxes when they began the offensive against Khafji. We contained the Iraqi offensive with very little effect on the rest of the air campaign. We flew just 267 sorties in those killboxes in 72 hours from January 29 to January 31. The 267 sorties totaled just 17 percent of the sorties flown in the 20 main killboxes in the KTO in those three days. We shot more Maverick missiles during Khafji than during the ground war.

4. *It Doesn't Take a Hero*, pp. 426–7.

Sadly, we also lost a gunship on the early morning of January 30. The crew was launched just before dawn, and got so engaged in working over Iraqi targets that they became visible in the dawn. One of the small SAMs got them—it was the largest single loss of life for the Coalition in the air war.

The Marines also had a bad friendly fire incident early in the battle. I could see just how it had probably happened; the ground controller talking the strike aircraft onto the target, and they were 90 degrees off, and hit two of their APCs. Tragic.

As the results from Khafji began to come in, we had significant new intelligence on how our enemy reacted to the war.

I told Schwarzkopf, "Remember my promise, if they try to move tanks in the desert, they die."

The only way you can keep a tank alive in the desert under air attack is you keep it covered and keep it camouflaged and don't run it and don't make it hot. Khafji was a case in point. The bad part was that nobody was interested in taking the lessons from this and applying them as we went forward. My only complaint was that the TACC had been too slow in attacking the armor. They had a "minding-the-store" mentality. Only Horner's personal intervention got the priorities straight: JSTARS retasked, all sorties in those killboxes diverted for the FACs, the gunships and other aircraft scrambled. There was another big lesson in air war execution.

Overall, Khafji was a stark revelation, or should have been. The Iraqi army could not execute maneuver warfare under Coalition air power. *'Saddam has less understanding of our air capability than I thought,'* I recorded in my diary. *'Khafji was fairly large for his size of army but execution was straight out of WWII. Night is our strength. Saddam continues to not understand LGB, IR weapons.'*

Schwarzkopf wrote later, "I concluded with great relief that the Iraqi army wasn't half as skilled or highly trained as it had been portrayed, and all we should really worry about in the future was their use of unconventional weapons."

Without a doubt, Khafji proved we could dominate at night and attack armored vehicles on the move at night, with air power. The bottom line: the Iraqi army would die in place or die on the move, their choice.

'Khafji sent a message difficult to ignore,' I noted on January 31. After that I kept reminding Schwarzkopf about it. Part of him wanted to understand, and a part of him wasn't anxious to understand. "Just remem-

ber," I said to him a few times, "if they have to move, they die. And I don't know how you can fight a ground war and not move."

It was some time on the 31st of January that Perry Smith, on CNN, referred to me as the "intellectual guru of the air campaign." All my guys watched CNN in the Black Hole. They had it on all the time, so I heard about it right away. That was a heavy title. They made up a black and white slide for my office door: "Home of the INTELLECTUAL GURU of the Offensive Air Campaign." I was pre-occupied with winning a war, not trying to build a legend. The sign disappeared from my door fast. But, I admit, I saved it.

My media reputation was spreading though, accurately or not. My favorite intelligence expert, Captain John Glock, passed me an excerpt from a letter his wife had written him.

"I saw General Glosson on CNN the other day," Donna Glock wrote her husband. "He seems like a very nice, even-tempered man. Do you enjoy working for him?"

That one I had to keep for my files.

Bomb Damage Assessment

Khalid and General Sultan were just clearing out Khafji when Yeosock briefed Schwarzkopf that the Republican Guard was at 99 percent strength—after 15 days and over 2,000 strike sorties. It was unbelievable. We'd put 458 sorties on the Republican Guard on January 29 and another 408 on January 30.[5] But it was clear we had serious problems on our hands.

In a nutshell, the BDA process was haphazard, with rules that kept changing; yet underneath it all, the other problem was that we weren't being as effective as we thought against fielded forces in the KTO. We'd have to do much better to make Phase III a success and get to the 50 percent degradation of Iraq's ground units.

Our BDA on the strategic targets was limited but for the fielded forces, the problem was more severe, and more complex. BDA consisted basically of whatever I could ascertain from the tapes from the fighters, or whatever McConnell gave me. For all practical purposes, the rest of the BDA was non-existent and a waste of time.

5. Lt. Co. William F. Andrews. *Air Power Against an Army: Challenge and Response in CENTAFs Duel with the Republican Guard,* (Maxwell AFB, AL: AU Press CADRE Papers, 1998), p. 46.

I relied heavily on mission tapes and reviewed tapes every day. I told the wing commanders to send me a cross-section of their tapes via the intelligence officers at the wings. A lieutenant from Combat Camera came over every day with the stack of tapes and she and I would go over them. From there, I often picked the ones I wanted to show the CINC, plus tapes to show the press.

The F-111s, for example, were getting the job done. On January 31, I had a list of the 48th TFW's successes to date as confirmed by review of their film:

143 HAS	6 K2 storage bunkers
24 bunkers	Kirkuk IOC
30 buildings	4 C2 bunkers
8 runway, 7 taxiways	H-1 IOC 7 communications center
5 large hangers	Tall King radar
2 POL sites	Entray radar
1 Scud (or so we thought)	Tikrit presidential residence
5 Bunkers	III Corp Bunker
4 storage areas	VI Corp Bunker
Basra assembly area	Shaibah communications center
2 culverts	Oil spill manifolds
Latifiyah liquid plant	30 direct hits on bridges

In fact, we were finding the F-111s worked best against bridges because they carried more bombs than the F-117s.

For compiled tracking of BDA, I got good information from Mc-Connell, whose sources included overhead satellites and other methods. CENTCOM also kept track. CENTCOM's count was reasonably accurate once it was finished, but it was about three to five days behind. That wasn't nearly fast enough for retargeting decisions. Which is why I say, from the execution standpoint, anything except the tapes from the wings and information from McConnell was a waste of time.

For example, I had to send CENTCOM J2 a memo on NBC targets. They'd claimed in a memo of January 31 that we had not struck or not damaged aimpoints at eight different target sites, which wasn't the case. In five areas—the Al Jarrah CW bunkers, the Salman Pak BW/CW bunkers, the Ad Diwaniyah BW bunkers, the Ad Nasiriyah BW bunkers and the Fallujah BW bunkers—all the sites were destroyed as of February 1. The BW bunkers at Karbala, Kirkuk and Habbaniyah tallied a mix of "destroyed" and "damaged." CENTCOM's BDA was just that far behind.

Meanwhile, ARCENT and MARCENT were in charge of tracking progress against Iraqi ground units. We'd talked about BDA before the war started but there was no formal methodology to keep things straight between ARCENT, MARCENT and the air component. I placed great faith in pilot reports backed up by gun cameras. We'd had gun cameras since World War II and "a picture is worth a thousand words." As pilots, we trained in the intricacies of dive-bombing and we were used to getting harsh grades from the ranges. In the F-4, if I was good, and I was having a good day, I could put a bomb right on target and the range called "shack" for a direct hit. But it sure wasn't like that every day. We knew a hit from a miss. Just as important, I watched the gun-camera video to see what happened after impact, if there were secondary explosions, etc.

The Army and Marines, however, had their own ways of counting. So did the national intelligence communities whose overhead sensors sometimes could not pick out destruction of a vehicle unless it was strewn all over the desert floor. ARCENT and MARCENT were supposed to count up how many tanks, APCs, and artillery pieces the air campaign hit and report it to Yeosock and his staff, but what exactly was a "kill?" The Army had all manner of terms for a hard kill (blown to smithereens) versus a "mobility" kill meaning the thing couldn't maneuver, and so on.

Schwarzkopf was aware of the problem. He joked at the staff meeting on January 29 that "vehicles must be on their back like a dead cockroach before J-2 will assess a kill." Then he told CENTCOM to use pilot reports for the tallies.

We thought they'd look at pilot mission reports and gun-camera video as we did and count up what had been hit. We thought wrong.

It was early February when Lewis figured out that ARCENT was counting *only* reports from the A-10s and *only* kills, not probables. That's the system the Army knew best. The only other time they'd count a kill was if imagery or signals intelligence confirmed it as killed or "probable." A "possible" didn't count, even if it and the mission report supported each other exactly. There was only a trickle of imagery, or signals intelligence, for the ground forces. So ARCENT threw out everything else.

And that was just for the A-10s progress! No other Coalition platforms were in the count. So if an F-16 or F/A-18 had a great day and claimed a direct hit on a tank, too bad. Outside of the A-10, ARCENT counted a hit only if imagery spotted it. Imagery was great, but overhead

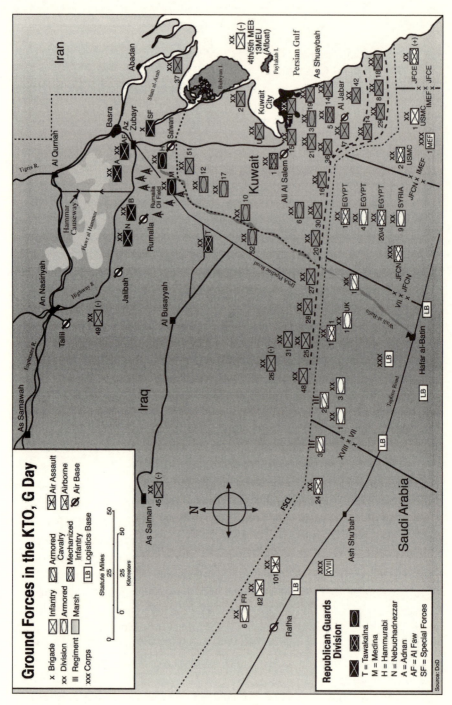

FIGURE 6

and medium-altitude sensors from the Defense Intelligence Agency (DIA) could not see anything except catastrophic kills and could tell us virtually nothing about hits on vehicles buried in the sand. In this case, only the strike aircraft's gun camera got close enough to see that a turret was blown sideways or tracks were crumpled. But the videotapes weren't getting back to Washington.

These BDA problems for the fielded forces targets hardly surprised me because of the trouble we'd had keeping track of the impact on the strategic targets—which were fixed in place, and far fewer in number.

The numbers looked bad. As far as Yeosock knew, the air component wasn't living up to the promises I'd made. At this rate we wouldn't achieve 50-percent attrition until the fourth of July.

ARCENT's BDA surprise gave no insight into what was really troubling me: I could see from the pilot reports and cockpit video that it wasn't all a feedback problem. Our strike aircraft were *not* attriting the fielded forces as efficiently as I wanted.

Buck Rogers looked over the F-16 tapes and saw they were using tactics that eroded results.[6] The F-16s were doing dive-toss attacks and attacking at shallow dive angles, like they'd learned for low altitude, but it wouldn't work at higher altitudes. No way were we going back down to low altitude but we had to do something. The F-16 crews figured it out for themselves when they saw their bombs miss.[7] The F-16s during the day just weren't able to find or hit them and destroy them as well as I had hoped they would. The A-10s operating at night with the Mavericks were better, but unless there's a sharp contrast for the Maverick's seeker, it's tough to hit a tank. If the Iraqis were not operating their tanks and getting them heated up, there couldn't be much of an infrared contrast. Many armored units now had their tanks buried in sand right up around their turrets.

Boomer Moves the Marine FSCL

Soon I also learned that the Marine Commander, Lieutenant General Walt Boomer, had moved the Fire Support Coordination Line (FSCL) in his sector without my knowledge. The FSCL was a control line placed as a safety measure for friendly ground troops, as shown in Figure 6. Inside

6. *Air Power Against an Army*, p. 40.
7. Ibid., p. 88.

the FSCL, friendly troops were present, either in fixed locations or maneuvering. Air strikes inside the FSCL all had to be controlled by someone in contact with the ground force units, usually, a Forward Air Controller (FAC) on the ground. The Marines were masters at controlling their own aircraft for support of their own marines on the ground.

In front of the FSCL, there would only be enemy forces, so air strikes could take place without direct control. The concept was simple in theory but, like many others, the air and ground tended to see it differently. Ground commanders wanted the FSCL out far enough to give them space to maneuver and advance fast during battle. Airmen liked a tight FSCL because more strikes could be poured into the area beyond the FSCL since they did not have to wait for a FAC to give permission to drop.

Of course, there was no big ground maneuver or advance going on in the Marine sector. The control issue was the fine point here. Boomer and I had an agreement that south of the FSCL, he could use his AV-8B Harriers and other organic Marine aircraft however he wanted. The FSCL was placed on the border of Saudi Arabia and Kuwait. It covered only Marines and Coalition troops.

Then, Boomer moved his sector's FSCL just up into Kuwait so some of the front-line Iraqi units poised on the border fell *inside* the FSCL, enabling him to attack them at will. He wanted to use his own Harriers to get more of what he felt was battlefield preparation started, with more intensity. By moving the FSCL, he'd be able to do that under the rules of engagement we'd laid down.

He passed the change back to CENTAF verbally on January 31.

It annoyed me. The catch was, by moving the FSCL so he could work it himself, Boomer had also closed it off to the rest of the air component. The Marines would be on their own trying to get those Iraqi units down to 50-percent attrition—if they could even get an accurate intelligence count of the damage they'd inflicted. Given the problems we were having, I doubted it would work. Their AV-8Bs also did not employ Maverick missiles or the 30 mm gun like the A-10 did at the time and that would be a disadvantage.

'*Next time, I'll go direct to the CINC,*' I noted in my diary. For now, rather than fight Boomer on this, I cautioned him at the CINC's staff meeting: "I'm concerned you're not going to have things attrited enough when the CINC gets ready to start the ground war."

No matter what the BDA rules, we'd all have to crank out better results, and fast. Yeosock's briefing just put the challenge out in the open.

In the last week of January, we started to innovate. First I directed the A-10s to go deeper. We all saw the A-10s as a true close-air-support platform, flying low, answering calls from friendly troops. I directed them to seek out interdiction targets in raids over the Tawakalna Division, the nearest of the heavy Republican Guard divisions.

Despite the phenomenon at Khafji, from the intelligence photos in other areas, I could see that we were not destroying enough tanks fast enough.

"Come up with something different," I told Joe Bob Phillips. "Figure out another way to do this."

Joe Bob was probably the best natural aviator I'd ever known. He had pure flying ability but he also was a bright tactical thinker. He was never given credit for the last point, and that was unfortunate for the Air Force. Joe Bob was a lot like General Carl A. "Tooey" Spaatz, the first Air Force Chief of Staff. Spaatz and Joe Bob didn't care about what they looked like. They didn't care whether the buildings were painted or not. They didn't care about pomp and circumstance. In Spaatz's official portrait that hangs in the Pentagon he sits slumped in a chair in a rumpled uniform. A cigarette dangles in his fingers. Spaatz only cared about your ability in an airplane and how you performed. Everything else was irrelevant. Joe Bob was just the same.

Early on, when I needed help, I called Tiny West, the behemoth commander of the Fighter Weapons School. Tiny was one of the best combat minds that ever put on a flight suit. I asked him to send weapons systems experts from Nellis and he asked, "Do you have a problem with Joe Bob being the team leader?"

"Not only do I not have a problem," I said, "he's a brilliant choice."

Now, in Riyadh, I wanted him to use the Nellis brain trust of weapons experts he'd brought from Las Vegas to find a means of destroying that Iraqi armor, and fast.

DECISIONS

As I waited for a better fix, I dealt with a rash of problems.

First, McConnell called back on January 31 with the news that our "successful" Scud strike briefed on TV had hit four Jordanian fuel trucks, not transporter erector launchers. Once again, CENTAF intelligence demonstrated their incompetence.

Next, I had a problem in my own units. F-15Cs on combat air patrol over Baghdad had indications of MiG-29s taking off. The pilots asked AWACS for a vector to the MiGs, but the AWACS was now too far south to monitor the Iraqi warplanes. The MiGs got away. McBroom at the F-15C wing was livid and rightly so. I directed Lewis to fix the AWACS CAP so it never happened again. "If necessary, I'll send AWACS north of the border continuously with an escort," I threatened.

This was also the day we heard that the Iraqis captured CBS News reporter Bob Simon and his crew. Sudairy had more word on that.

"They are going to move him to Baghdad with the other POWs," Sudairy said. I fed that back to McConnell, who had no information on the move. Sudairy did not know the time of the move, or where the prisoners would be going. It made me uneasy, and I hoped Sudairy or McConnell would be able to tell me more before long.

Improving Results in the KTO

By February 3, Joe Bob was ready with ideas for how to improve our results against the fielded forces in Kuwait. He brought me three recommendations:

192

• Try 500-pound laser-guided bombs (LGB) on the tanks.
• Implement airborne Forward Air Controllers.
• Stop the F-16s from "pickling" too high.

Of these three, the last was the easiest to implement. The F-16s were showing disappointing results except for a few at night. Part of that was because they were hitting the "pickle" switch to release their bombs at an altitude that was too high.

I'd told them, "Until the ground campaign starts, I don't want any of you guys pickling below about 7,000 feet." Well, somehow they interpreted that guidance to mean that they were supposed to pickle so as to pull out of their dives above six or seven thousand feet. Their accuracy was out the wazoo. To pull out at 7,000 feet, they were pickling around 10,000. Some units were pickling above 20,000 feet! I wanted them to pickle at 7,000 and that meant they pulled out of their dives down at 5,000 feet.

The other thing that made the F-16s, A-10s, F/A-18s and other non-precision aircraft more accurate was the use of Killer Scouts.

"We need to go to FACs," Joe Bob said. The trouble was, we didn't have any. Forward Air Controllers in Vietnam scouted the battle area to identify targets such as enemy troops, vehicles or artillery, and passed them on to strike aircraft waiting nearby. The OV-10 was a slower-flying plane giving the observer more dwell time; F-100s were "Fast FACs" moving rapidly to scan an area, lowering risk. The Air Force was once full of pilots who knew the airborne FAC job, but I didn't have any in the Gulf.

Either way, I suddenly remembered the other problem was that Horner hated airborne FACs with a passion. He'd had a bad experience with them in Vietnam.

I called back to Major General Billy Boles in personnel to do a quick run for us and find out who was in theater that had previous FAC experience of any kind. Boles kicked out the names, and then I was able to tell Cash Jasczak where to look. Cash already had volunteers from his own unit. That's how we were able to put the people together as fast as we did.

Next, we needed to divide up the battlefield and focus on it as shown in Figure 7. The killbox squares extended over Iraq and Kuwait and up to 20,000 feet. Each 30-by-30-mile grid was a killbox named with a letter designation such as AE, where much of the Tawakalna sat.

I decided to rename my FACs the "Killer Scouts." In each box or group of boxes, you'd have a Killer Scout. That killbox set would be the responsibility of two or three daytime Killer Scouts and two or three

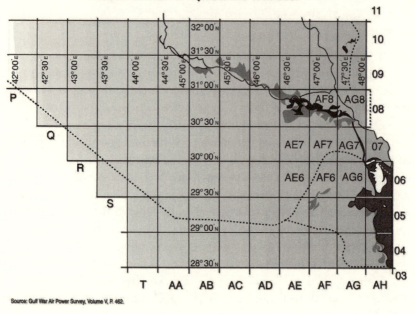

Kuwait Theater of Operations' Killboxes

Source: Gulf War Air Power Survey, Volume V, P. 462.

FIGURE 7

night Killer Scouts, and it'd be the same guys going over and over. That way they would learn the topography and distinct features of the killbox enough that they could systematically go about digging the tanks and the artillery and the supplies out of that area, instead of just depending on satellites and JSTARS to pick up stuff that looked interesting.

Once they put a Killer Scout inside of a killbox, and started seeing a spike in effectiveness, they all fell in love with it instantly.

Now, in reality, the Killer Scout system worked great in some cases and not so well in others. It depended on the abilities and experience of the Killer Scout himself. Some were more adept, especially the dozen or so who'd been FACs earlier. Those guys were really good at it. The others were starting from scratch, and had never been trained, so it took them a little while to pick up all the techniques of how to talk the eyes of the pilot onto the target so he could drop his bombs. But compared to the first few weeks, these Killer Scouts were phenomenally successful.

Tank Plinking

Tanks were Joe Bob's coup de grace. He suggested we use the F-111 and its Pave Tack laser targeting system with a 500-pound laser-guided bomb, the GBU-12, against individual Iraqi tanks—a technique we later called "tank-plinking."

"Have you talked to anybody about any test we've ever run on trying to hit a tank with a Mark 82 or Mark 84?" asked Joe Bob.

"No," I said, and I hadn't. "But you know, now that you say that, I do remember some discussion about the relative accuracy of Mark 84 versus Mark 82s."

Both the 2,000-pound Mark 84 and the 500-pound Mark 82 bomb bodies had the same laser-guidance kit attached to them to make them into precision weapons. Even though one was four times heavier, they had the same ratio fins on both of them.

Joe Bob and I discussed it from every possible angle.

"Just from a plain physics standpoint, if you have the same guidance kits and the same fins on a bomb that weighs half or less than the other projectile, it has to be more accurate," I said. Joe Bob agreed.

"If you're thinking about this," I told him, "why don't we get the 500-pounders? We've got some, and the Navy's got so many of them you could make a bridge across the Euphrates River with them."

A short while later Joe Bob came back with his findings.

"Okay, I want 500-pound LGBs," he said. I give Joe Bob credit for it because he came up with the idea. All things being equal, the smaller, 500-pound bomb would hit closer to the laser spot target just because physics dictated it would have less momentum with which to drift off course. A 500-pound bomb would be more than enough to blow an Iraqi tank to bits, even if the tank was half-dug into the sand.

After talking to Joe Bob I immediately called Tom Lennon at the F-111 wing. We'd never tried a technique like this before.

"Remember the old days when we used to do buddy-lasing in the F-4?" I asked Lennon over the phone. The first laser-guided bombs used in Vietnam required one aircraft to fly around the target and designate the laser spot, while his buddy in the second aircraft released the bomb. "I want you to go 16,000 feet and fly in a circle." I told him. "I want you to pretend that you aren't dropping a bomb, but you are buddy-lasing. That's the kind of arc I want you to take around the tanks.

"As you get in the envelope to launch, you can take your time. I want you to launch at those tanks one at a time using buddy-lasing."

Lennon thought it was the dumbest thing that I had ever asked him to do. His reaction was so visceral that as we were talking, it occurred to me how to make sure he did what I wanted.

"Now, I want you to fly this mission yourself," I told him. Lennon was skeptical, but he said he'd give it a try. With Lennon, I knew I'd get an impeccable picture of what was happening. No way would he come back and say it was pretty good when it really wasn't. Second, I knew he'd bust his ass to make it work.

Two days later, he once again confirmed that he could make anything happen and proved the brilliance of Joe Bob's idea. On February 5 Lennon and a wingman flew the first F-111 vs. tanks mission over the Medina division of the Republican Guard. As soon as he landed, he called to say:

"Unbelievable, I got seven out of eight direct hits."

"Great," I said. "Destroying tanks is your number one priority until further notice."

Then I telephoned Hornburg and directed him to test his F-15Es against tanks, the same way. His F-15Es had just 12 laser-targeting pods in the whole theater, whereas all the F-111s could self-designate. But, because of its maneuverability and load, the F-15E was even better suited for the mission.

Tank-plinking was a breakthrough, and one we needed. *'The number one shortfall at this juncture: attriting tanks,'* I wrote on February 5. *'Killer Scouts will help, but significant change will require F-111 and F-15E success with GBU-12.'* We had about 2,000 GBU-12s in theater at the time, I calculated, with more on the way.

Soon Hornburg called to tell me he was going to do some of the tank-plinking with buddy-lasing because of the demand for sorties that I was putting on him. I said, "Whatever you want to do, as long as you have success." He was always thinking and working to carry more of the load. My problems were his problems—what loyalty.

We had two ways in addition to the pilots' mission reports and video-tapes to verify that tank-plinking worked. First, the Army verified it. Under Horner's deal, they got to count. We worked a deal so that as long as the Army ground liaison officers verified the kill, ARCENT would accept it. Their tallies showed right away that more tanks were being destroyed.

My second source was McConnell. "Buster, I'm seeing a lot more tanks that have tracks blown off of them or the turret blown off," he told me. "So obviously your tank-plinking is being effective." One of the best telltale signs was the overhead imagery that clearly showed Iraqi tank crews sleeping out away from their tanks. You could see all of the Iraqi soldiers lying out on the ground at night. They wouldn't get near the tanks. (We found out after the war that on occasion, the F-111s and F-15Es blew the tanks into pieces so small that the imagery analysts couldn't tell a tank had ever been there.)[1]

Ultimately, the numbers of tanks destroyed before the ground war—based on Army counting—showed the success of tank-plinking. The official Pentagon report after the war, stated that Iraq had 4,280 tanks of which 1,772 were hit prior to the ground war. (For APCs, the score was 948 out of 2,880 and 1,474 out of 3,100 for artillery.) I still felt the Army was under-reporting but I understood Horner's motives for letting them keep the count, even if we were at their mercy.

We also used tried-and-true techniques. 'B-52s turning the heat up on infantry divisions.' I noted in my diary on February 3. The front-line infantry divisions arrayed along the border were particular targets. Filled with conscripts, they were vulnerable to the physical and psychological effects of relentless attack. Schwarzkopf wanted to make sure they were miserable and eager to surrender. We'd select different divisions each day, and sometimes we'd go from infantry to mechanized. Soon the assessed strength of these divisions plummeted.

While I wanted the armor to go away fast, there was an art to this. For example, in the last three days before the ground war, the F-117s would take out the T-junctions to all the pipes that led into the fire trenches, so they couldn't put any oil in them. If we did it any sooner, the Iraqis would have had time to repair the T-junctions and refill the fire trenches.

Artillery also had to wait because it was so easy to replace. With artillery, you can throw it on a truck and drive it down to the battle area. Most Iraqi artillery was not sophisticated, self-propelled artillery (although they did have some of these.) If we destroyed it too early, there was a good chance that they could go back into other areas in the northern part of Iraq and around Baghdad and pull new artillery down toward Kuwait. Even if we destroyed it a few days before the ground war, and

1. GWAPS picture, p. 39 in Vol. 2 Part 2.

they started to replace it, they'd get right in the middle of trying to move it and we could pick them off from the air. Much better to wait.

Where we did not want to wait was in hitting specially selected units and their equipment with strikes planned to degrade the units below 50-percent effectiveness.

Weather

On February 3, I was alone in my office when Jerry Riley came to me with the latest long-range weather forecast. He painted such a dire picture for the next three or four days that I wasn't sure how much we were going to be able to accomplish. *'God, we ask your power to remove these clouds,'* I wrote in my diary, in all capital letters.

It was getting harder every day that went by because I knew the days were numbered: I only had a finite amount of time left to meet the goals that only the air campaign could accomplish. The NBC targets bothered me most. Our objectives were to get Iraq out of Kuwait; there'd never been serious discussion of occupying Iraq itself. I figured that we weren't going to send troops up to these areas, so I had to get rid of whatever was going to be dealt with via the air campaign. There were many targets that I didn't want to leave intact after a campaign. We had no choice. These targets were not in the path of the land campaign. I knew the Army and Marines and Coalition forces would take care to destroy whatever key facilities or equipment might be in their area, but their objectives were in Kuwait. They weren't going all over Iraq, and my fighters and bombers were. We weren't going to have a division at the Baghdad Nuclear Research Center or at Salman Pak. Whatever we accomplished there, we had to do with air power.

All this left me with a different sight of the unfolding battle. It came to a head when Schwarzkopf pulled me aside after the staff meeting on the night of the February 4.

"We're approaching your 21 days," he reminded me.

Here we were, at Day 19. But he was totally disregarding the weather. We'd had nowhere near 21 days of effectiveness.

So in self defense that evening, I reminded him weather was holding us back.

"That's part of war," he snapped.

The CINC and the Ground War

The next day, the weather was just as bad as Riley said it would be. *"Weather is an absolute albatross,"* I complained in my diary notes. *"After 18 days, we are effectively at day 10—maximum."*

The afternoon was full of irritations. Britain's Special Air Services (SAS) had called in a strike on a Scud, and destroyed it. Then McConnell informed me that it looked like the Scud might have been a fake. We were inserting American special operations forces along Highway 12 to join the Scud hunt alongside the SAS. At least this time the special operations snake-eaters had told us where they'd be so we could avoid putting air strikes on top of their heads.

Obviously I was feeling more pressure and tension myself. Here I was, trying to reach our objectives and yet satisfy what the CINC wanted as far as the ground war was concerned and the weather was really going to pot. And I was running out of time and I knew it. So I didn't need anyone wasting my time.

In this foul mood, Deptula came to me with one too many questions about the upcoming plans. You can tolerate that if you've got plenty of time. I was past the point of tolerance. *"Deptula starting to reluctantly follow my direction . . . directed him to maintain my focus or else,"* I grimly noted. I told Tolin to give that part of the ATO closer scrutiny.

Then I really lost my temper. Secretary Cheney was to arrive in the theater for a visit on February 8. He was going to see several units, and meet with Schwarzkopf, but there were no Air Force bases on his itinerary. That did it. I called one of Cheney's special assistants.

"What is going on?" I asked. "The Chairman is at it again. I don't want the SecDef to come into the country and not visit any Air Force bases! Specifically, I want him to go to the F-117s. They're carrying the war. That's what's happening out here. They're the ones we're riding on. Why wouldn't he go down there?"

Cheney's office called right back. "Let's not worry about it," they said, trying to soothe me. "Secretary Cheney has not seen the proposed itinerary, and it will be corrected."

After all this, my frame of mind was not one of exuberance. It was time for me to step back for a moment. I took out my diary. *'Personal How-Goes-It for Day 20,'* I wrote.

'The strategic plan has worked—but not without turbulence.

Weather impact exceeded expectations
Iraq in disarray—approximately as anticipated
Scuds . . . intelligence and location shortfall greater than imagined
Attritting armor a disappointment.'

Then I graded the system performance to date. The F-117s, F-15Cs and F-111s all got a plus for superior performance, as did the RC-135 Rivet Joints and, of course, the tankers, now that we'd figured out how to schedule them. The F-15E, F/A-18, F-14 and the British GR1 all got a level mark, for performance as expected. I was disappointed with the overheads, the A-6s and the AWACS. The F-16s got a double minus. They were flying sorties, but they weren't accomplishing very much.

For intelligence, McConnell was the saving grace. *'His impact cannot be overstated,'* I wrote.

As for the Iraqis, their air was very weak—as anticipated. So were their ground forces, which I'd stated over and over again, but they'd proved it at Khafji.

Then I reviewed the performance of my wing commanders and staff so far. A few were disappointments. Most were doing very well, and I felt they'd have a good shot at promotion to general, such as Whitley, Lennon, Boomer, Parsons, Huot, Jasczak, Sharpe, and Sawyer, as well as Baptiste and Rogers on my staff. Hornburg looked like a potential three or four-star to me, and maybe I was biased, but so did my trio: Tolin, Lewis and Deptula.

I'd gotten a call from Boles about personnel—discussion about the latest one-star promotion list, and follow-on assignments policy after the war. It set me to thinking. I felt I'd better make notes to refer to, so I could take care of my people when this was over. If you don't jot these things down, your memory becomes too general over time. If you take a minute to put it on paper somewhere, privately, it will honestly reflect what you believed at that time, based on what you saw.

If you take care of the people, the mission will take care of itself. (That's true as long as the people understand the mission. If they don't understand the mission, it won't get accomplished.) But, by and large, if you really take care of the people and the people know you're taking care of them, if they know that you're working to make sure that they get every opportunity to do as well as they can and they will be rewarded accordingly, the mission will take care of itself.

I've always felt that you only have two major responsibilities: make sure the people understand the mission and take care of the people. Do those two things and you'll like the results. Over time, in every command I've ever had, that proved to be true in spades. I've had commands where things were not going very well when I took them over but they turned around and the success speaks for itself. That's the same attitude I had as the Director of Campaign Plans and Commander, 14th Air Division. Planning and executing war is what our profession is all about. The wing commanders and the senior guys on my staff were really controlling and making the day-to-day decisions. When the shooting stopped, I didn't want these people to be just thrown into a pot like all the other Joe Blows all over the world that for whatever reasons weren't part of this action.

I was determined to take care of these people. That's me. I won't change. I just think that's very critical. People forget that. People start believing their own press clippings, and try to impress the world with how bright they are, how tough they are or how great a strategic thinker they are. In all honesty, at least 90 percent of what they do and say is a result of somebody else's ideas, intellect or determination. And when a person doesn't give appropriate credit to his people, it's really a sad sight. You see it over and over and over, but that doesn't make it right. I would hope more people would focus on taking care of people rather than just using people.

Thinking about future glory for my staff nudged me out of my mood.

Setting the Date

I expected the CINC to turn all his attention to the ground war within two or three days, but it happened faster than that. "The Chairman's pushing me to start the ground campaign," Schwarzkopf said to us all at the staff meeting on February 5. "We need to get more serious about battlefield prep." I never liked that terminology because we'd been "preparing the battlefield" since Day One. Or as Deptula liked to say, "We are not preparing the battlefield. We are destroying it." He was 100-percent correct.

"We may have to start the ground war between 7–10 February," Schwarzkopf ventured.

'*Criminal!*' I scrawled in my diary.

This was a shock. There was no reason to push for a ground war in a few days. Schwarzkopf's stated goal since August or September had been to achieve 50-percent attrition on Iraqi army units prior to the ground war. With Powell itching to start sooner, it put Schwarzkopf in a tough spot.

Powell was one of the most politically effective Chairmen the nation's ever had. It was very disconcerting, because Powell was a wonderful person as an individual and he's a tremendous family man. I have the utmost respect for him on a personal basis. But to have him pushing to start the ground war prematurely was disconcerting.

At work, Powell wanted whomever he was advising to follow that advice, not use that advice to make the decision you thought correct. He and Schwarzkopf had already had heated moments. Only a person with suicidal tendencies would want to get crossways with him. If Powell was pressuring to start the ground war, this was a serious problem.

No matter when the ground war started, we had a lot of coordination issues to sort out immediately, and first among them was apportionment: how much of the air resources went to destroy targets facing the ground forces, and how those sorties were assigned to the Corps areas. Overall, we knew the goal—50-percent attrition—but I had one view about how to accomplish that and the ground commanders had another. They were screaming for more air.

Horner and I talked it over.

"The CINC's going to put Lieutenant General Cal Waller in to arbitrate between the Marines and the Army and the allies on who gets what," Horner told me.

"No," I countered. "He's going to arbitrate on what they submit as a request. He is not going to arbitrate what we attack. That's your decision. You are the JFACC."

Horner shrugged it off. "We'll attack whatever."

"Please," I said, "there may be times when we either have already destroyed it or it is no longer a valid target. There are a lot of reasons that we're not just going to blindly go bomb everything he puts on the list every day."

Horner agreed with that, so I didn't say any more to him. Ultimately, Schwarzkopf's opinion overrode all the air and ground commanders. A day or two later, when I was talking to the CINC about something else, I told him, "I've got to talk to you privately." We went into his office and I continued.

"Sir, you are holding me responsible for carrying out your air campaign. I can only do that if I have the authority to say 'no' going forward, as I have had up until now."

I was worried about Waller handling the apportionment job, which I mentioned to Schwarzkopf, but it wasn't my call. Waller would put together a list of 50 to 75 targets each day that had been selected by the ground forces. However, I couldn't just blindly commit to hit each and every one, for several reasons.

"What if the target has already been destroyed? What if it's moved, or if something has happened and it's no longer significant enough to be a target? We all had intelligence problems and the ground commanders could not always double-check a target before they put it on their list." They were best at tracking radio communications of an enemy on the move, and they split up the responsibilities for maintaining the ongoing list. It just wasn't an efficient cycle from their side. We'd seen that before. It was unclear how good their internal feedback loops were on the status of nominated targets.[2]

"But here's the one that troubles me the most," I continued. "What if some of the nominated targets on Waller's list are not consistent with your direction to me personally? You told me not to let a single bomb drop for the foreseeable future west of that particular location near Al Salman and west of the wadi because, you said, 'I don't want to give them the indication we're preparing for anything.' You know Luck's going to want some bombing out there."

Lieutenant General Gary Luck might well nominate targets in or around the path of his advance as he readied the XVIII Airborne Corps to move into position for its big sweep west once the ground war started. But if the targets were in an area designated off-limits by Schwarzkopf, I didn't want to hit them.

I made my case as strongly as I could but I was afraid of the answer I might get from Schwarzkopf. My next words were chosen carefully.

"Unless you tell me differently, I'm going to ignore any request that Waller makes that violates your direct guidance to me, or where the conditions have changed and the intel that he was using to make that decision is no longer accurate, or the target is no longer there."

"Fine," said Schwarzkopf.

"Okay. That's all I need. Now Waller's going to come to you screaming," I cautioned Schwarzkopf, "because I can tell you already from looking at the dry run they did yesterday, about 25 percent of the things he's put on the target list fall into one of those categories."

---

2. *Lucky War: Third Army in Desert Storm*, p. 187.

"You're kidding," Schwarzkopf said.

"I wish I were."

"Okay," he said. "You don't do anything that I've told you I don't want done, or if it looks like the intel they used is incorrect."

Schwarzkopf backed me up all the way. For the rest of the war, of course, Waller detested me.

My frank discussion with Schwarzkopf was hardly the end of the matter. Every day, Lewis, Deptula, Tolin and I sat down with Waller's list. I'd just mark off everything that was contrary to the CINC's guidance and the targets that had changed long before they'd made the list.

With Horner's approval, I refused to attend Waller's targeting board meeting. Corder went instead. Corder would provide Horner and me with a list of Waller's desired targets after his daily meeting.

One day, about a week later, Corder said, "Waller's just screaming that we're not supporting him."

"Tell him to give us specifics," I replied.

Corder brought back Waller's list. There were 27 targets out of 63 that I had not hit. Waller had them all circled.

"Now, I'm only going to do this one time," I said to Corder. "I'm not going to do it again and again every day, because it's going to take a lot of time."

I called in Tolin and he got three other guys together. "You see the ones he's got circled?" I asked Tolin. "I want you to put down why we didn't hit it and if there is a photograph, or overheads or anything to verify, include that."

Tolin and his team reviewed the list and I took it over to Waller. Out of the 27 targets, I showed him that any person with a pea for a brain would instantly have left them off because intellegince of 24 or 25 of the targets was completely outdated. Two were questionable. To my surprise, Waller tried to make a big issue out of those two, and ignore the fact that 24 or 25 of the nominations were absolutely ridiculous.

Years later, Waller claimed that in that meeting he called me a "duplicitous bastard" and threatened to choke me.[3] The truth was he didn't say anything of the sort. If he'd said that to me his next comments would have come from a prone position on the floor.

The deep lesson was what I knew already: When you have the right relationship with the CINC, minor problems are never significant. If

3. *The Generals' War*, p. 321.

you've performed for him and you've been successful, then he's going to trust you. At this point, in early February, there was nobody the CINC trusted more than me, because I'd done everything he'd asked and I never let him down, not once. It was that simple so I continued to deal with Waller as the CINC had directed—end of subject.

Target Growth

Schwarzkopf was starting to focus almost exclusively on the potential ground war. He agreed I could continue to use 50 percent of our F-111s, F-117s and F-15Es on the hardest, fixed, strategic targets. As much as possible, except for the tank-plinking, I focused them on the NBC sites, weapons labs and similar key locations. Yet we were struggling to keep "nice-to-have" new targets off the list.

Still, there was growth in the total number of targets, but it wasn't really beneficial in meeting the military objectives, at least in my opinion. For example, it was rare that we would have a new NBC target. Occasionally we picked up a few, but not like we should have. And it was the same way with alternate communications nodes. We picked up a few targets here and there. Overall, we weren't finding more strategic targets, at least not to the extent I'd expected. I thought that once we started taking their electricity and their telephone communications away and drove them to other means, that the target list would grow significantly, but it didn't happen. I also thought that we would pick up more movement of potential NBC-related activity once the war started. It just didn't happen, and it hurt our efforts. (As we learned from the United Nations inspectors after the war, we just were very inept, from an intelligence standpoint, on the NBC targets.)

We tried so hard sometimes we outfoxed ourselves. Late on February 3, McConnell called with a hot prospect.

"There's a refrigerated van parked outside a school in Kuwait City," McConnell said. He believed it could be a storage van for chemical or biological weapons.

"Do you believe that just because it's refrigerated?" I asked. "Is that what we're basing this on?"

"Yes."

"Look, I'll get in touch with the Kuwaiti resistance and find out if anybody is in that school. If nobody's in that school, then I'll take it out. If the school has children inside, I'm going to get one of the Kuwaiti resistance to go over and find out what's inside the van," I said.

McConnell got to it first, verified there was nobody in the school, and we took the van out. Turned out it was a refrigerated meat van for the Iraqi troops.

McConnell and I had also been sharing information on the whereabouts of Saddam. Once Sudairy told me his sources thought Saddam would be at a specific location, but McConnell was able to track it down and determine the tip was inaccurate. Yet, Sudairy was one of the best resources we had on sensitive targets.

I went ahead and destroyed the target just to show Sudairy I'd destroyed it, and let him see the post-strike photograph.

"My intel people tell me that we didn't get him," I said to Sudairy. "But I want you to keep working this as hard as you can."

We weren't closing in on Saddam, but our other mid-war innovation was working well against the Iraqi army. The first indications on February 5 were that the Killer Scouts had racked up a great success. But we were innovating on the fly and a lot was riding on making the concept work. Monitoring and tweaking it was vital, so I told Joe Bob and Lewis to stay on top of it. Joe Bob with his innate fighter pilot sense looked at the Killer Scouts through one set of eyes. As for Lewis, he would take an analytical approach and look at the Killer Scouts in a slightly different way. I wanted the benefit of both viewpoints.

It was very interesting. Over the next few weeks, I never talked to Rick and Joe Bob at the same time on the Killer Scout issue. I made it a point to talk to them separately. They never once had a disagreement on how it was going and where we were. They both pointed out similar problems every time they would occur, to the point that one time I thought maybe they were colluding.

In fact, they were just working together well and they had the system humming. They quickly refined the concept so that each Killer Scout handled only two killboxes. Later they subdivided each killbox into four quadrants. Every day, they'd come to me to recommend which boxes were going to be most actively pursued that night, depending on which Iraqi divisions our collective intelligence input said was least attrited. The killbox system worked extremely well for the A-10s. Given their stacks of Maverick missiles (they had first priority in theater for them) and their extensive training, the A-10s were doing very well. To be sure, they felt some frustration with the deep air interdiction and SEAD missions, but the crews understood the need, and got the job done.

Employing the Killer Scouts really leveraged the F-16s (which Joe Bob and Lewis had both flown) and improved their effectiveness in daylight. One of the F-16 squadrons described it as "an order of magnitude increase in effectiveness, compared to a week ago." With the Killer Scout system, F-16s had multiple passes into lucrative targets vs. "five frenzied minutes and one pass into I don't know what" under the old method. "Seventy percent of my passes are vehicle destruction or secondaries," reported another pilot. "Most of my guys are smiling now," said their commander.

They also loved the double turn at King Khalid Military City airfield (KKMC), close to the border. The F-16s from Al Minhad, UAE, flew their first mission, then landed at KKMC, 70 miles short of the Saudi border with Kuwait. At KKMC they'd refuel, rearm, and take off again for another bombing mission in the KTO. KKMC turned them again for their third mission of the day, and then they flew home direct to Doha. These multiple short missions with high payloads generated good results in the KTO. The crews were fighting each other to fly it, I reported to Horner on February 6.

That day included an intriguing tip from Sudairy.

"The 5th and 3rd Corps commanders meet daily in Basra," Sudairy confided. "At the naval academy. In the early afternoon."

Sudairy was concerned about the brutality of the Iraqis in Kuwait. I agreed with him. The reports we were getting were horrible, and I had to ask for Sudairy's help.

Unless we had very specific, advance information, our options were limited. If we knew a group of senior Iraqi military or intelligence forces were meeting, we could take out the meeting place at liberty. You can take out barracks and things where the soldiers carrying out the dictates are living. But those are about the only two things you can do when a nation-state that you're trying to help still has a tremendous amount of people in a city. The last thing I wanted to do was go after every chit of information and end up bombing Kuwait City at random. Do that and you'll kill more innocent people than the Iraqi security services will.

So I pressed Sudairy for more details. Tell me who's running the meeting in Kuwait City and where does he hold his meetings? Where's his office? Is he moving around? What is he doing? I kept beating up our intelligence people, trying to get that information too. Sudairy's naval academy tip was just the sort of advance information that we might be able to use to schedule a strike.

I called McConnell and asked him to try to confirm who was going in and out of the building Sudairy had described. (Ultimately, we were successful in interrupting some meetings and we took out a couple of barracks complexes near the airport, but we never got the top guy. We got his chief of staff, but we just were never able to get to the top guy.)

Around midnight Saudi time I talked to General McPeak in Washington. He thought the ground campaign was going to start between February 21 and February 25.

"Why don't we just be patient?" I complained to him. "Why are we rushing?"

"The Chairman will force it, ready or not," McPeak said.

Coming on top of the sour weather predictions, this was not good news. When you arbitrarily double the number of ground troops in a combat theater for no rational reason you must ensure they are used, I thought. I could think of no other reason to hurry. It left me wondering again why he'd doubled the forces.

Finally, we were making progress toward the 50-percent attrition. When the Army complained in late January, Lewis started keeping a daily spreadsheet of the ARCENT and MARCENT counts showing how our air strikes had attrited each Iraqi unit. The total strength of the Republican Guard averaged 84 percent on February 6—dragged down mainly to the plastering of the Tawakalna, assessed at 55 percent strength. Infantry units in ARCENT's area were at 79 percent strength. The trend was going in the right direction. By this time, Lewis had calculated we were attriting 2-percent of the tanks, APCs and artillery per day. By projecting that out, 50-percent attrition was expected to occur on February 21. In actuality, we started on February 24, and 65 percent overall. MARCENT attrition lagged, with an overall estimate of 90 percent for all the Iraqi units in that sector. This was the count Schwarzkopf would use for his final decision on going to war.

At Schwarzkopf's meeting later that day, February 6, Schwarzkopf said he would brief Cheney and Powell on the probable start date for the ground campaign during their upcoming visit.

They weren't the only ones packing their suitcases. McConnell faxed me a note from Pete Williams, Cheney's witty and skilled press secretary. It said:

Mike—

As the attached memos say, the Iraqis have granted more visas to Western news organizations, who will be entering the country Thursday from Jordan.

The news organizations ask that we not blow them up.

—Pete

McConnell mentioned later that the ground war was the big topic in Washington, too. Secretary Cheney believed the ground war was necessary.

"Sooner rather than later," McConnell said.

Now there was no question where the senior leadership was headed. I sensed Powell's influence. In fact, the only exception was Cheney's deputy, Paul Wolfowitz, who had said he thought the ground war could wait until the end of March. He was the lone voice for getting the maximum out of air power before sending in the ground troops. Yet I understood Cheney's instinct. It was both a political and a military decision. Cheney decided there was no way Saddam was ever going to give up and so we would have to do some sort of land maneuver to get Iraq's forces out of Kuwait, so let's do it and get it over with. Had I been in Cheney's position I honestly believe I would have made the same decision.

McPeak called back to complete our earlier conversation. This time, the Chief of Staff mentioned that Secretary Rice had taken a briefing to Cheney, and believed Cheney was a supporter of staying with air only for a few more weeks.

"That's not what Cheney is telling the White House," I told McPeak. "McConnell told me less than two hours ago that Cheney wants to go ahead and start the ground campaign as soon as we reasonably can, and McConnell has never been wrong about Cheney's intentions." Once Cheney made the decision, the die was cast.

My whole objective was to make sure that we destroyed as much as we could and make the ground effort as close to a police action as we possibly could.

Ground action of some sort would be required unless one thing happened: if Saddam himself happened to be killed. Free of Saddam, I believed the Iraqi people would have a euphoric reaction, take back control of their country, and call back the troops from Kuwait. That was the only possible combination for accomplishing all our objectives without risking lives in a ground action.

From what I was hearing, Secretary Rice was adamantly against the ground campaign, and it brought out an important point. Deptula talked to him on February 6. Rice believed, just as I did, that if we were to focus our efforts and turn up the heat on trying to kill Saddam then the Iraqi people would take over. Yet nobody ever laid that case out directly to Cheney. What I should have done was work the issue through Wolfowitz that, for the air campaign to end everything, Saddam has to go away. It was that simple. It wasn't about Army vs. Air Force or any of that crap.

To do that, we'd have needed a Special Forces team on the ground or a CIA team to assist with location. We just weren't getting enough intelligence to be able to do it any other way. The fact was none of us approached it that way at the time. We always assumed there was going to be a need for at least a police action by the ground forces. So the Secretary of Defense did not get the best advice during this critical time.

We were all convinced that the Kurds and the Shiites were going to overthrow Saddam the day this was over if the Coalition made him as weak as we could possibly make him. We permitted the intelligence community to sell us that bill of goods. I bought into that. Ironically, so did President Bush and all our other senior leadership, including Cheney and Powell, and we were all wrong.

Meanwhile, the weather was still throwing us every evil variation possible. Fronts stalled unexpectedly then picked up speed. By four o'clock in the afternoon, the weather forecast from the previous day, when you planned the missions, might be completely wrong.

As this went on day after day, we could not afford to scrap any more missions. So I moved them around, aggressively scheduling them immediately behind, between or ahead of weather fronts. For example, say we'd planned to focus the first four hours of the night from 8 to midnight on Baghdad, then the second part of the night, from midnight until 4, on another site, maybe Tallil to the southeast of Baghdad. All of a sudden the weather is socked in over Baghdad, so the missions for the first four hours can't go. But the front was moving off to the east, so Tallil's open early. I switched the segments around at the last minute.

All the missions were pre-planned. One fighter pilot hands it off to another and in 15 or 20 minutes, he reviews the target materials and makes it his own. If the fighters swap, then there are no ripple changes to the tankers, communications, etc. If they can't do that, then we're not training fighter pilots right. That's what I told the wing commanders.

It didn't seem like a stretch to me, but it did to others. After a short

July 1990, General Glosson departing from Andrews Air Force Base for Middle East.

October 1990, General Larry Henry, center, inspects readiness of decoy drones used in first three hours of 1991 Gulf War.

October 1990, White House Chief of Staff John Sununu, General Glosson, and Secretary of State James Baker, preparing to leave White House after Gulf War briefing with President H. W. Bush. (Official White House Photo)

December 1990, General Glosson, front right, discussing pending war effort with his 14th Air Division Fighter Wing commanders.

January 1991, General Glosson with F-16 pilots assigned to the Gulf War campaign.

January 1991, General Glosson and Lieutenant Colonel Dave Deptula updating General Norman Schwartzkopf, facing map, on attack planned for first six hours of air campaign in Gulf War. (Official CENTCOM Photo)

February 1991, Lieutenant colonels Dave Deptula, left, and Sam Baptiste preparing Air Tasking Orders on Day 23 of Gulf War.

February 1991, General Glosson discussing targeting changes with Admiral Mike McConnell in the Pentagon and F-111 Wing Commander Tom Lennon at Taif Air Base, Saudi Arabia.

February 1991, Colonel Tony Tolin directed changes to F-117 targeting on Day 17 of Gulf War.

February 1991, General Glosson and Lieutenant Colonel Dave Deptula making late changes to air attacks on Day 24 of Gulf War.

February 1991, TACC staff discussion with General Glosson on latest mobile Scud locations.

February 1991, General Glosson and Lieutenant Colonel Rick Lewis review KTO targeting strategy.

March 1991, General Glosson refuels in F-15E during inspection flight over Iraq from Basra to Baghdad and over burning oil fields in Kuwait.

March 1991, General Glosson prepares to leave Riyahd. With him are Lieutenant Colonels Rodgers Greenawalt, center, and John Turk who were among the "Black Hole" planners.

March 1991, General Glosson and Saudi Air Force Brigadier General Ahmed Sudairy. (Official CENTAF Photo)

UK fighter pilots returning home after release from Iraqi POW camp included Simon Burgess, seated, and, standing left to right, John Nichol, Bob Ankerson, Rupert Clarke, official escort Chris Lunt, Robbie Stewart, and Dave Waddington.

while in the severe weather disruption of February 3–7, the wings were starting to show the strain.

Tolin and Lewis sought me out and told me all the changes were just creating too much turbulence for the units.

"Oh, bullshit," I said. "They're just accustomed to being treated like a bunch of prima donnas and they want every ATO to be in granite."

That was just frustration on my part. I was blowing off steam, and Tolin and Lewis took it right. They waited three or four hours and then re-engaged just as they should have. They were both tough as nails.

"Look, we've got to do something to give ourselves the flexibility to react if the weather improves in some location, but we can't totally disrupt the wings," Lewis insisted. With the tank-plinking assignments, and the bad weather switches, the changes were too much. What Lewis did not know was that Hornburg had reminded me about an hour earlier that I had directed each wing commander to call me if we were pressing too hard.

I told Lewis we would reduce last-minute changes and put some F-111s on alert so that I could verbally task them and their weapons loadouts.

"That's a good idea," Lewis said. He'd flown F-111s. "They're used to sitting alert," was his throwaway comment.

I called up Tom Lennon. "Put eight airplanes on alert. They'll be tasked on the ATO every day. You'll go on alert at the time directed. You'll come off alert when Tolin or I give the release. The mission will be verbally directed by me or by Tolin. Nobody else. So if anybody else calls you and tells you to do anything different, ignore it."

Once again I was so glad that I had the double hat—campaign planning and commanding all the fighter units. That's why I could do that. Changes were mine to approve and execute.

Keeping the F-111s on alert gave me flexibility to keep the pressure on. It didn't mean that was the end of the changes. If the weather was down over one target area but clear enough somewhere else, I wasn't going to let the F-117s sit on the ground and miss a whole night's activities, if there was any break in the cloud decks and anything worth taking out anywhere in Iraq, which there certainly always was. But it minimized the chaos.

My staff wished all along they could get closer to the action. My star F-117 pilots were Tolin's protégés—I knew he'd rather be flying with them than yanking around their target coordinates. Deptula would have loved to be up in that Baghdad CAP in his F-15C. All the weapon systems representatives in the Black Hole desperately wanted to get back to their units to fly missions. "I'm still current!" they'd lament. For some, like Eskridge, I let them go back to fly a few sorties. On February 9, I gave Lewis time off for a 15-hour mission with the Western AWACS. "That's as close to combat as I'm going to get," he begged. It was uneventful. He looked glad to be back in time to get to work on the briefing charts for Schwarzkopf the next afternoon.

Cheney and Powell Visit

Cheney and Powell were scheduled to arrive on the evening of February 8, and Horner would lead off the full day of briefings on February 9. For me it ended up being a 36-hour day and one filled with significance.

Schwarzkopf directed each component commander to give the Secretary of Defense his personal view of where they were in their area of responsibility. I especially wanted to get Horner to mention the weather situation, our progress on armor attrition, and the status of NBC targets.

One operational assessment Cheney and Powell weren't going to see was Lewis' track of overall aircraft effectiveness. If we were to improve our ability to attrit the Iraqis, Lewis set out to find the raw rate of effectiveness we could expect, leaving BDA counting rules aside. He strung together all the variables in the chain from generating the ATO to the bomb's impact: weather cancellations, maintenance cancellations, pilot missed the target, missed refueling, everything in the mission that could lead to the lack of a bomb on target. He handed me a slip of paper with the results: F-117 effectiveness was 50 percent; F-111s were 30 percent and all others were at about 15 percent. For the F-117s, that meant we could count on about one mission in two to hit the target.

That was low, and in all honesty, it surprised me. I thought we were about 10 to 15 percent better than that in all cases. Compared to other conflicts, it was probably excellent. In some of those early World War II massed bombing raids they couldn't even locate the right city. But considering the technology we had in 1991, I thought we should certainly be able to do a lot better than that. Yet, given the weather problems especially, I felt Lewis' numbers were probably realistic.

Once Rick and I went over this, I had to make some immediate changes. Because of the numbers, I had to double the F-117 sorties for each target. I directed Deptula to double everything: If we'd planned to put one F-117 and two bombs on a target, that same target now got two F-117s and four bombs. We had always doubled F-111 targets anyway, so that wasn't going to get any better. With the other platforms, I decided we'd wait on the BDA and then go back and strike if we had to.

Deptula, Lewis, Rogers and I met for an impromptu doctrinal discussion on where we stood with the Army and apportionment during Phase IV. Afterwards, Deptula told me he'd talked personally with Secretary Rice and that Rice would urge Cheney not to rush into a ground war. For most people, this was a parochial issue: air power vs. ground power.

'I abhor this attitude,' I wrote in my notes after our discussion. *'The issue is how to accomplish our objectives with minimum loss of life . . . rushing the ground campaign is not the answer . . . but that is where we are headed!'*

McConnell reconfirmed that both Cheney and Powell were in a "let's-get-it-over-with" mindset when they'd left Washington to fly to Riyadh.

I debriefed Horner on McConnell's telephone discussion and then went to see Schwarzkopf. "I just got a report that the SecDef and the Chairman are thinking 'let's get it over with' so they're probably going to try to rush you into starting the ground campaign before you're ready," I told the CINC.

"I'm not going to let that happen," he assured me.

Later at the staff meeting, Schwarzkopf turned to me and said, "Buster, we will likely get a lot of air-supporting-ground-campaign questions tomorrow."

Horner and I were both expecting those questions. Then, Schwarzkopf mentioned that the Chairman was trying to minimize attacks on Baghdad. Powell wanted us to stop attacking bridges, Schwarzkopf said. I reminded him of the fiber optic cable strung along one of the Baghdad bridges. We wanted to take that out shortly to help force the Iraqis off the landlines and back to communications we could intercept. Schwarzkopf promised to discuss it with Powell, but his body language caused me to write down *'CINC's heart not committed. He's focused on the ground campaign.'*

I suspected the Navy might surface a few complaints to Cheney and Powell. Vice Admiral Stan Arthur would be briefing the maritime component status. Rear Admiral Conrad Lautenbacher—we called him Connie—had raised Arthur's concerns again at the nightly staff meeting about the Navy not getting enough tanker support. Connie was from the surface Navy. Arthur, an airman and the Maritime Component Commander, stayed out with his command ship, so Connie was the liaison. Navy tanker support had been an issue for a while. Early on, Lewis found the Navy strike aircraft from their six carriers were taking up way too many tankers for the number of bombs they were dropping. Typically, the land-based aircraft had 20 percent support aircraft, whereas the Navy liked about a 40:60 ratio of support to strike. He cancelled two or three Navy strike packages while sorting out the fracas. Lewis had overdone it. I pointed out that all he had to do was to get those targets closer to their locations. Still, at this point in the war, the potential threat did not warrant the large number of air-to-air aircraft the Navy included for every attack mission. Plus, we had CAPS and SEAD everywhere for all the packages, including the Navy. So, I refused to give them tankers for their support aircraft.

As for Horner, he had the leadoff slot. We set up a run-through of the briefing he planned to give to Cheney and Powell the next morning. He covered the progress to date, but I wanted him to play it differently. Horner didn't want to make weather an issue. I had no idea why. Perhaps he thought of it as complaining or whining. Horner was set to discuss the NBC targets, but I also wanted him to cast the armor attrition as a go or no-go variable, which is what it was to Schwarzkopf. Although my guys had built the briefing, I thought there was too much telling the SecDef and the Chairman what they knew already. I was itching for Horner to lay the hard issues out on the table. I wanted him to say, 'This is where we stand, and this is what changes we'll be making as we push the ground campaign, and this is how we're going to support the ground campaign.'

"I'm not interested in walking out on limbs," Horner replied.

'You got to be shitting me,' I wrote in my diary notes so I wouldn't say it aloud. Obviously, I was frustrated after the practice briefing. I continued with my diary:

'Glossonisms . . . there are only two principles of war: 1. Winning and 2. Minimum Loss of Life.' Everything else is just a means to an end.

The next day, February 9, Horner started the briefings, followed by Yeosock, Boomer from the Marines, and Arthur. Boomer complained about too many attacks near Baghdad and not enough on the Iraqi forces in his sector. Burt Moore, CENTCOM J-3, briefed on the timetable for launching the offensive and Army Major General Gus Pagonis discussed the major logistical feat of moving into position to cross the two corps, which they'd just completed over the last three weeks. The bottom line was that the ground forces needed 12 more days and then they could attack.

To me, the most interesting note in Horner's briefing came from Powell. Horner briefed that we were running steady at 2-percent attrition of the Iraqi ground units per day.

"Our greatest fear is that as we attrit them at 2-percent per day, they will run and we won't be able to destroy his Republican Guard and armor," Powell said. All the politicians will be screaming for us to stop, he added. The thought process that went into that statement startled me. He had it backward. *'The sure way to have Iraqi ground troops and armor run north is to start a ground campaign,'* I jotted in my notes.

The ground campaign date was briefed for February 23–25, unless there was a presidential decision to delay it.

At this point, Wolfowitz suggested we could wait until the end of March and let the air campaign run its course. Wolfowitz had a point, but from the atmosphere in the room, no one else was interested in that option.

'The unbelievable part of this to me . . . Chairman and CINC do not appear to have learned anything from Khafji,' I wrote in my notes right after the meeting. *'Air can devastate moving armor . . . Iraqi ground troops are waiting to surrender . . . why not give them a chance to do exactly that without risking soldiers' and marines' lives?*

'God, please guide their thought process! Let your guiding hand protect the young soldiers and marines.'

The four-phased plan had been clear from the outset. We weren't finished yet with the Phase I strategic targets. Deptula was dealing that very day with a batch of new imagery showing there were bunkers we hadn't even touched yet. Phase III attrition wasn't where it should be. Why the jostling to get started with Phase IV? We had to have a sound strategy for nailing the Republican Guard. Either the air war could continue, attriting at 2-percent per day, or when the ground war started, hopefully the Republican Guard divisions would maneuver and we could destroy them in detail as they moved.

I felt like we were losing sight of the ongoing need to adapt while executing the war. We'd had to catch up fast in the air war—tank-plinking, Killer Scouts, restriking bunkers, double-targeting the F-117s. Khafji was the big signpost for how to adapt the whole air-ground strategy. But apparently, we were going to ignore it, even though it was the best, freshest operational intelligence we had on what Iraq would do.

Finally, what did Powell mean about politicians screaming for us to stop? It disturbed me, and with good reason, as we'd discover later.

Cheney, Powell and Schwarzkopf went off by themselves after the day of briefings finished. According to Schwarzkopf's account of this private meeting, he recommended to Cheney that February 21 be the start date for the ground war, "But I've got to have three or four days of latitude because we've got to have clear weather to kick off the campaign."

President Bush approved of the 21st. A few days later, after briefings with Boomer, Schwarzkopf shifted the date to February 24 to give the Marines time to reposition so their attack would breach a less heavily defended part of the Iraqi lines some 20 miles from their original breach point. As Schwarzkopf told it, Powell protested when Schwarzkopf advised him of the change. "I hate to wait that long. The President wants to get on with this," Powell told Schwarzkopf.[4]

The last stop on Cheney and Powell's trip was the F-117 base at Khamis Mushait. I was delighted that they'd taken time to visit the F-117s. They spoke to the pilots, maintainers and the troops who assembled the bombs. Cheney and Powell each wrote a slogan on one of the bombs. Cheney's read, "To Saddam, with fond regards."[5]

It seemed that the Saudis, too, were ready to move to the ground war. Sudairy told me he was concerned the air campaign was starting to drag. He never confided where that comment originated from, but one thing was for certain, it was an out of character remark for him. Did it come from a higher authority? I never knew.

"We must have Saddam gone, and return to normal life," Sudairy said. "The war needs to end."

4. *It Doesn't Take a Hero*, pp. 434–436.
5. *The Generals' War*, p. 324.

CHANGING FOCUS

"The air campaign is approaching the point of diminishing returns," Buster Glosson was misquoted in the *New York Times*.

My philosophy on dealing with the press was simple. I once told a reporter during the war, "Look, when I have a deep background discussion with you, it's because I believe American citizens make good decisions when they're informed. The way they make bad decisions is when they're uninformed."

To this end, I had a conversation with Schwarzkopf one day when he was complaining about some of the inaccurate things being said back in the United States about the war. We both felt sometimes that the press inadvertently misrepresented what was happening.

"I can help deal with that," I told Schwarzkopf privately. "I will never deal with it in a way that would be embarrassing to you, but I'll make sure that the truth gets out."

"Good," he said.

I took a lot of license from that one word. I frequently communicated with reporters from the *New York Times*. I believed Michael Gordon and Eric Schmitt were two of the newspaper's best. Also, if a story was printed in the *New York Times*, everybody read it and everybody reprinted it. The one misquote about the air campaign notwithstanding, they reported things more factually than other papers, with a minimum of sensationalism.

This time they'd gotten it wrong. What I actually said was we would eventually reach a point of diminishing returns unless Saddam surrendered. I estimated that point would come prior to mid-March.

Evidently Sudairy read the *New York Times.*

"How is the campaign going?" Sudairy asked me cautiously.

I couldn't resist the opening. "When your enemy is experiencing total chaos you don't need intel, news media or politicians to tell you how the war is progressing!" I told him.

He laughed.

"How would you feel about now if you were Saddam?" I teased Sudairy.

"My future would not look too bright," he said. That was Sudairy, with his wonderful, understated way. It was the first time I'd seen Sudairy laugh.

Priorities

With the decision to launch the ground war in two weeks, our focus shifted. I still felt the decision concerning the ground campaign was not correct. *'But—it is the decision!'* I hand-wrote at the top of my diary sheet for February 10. *'Air focus must change—review with Tolin and Lewis.'*

The rest of my diary page became my private memory jogger:

• Timeline (assume 24th is ground start date) . . . maximum one week
• Track: Armor, Artillery, C3 individually
• Bridges . . . choke and exit points
• % Iraqi Divisions destroyed . . . especially Marine area
• Chem Bio—turn up heat on Intel (McConnell)
• B-52s . . . maximize psychological factor
• F-117s on C3 and NBC
• Iraqi bases with air to ground capability . . . daily updates . . . close no later than 23 Feb
• A-10 . . . total focus . . . ground troops . . . <u>No Distractions</u>
• Review "friendly fire" precautions
• Review "Pointer" responsibility
• Discuss night A-10 ops with Sharpe and Sawyer (have Lewis monitor)
• Hornburg . . . F-15E QRF

• TACC concerns . . . discuss with Horner . . . (<u>Tolin and Lewis must stay on top of it</u>)

• FSCL movement . . . discuss with CINC

I also noted that I wanted to maintain pressure on Baghdad to the maximum extent possible, primarily with F-117 attacks on NBC, C3 and bridges.

Finally, it was time to discuss the change of focus with the wing commanders. Taking more risks now was not only okay, it was expected. They had to increase their intensity as we ramped up to February 24.

Meanwhile, I had to deal with "Baghdad Billy." Baghdad Billy did not exist, but way too many of my 14th Air Division pilots, believed he did.

The myth of Baghdad Billy started when the EF-111s thought they'd seen a lone MiG operating at night. Every time the reports came in, it turned out it was only our own F-15s that were somewhere in the area. For example, I had the F-15Cs capping Baghdad. The rumors of Baghdad Billy spread through the F-111 community and beyond and peaked in the first half of February. The Iraqi Air Force—what remained after the bulk of it bugged out to Iran—was barely flying. Yet somehow Baghdad Billy became accepted wisdom among the F-111 aircrews. One F-111 pilot wrote a ballad about it that began:

> I'm an F-111 jock and I'm here to tell
> Of Baghdad Billy and his jet from hell . . . [1]

To make matters worst, the CENTAF intelligence shop had duly collated the rumors and put them into a bulletin passed around to the wings without my knowledge.

On February 11, we even got a report from a B-52 tail gunner who thought he saw a MiG at night. You know what the odds of that are? Even if a MiG was there, the odds that a tail gunner would see him were infinitesimal.

That was the last straw.

'*Baghdad Billy . . . figment of F-111 imagination,*' I wrote at the top of that day's notes. '*Must stop before someone flies into the ground.*'

Too late. That very night, an EF-111 shot off flares, made S-turns and otherwise "evaded" some threat or bandit he thought was there and flew into the ground, all within view of a pair of F-15Es returning from a

1. *Every Man a Tiger,* pp. 363–365.

strike mission at 31,000 feet. Investigation would show there were no enemy aircraft in the area at the time. When I found out intelligence had been spreading this crap rumor too, I can't tell you how angry I was. These were my units. The 14th Air Division was mine and I was responsible for the lives of these pilots. We lost two lives totally unnecessarily. I chewed out Chris Christon, the CENTAF chief of intelligence. He'd been aiding and abetting this rumor and now two people were dead. I directed Lennon to put a stop to the Baghdad Billy rumors immediately.

Reviewing the Shift

The start of the workday on February 12 brought a major review of the shift with Deptula and Rogers. In the days remaining I had to make sure the strategic air campaign continued to hit targets to meet the President's objectives. We also had to take special care to cover Schwarzkopf's priorities for he was now totally consumed with the upcoming land campaign.

I always tried to make sure we were focused on what the CINC wanted to hit. Schwarzkopf gave guidance every night on his priorities. If we had the resources to hit what Schwarzkopf wanted and what I wanted to strike too, I'd do both. If not, the CINC's guidance came first. From the B-52 strikes on night one onward, I never failed to bomb a target the CINC wanted hit.

With the land campaign approaching I wanted to ensure there were no oversights. Soldiers and Marines were going into harm's way. A mistake could be catastrophic. That's why I now had both Tolin and Deptula on the daily master attack plans.

That took care of strategic targeting, but for the bulk of the sorties planned by the KTO cell, it was time to change the way we did business.

KTO targeting strategy belonged to Sam Baptiste. Every afternoon, Corder would come back from the Joint Targeting Board, a meeting headed by Waller, with a list of targets the Army wanted to hit. As I discussed previously, we still had to look it over carefully. The Army, in many areas, had the most sophisticated methods for picking out key targets. From the counter-battery radars to their expertise in identifying the Iraqi order of battle, the Army specialized in what they called "intelligence preparation of the battlefield."

However, I knew the Army was not always attuned to air strike requirements. Sometimes they'd nominate a target they'd found days or even weeks earlier, but they would not provide updated information. Too often, as we looked over the target nominations while planning the strikes, we found many of the targets selected by the Army had been moved or already hit. Other times—as with front-line artillery—a target a division commander was itching for us to hit was a target Schwarzkopf did not want touched until later.

The first thing I did each afternoon was review the Waller target list with Deptula, Lewis and Tolin. Consistent with Schwarzkopf's guidance, I would circle the targets I wanted attacked. Then I'd go to Baptiste in the KTO cell and tell him to hit the targets I've indicated on Waller's list.

After that, Baptiste was basically solely responsible for the daily ATO in support of the Kuwait Theater of Operations, and the lion's share of these strikes hit ground force targets prioritized by the land component. The major exception would be that if I put F-117s, F-111s or F-15Es into the KTO, I'd get more involved and use them to go after targets in the KTO the CINC or I wanted to hit. I would often pull a half-dozen or a dozen F-117s off the Baghdad targets if the weather was bad, in which case Deptula scheduled those sorties and informed Baptiste.

It was mostly Baptiste's show, and what a show it was. On a typical day such as Day 27 we logged 247 strikes on the "strategic" target categories and 1,022 on forces in and around the KTO. The aggregate number of strike sorties for the whole campaign was even more dramatic: 9,731 for the strategic cell versus 31,578 handled largely by the KTO cell.[2]

However, this system of handing it all off to the KTO cell would not work for air support during the ground war, which would almost certainly be a stew of changing targets and demands for support. I had to provide Baptiste with more of the big picture and I had to make double sure the TACC would execute the plans properly. With ground forces moving and the Iraqi army running north, we weren't going to have any margin for error.

Having an overall view of the strategic effort was the only way for good decisions to be made fast. I had every one of the airborne commanders on the AWACS briefed every night by myself, Tolin, Lewis, Deptula or Rogers. The ACEs understood the objectives—most of them had been part of the planning process and knew how things were supposed to come together.

2. GWAPS, Vol. V, pages 531 and 517.

We had many loose ends in the target set to tie together before the start of the ground campaign, or "G-Day." North of Basra just over the Kuwait border in Iraq, for example, there were numerous river barges. The Iraqi army might use the barges to move supplies, troops, whatever. Initially I'd given the F-16s the mission of destroying the barges, but without precision, the results were not satisfactory. So on February 12 I called Tom Lennon at the F-111 wing.

Lennon proved over and over he was an outstanding warfighting wing commander. He was tough on his pilots but I liked his results. "Take a few of your airplanes, two or three or four, and every night make sure that you take care of the barges on the river north of Basra. I don't care if they're moored or moving. If you see them, blow them up," I told Lennon.

On February 12 I also directed Lewis to start putting together a Close Air Support plan with the emphasis on avoiding friendly fire.

The TACC operated like your classic black box—innovation and original thought were not their strong suits. Khafji and other events were all the evidence I needed. In the last days before the ground war, I had to make sure once and for all the TACC staff wasn't making changes to the ATO with no idea about the impact of the changes.

I went to Horner. "The TACC is just not competent," I told him. "I need your authority to sign off on every execution change sheet." That would be in addition to the pre-planned changes.

Horner told me he thought TACC was more confident than I did.

"At day's end you may be right, and I'm wrong, but it's a risk you can't afford to take," I argued.

Horner agreed with that, and so my request was approved.

End of the Strategic Campaign

Under Horner's aegis everything could usually be smoothed out. But when Washington, and especially Powell, got involved the outcome was never certain.

Schwarzkopf's plan called for transition to Phase IV when Phases I through III were in hand and we got to the 50 percent attrition goal. However, now that there was a date for the ground campaign, it seemed Powell was shifting his focus faster than anyone. Yes, getting the Iraqi army out of Kuwait was the major objective, but the President's other objectives such as setting back NBC production were not in the bag. Yet Powell was starting to give Schwarzkopf serious grief about any strike activity around Baghdad no matter what the target, and Schwarzkopf was passing it on to us.

Bombing Baghdad for whatever reason was no longer important to Powell. Never mind that Baghdad was the only major city in Iraq and Saddam had most of his weapons research activities in the city or on its outskirts. Powell just didn't see it that way. He did not accept what Mc-Connell was telling him about how weather had induced slower progress in destroying potential weapons of mass destruction sites. Also, he brushed off comments about the importance of destroying critical elements of Ba'ath Party headquarters and Saddam's home base of Tikrit.

Saddam played up his ties to Tikrit to enhance his control, and it was the heart of his political support. Powell was unwilling to accept the strategic significance of decimating Tikrit. In all honesty, it was like a denial of the tribal heritage of the Middle East region from the days of the Ottoman Empire on. He refused to believe in the impact of the tribal mentality on Iraq as a nation-state. He bought the impact of the Sunnis and the Shiites and the Kurds, with their different political and religious agenda, but he didn't give the same emphasis to the tribal heritage.

Even more vexing, Powell wasn't acknowledging the impact of the air campaign on Iraq's forces. Since he was the person most often updating the President, the old adage about "whomever presents the information controls the message" had an ominous ring.

Powell's inputs were limiting the ability to execute the strategic campaign. The next day, February 12, I wrote in my diary: *'History should reflect the strategic air campaign was officially terminated on 13th February.'* Powell might deny it later, I seethed, but he had already clamped down on our master attack plans.

Al-Firdos

We'd been at war for almost a month and the Iraqi army was showing signs of wilting, yet some things were business-as-usual. In Baghdad, Peter Arnett continued to broadcast from the Al-Rashid hotel. In the basement of the hotel was a fiber-optic cable. Arnett denied it, but Schwarzkopf and I felt he was being duped. The Iraqis said there was no cable there, but had Arnett gone down and looked for himself?

Arnett was being censored. He was very professional and would always include the disclaimers that CNN's reports were being cleared from Baghdad. But in the next 24 hours following Arnett's report from Baghdad, snippets of Arnett's report would be excerpted by CNN without Arnett's disclaimers. It was the manner in which CNN handled the short clips that concerned me. By deleting the disclaimers, they were in effect showing the censored information to the American people as fact. It felt unethical to me. Schwarzkopf and I discussed it privately on February 12, but there wasn't much to be done. I still wanted to take out the fiber optic coaxial cable nodes in the Babylon Hotel and the Al-Rashid hotel, but with all the foreign reporters living there, including the new arrivals who'd come through Jordan, it was not going to happen.

At this stage the Iraqis still had strong communications lines. Deptula was working on a new plan to neutralize more of their C3 targets. McConnell told me that the Iraqi command, control and communications were still operating pretty freely down to the battlefield area. Primarily that was because they'd laid the fiber optic cables along the oil pipelines.

As Horner and I drove to the nightly staff meetings, we saw all around Riyadh well-lit streets and normal activity. Glenn drove us, with a bodyguard from the Air Force Office of Special Investigations. *'You'd never know there was a war in progress on the streets of Riyadh,'* I jotted down on February 12.

I sure felt it though. *'I am physically and mentally exhausted . . . will force myself to get more sleep next couple days,'* I pledged in my diary. One day after the Secretary of Defense visit, when lack of sleep made me particularly brusque, Tolin dragged me out of the Black Hole and walked with me to my quarters.

I'm better off sleeping four hours one night and eight hours the next night than I am sleeping six hours every night. I can sleep six hours and just get more and more fatigued. But I can sleep eight hours one night and wake up feeling refreshed as though I'd slept for a week, and I'm ready to do anything for as long as it takes.

I knew that about myself. When I started feeling like this and things weren't that hectic, I'd walk out just a little bit early in the morning at maybe 5 o'clock before Horner came in, and I'd tell Rogers to tell Horner that I just had to get some sleep. I'd try to stay in bed 'til at least 1 or 2 and get up and come over around 3 o'clock in the afternoon. I wasn't able to do that very often, but occasionally I'd just have to pace myself.

The telephone in my room rang mid-morning on February 13 and jarred me awake. It was Deptula.

"Sir, you need to turn on CNN. They're saying we bombed a civilian shelter. The CINC wants you to telephone him ASAP."

"Get together all the planning material," I told Deptula. "Do not answer any questions until I personally review it." Then I talked to Tolin and told him to call Lewis into work too, since he was working the same shift I was.

CNN was reporting the deaths of between 50 and 400 Iraqi civilians—many women and children—in a bunker somewhere in Baghdad. Camera crews filmed the sunlight filtering into the ravaged interior of the bunker while bodies were piled up outside. It was a gruesome sight.

The first thing I did was call McConnell, even before I called the CINC.

"As far as we're concerned it was a military target," McConnell said. "You and I both monitored the target and you, rightfully so, took the intelligence you had and struck the target because it had all indications of being military and associated in some way with the communications in Kuwait."

"Yeah, I know that," I told him. "I'm not second-guessing myself. I just want to make sure that there's not something that we failed to see or didn't know. If it is, I'd like to know what it is."

McConnell had nothing to add. I phoned Schwarzkopf.

"The Chairman's uptight, but the SecDef is okay," Schwarzkopf told me. "Gather up all your info and bring it over here. The Chairman is going ballistic."

I told him it would take a couple of hours to get the data together, which he told me was all right.

I quickly told Schwarzkopf what I knew right then. "The target was a communications node being used by Iraqi intelligence concerning Kuwaiti activity. It was a shelter that had been reinforced and upgraded with communications. We'd been monitoring it for about a week." In fact, we'd seen senior officials visiting the shelter every night. The people who had been arriving were people in limousine-style vehicles with drivers—not exactly Iraqis off the street.

Just then Schwarzkopf broke in and said he had to take a call from Powell. I got off the phone and Deptula, Lewis and I started putting a folder together with all the information from A to Z we had on Al-Firdos. They made one copy for Schwarzkopf, one for Horner and one for me.

The Al-Firdos bunker (Target L30 in our master file) was one of a group of 10 leadership bunkers in the Baghdad suburbs. Two GBU-27s dropped by two different F-117s hit the same spot on the roof of the hardened bunker shortly after midnight on February 13. Unknown to American or British intelligence, inside on the upper level about 200 to 300 civilians, including 100 children, were using the bunker as an air-raid shelter.[3] Saddam himself was avoiding hardened command posts like the plague but for whatever sad reason, Iraqi families were inside Al-Firdos that night.

I took the information we had over to Schwarzkopf's headquarters. The CINC was tough as nails on the issue. He knew the CIA and DIA had both repeatedly validated the target.[4] We both regretted a situation like this, but it was part of war.

"The Chairman's really worried about this image," Schwarzkopf said. "He's going to minimize Baghdad bombing from here on."

"We need the SecDef to stand tall on the bunker issue," I told Schwarzkopf. He said he'd work it. I made the same call to General Mc-Peak, telling him the Chairman was wavering. "Don't worry, I'll work it," McPeak said.

When I had a minute to reflect on it, I found I wasn't completely surprised. One of Saddam Hussein's real strengths had always been his ability to maximize press opportunities. Now the Coalition had been cast in the worst possible light. I also believed there was something about this tragedy that did not add up. I had been watching the bunker on a daily basis for more than a week, and I knew that late every night limousines were driving up there and people were jumping out to open doors for people. That meant the bunker was no regular building, especially since this late-night arrival was happening repeatedly. We also had indications that communications coming out of the bunker were being directed toward the intelligence and security forces operation in Kuwait.

Even more puzzling, why were civilians in a bunker? At this point in the war, how likely was it that people would go to a bunker on their own when they could very easily see we were only bombing things of military significance in Baghdad. In other words, the safest place to be in Baghdad was in an apartment complex or in a housing area.

3. GWAPS Vol. II, Part 2, pp. 282–284.
4. *It Doesn't Take a Hero*, p. 435.

I still don't know to this day why the civilians were in the Al-Firdos bunker. Was one floor of the bunker really being used as a bomb shelter for people to stay at night or not? For civilians to go to a shelter that had any connection to the military would, in my opinion, have taken a little bit of orchestration. I suspected, and still do to this day, that that's exactly what happened. Saddam did it on purpose. Saddam wouldn't have cared about the fact that a lot of the people that were killed were dependents of the military and the intelligence service. That fact was irrelevant to him. All life, except his own, is irrelevant to him.

McConnell called later with the news that the President supported our findings that Al-Firdos was a military target. Cheney was very firm on that point. "The Chairman will probably restrict your targets in Baghdad," McConnell finished.

"Yes, he's already said that to the CINC," I told McConnell.

"This will pass. War is not perfect. People die. Some intentionally, some unintentionally," I said. We had to get on with it, and McConnell and I moved to talking about the C3 workarounds.

At Schwarzkopf's staff meeting that night, Al-Firdos was the major issue.

"This was a military target," Schwarzkopf announced to the group. "There is no doubt about that. I'm not sure why all the civilians were inside. And nobody here is going to make any comment to the press," he warned.

I called McConnell after the CINC's meeting for our routine debrief.

"There's some stray voltage inputs coming into the SecDef from some of the political appointees on the staff," McConnell remarked.

He could take the heat and not even feel it. Cheney was a tremendous leader and he was even tougher when he had to deal with adversity. He knew and accepted that any time you engage in any kind of military operation, things are going to go wrong. He wanted results and he wanted the mission to be accomplished, and he was tough enough to live with the decisions that were necessary to make that happen. Wolfowitz also was tougher than nails. So were Steve Hadley and Scooter Libby on his staff. But a lot of the others on the staff left a lot to be desired when it came to being tough when things went wrong. It takes a special fiber. It's easy to be glad-handing and smile when things are going right. When the shit hits the fan, it's tough for some politicians and senior military officers to stand up and be counted. It wasn't tough for Cheney.

As usual, Sudairy had the last word, in his inimitable way.

"We have no problem with targets," he said. "Only, Saddam would be the best one."

That evening, Sudairy turned philosophical, and discussed how the relationship between Saudi Arabia and the United States might be after the war.

"I am not sure this war will change it significantly," Sudairy said. He went on to tell me how the Muslim Brotherhood's hold on Saudi Arabia was more pronounced and more total that any American could understand.

"What do you mean by that?" I asked.

"You know the eastern province has all the Shiites," he said. "I don't know what percentage of those are of the radical Muslim brotherhood but I've got to tell you it's 80 or 90 percent. The same thing's true over near the Yemeni border." That was just south of where we had the F-117s at Khamis Mushait.

"Near the mosque in Medina and Mecca, look at the Shiites on the east and look over near the Yemeni border, it's more Shi'a than anything else," Sudairy said. "You start to get a picture of Saudi Arabia." What he was illustrating was how much of the area was controlled by the Muslim Brotherhood.

"That's why you see the leadership make decisions sometimes that you'd find it hard to understand and hard to accept," he explained.

I've thought about his conversation with me many times in the recent past, because it was so telling. That's why he thought it would be very surprising if the relationship between our two nations changed significantly even after Desert Storm.

Balancing Act

Al-Firdos was the nail in the coffin for the strategic campaign. I now had to get every target approved. This was a problem. In line with our theater strategy, I'd deliberately waited to hit some targets, like bridges, knowing the F-117s and F-111s could take them out at will. By waiting we left Saddam no time for repairs or workarounds. For other strategic targets such as communications, we weren't having the success I wanted, and we needed to hit new targets we'd discovered or in some cases, restrike targets.

Powell did not seem to grasp this, as he later wrote in his memoirs:

"Did we still need to pound downtown Baghdad over a month into the war? How many times could you bomb the Ba'ath Party headquarters, and for what purpose? No one was sitting there waiting for the next Tomahawk to hit." The Ba'ath Party headquarters was a critical communications node that was hardened. Our purpose had nothing to do with people. McConnell clearly stated that to the Chairman on two occasions.

The fact was we had some very important targets near Baghdad. For example, McConnell advised me on February 14 that they'd spotted the Iraqis moving equipment out of the Tuwaitha nuclear research center. We obviously hadn't destroyed enough of the center. Valuable materiel remained, enough that the Iraqis were trying to haul it away on trucks. We'd have to plan to strike it again even though it was in the Baghdad area, where Powell didn't want us to bomb. We eventually hit it again with B-52s to create as much rubble as possible.

The efforts we were making were to transition the air campaign into a supporting campaign for a land effort while still keeping enough focus on the strategic side to deal with the C3 and the NBC targets.

The CINC at his staff meetings said: "I want every airplane dropping bombs in the Kuwaiti theater, in Kuwait, or around Kuwait. I don't want airplanes dropping bombs anywhere else."

At the CINC's February 15 meeting, the majority of the discussion was on the ground campaign with only a brief review of Baghdad targets. *'He is 100% correct in his focus, but if only we could optimize with pressure at critical nodes, not limited to Iraqi divisions,'* I wrote in my notes.

So after one staff meeting I went up to him and said, "Sir, I know you want the major thrust in Kuwait and that's what I've been giving you. But I've got to keep a few F-117s and F-111s doing other things, if nothing else trying to break up this command and control and communications down to the battlefield from Baghdad and to destroy stuff that we know they're moving out of areas we bombed where there's nuclear equipment, chemical and biological equipment they're trying to save."

"I understand that," he said. The greatest thing about Schwarzkopf was that he was not a micromanager. If he had trust in you and you performed, he let you run as hard and fast as you could run. Schwarzkopf trusted me based on results, so he wasn't about to get into the decision-making process that I used to get the results he wanted.

But my problems were not over. On February 16, Saddam blinked. He offered to withdraw from Kuwait—but only under a list of onerous conditions, which President Bush properly labeled "a cruel hoax." Still, diplomatic activity coming up on the net after all these weeks threw in a complicating factor. I felt just like when the war started that we might not have much time to finish our task.

I was frustrated all over again at Powell's micromanagement of the Baghdad-area strategy and I poured it out in my diary on February 16. *'We are now only servicing targets the Chairman okays. No thought or strategy . . . Today is the first time I have been told that what is military correct can't be executed . . . Really sad.'*

Powell wouldn't permit Schwarzkopf to take out the bridge carrying the fiber optic communications cable from Baghdad to the other major cities in Iraq.

Quickly, I pieced together what was happening. Each night I'd brief the Baghdad targets to Schwarzkopf. After each meeting, McConnell told me, the CINC had to get Powell's approval of the Baghdad targets via an informal phone call. Schwarzkopf did not like this "Mother, may I" approach to fighting a war. McConnell usually gave me a heads-up when Powell said no to specific targets. When the CINC would call to say, "Let's not hit this target," most of the time I had already cancelled the sortie based on McConnell's input.

From where I stood, Powell was fast becoming the L.B.J. of the Gulf War. I tried to work around the restrictions so we could execute the CINC's strategy. I took a map and put a dotted circle with a three-mile radius around the exact center of the city and anything inside of that was the city of Baghdad. Anything outside of that circle was not "Baghdad." That also went on the briefing chart Lewis drew me for Schwarzkopf each night. The second time I used the new chart, Schwarzkopf asked me later in private: "How do you think Powell would define Baghdad?"

"I don't know," I said, "but I'm not going to ask."

Schwarzkopf just smiled. "Make sure everything we strike near Baghdad is really important," he said.

I promised him I would and ended the conversation by saying, "Thank you."

I also chafed at Powell's arbitrary restriction because I did not want the regime in Baghdad to get the idea that the war was over for them. The last thing I wanted was for Saddam and his top henchmen to sit back in their Baghdad offices and relax. On February 17, I directed Deptula to stretch out the window of time for the Baghdad attacks. Since we were sending so few airplanes to Baghdad now, I told Deptula to intermingle airplanes and cruise missiles and spread the attack over a 10-hour period. I did not want Baghdad to say, "Oh well, this is the 20-minute strike for tonight."

The same day, I directed Tolin to start destroying the key bridges, track the destruction and monitor what the Iraqis were doing to bypass bridges we'd taken out. The bridges on the list were critical to the ground campaign because they extended Iraqi lines of communication into the KTO. No bridges meant no reinforcements. I didn't want the Iraqis to be able to replace any of the bridges. When you have the confidence and the technical ability, you can do that.

Through this time, my main concern was to use the strategic air campaign to eliminate the NBC targets—if we could only find them—and if possible, to get Saddam.

When I sat down and thought about it, I knew there were only two elements of the strategic air campaign, and of the war itself, I had any doubts about. One, I knew the reliability of the intelligence determined success against the NBC. For example, on February 18—the same day I sat down to think about the strategy—McConnell told me we'd need to work over some of the chemical and biological weapons targets again. We'd only hit three of the cruciform bunkers at the site McConnell referred to, and he reminded me there might still be NBC weapons there. These bunkers were tough to get into because they had sand, cement, gravel and who-knows-what-else layered over the top. Cement hardened the bunkers, while the looser sand and gravel was there to throw off our calculations about where to set the fuses. We knew these were scary bunkers because we'd hit one north of Baghdad earlier and it had thrown a fireball nine to 10 thousand feet into the air. The next day we had scattered intelligence reports that an unusual number of people had checked into area hospitals with what appeared to be symptoms of exposure to chemical or biological weapons. We had no way to assess those reports, but we darn sure wanted to eliminate those bunkers before Saddam decided to use whatever might be in them on our ground troops.

I needed more photos! The lack of intelligence remained unbelievably bad.

The second thing was I knew I would only be successful in getting rid of Saddam Hussein if intelligence was reliable. From Day One I knew those two issues were to me the long poles in the tent. From day one these were my number-one concerns, the things that made me wonder, what's the geopolitical landscape going to look like when this war is over?

I was never as concerned about how much of the Republican Guard would be left, how much of the army or air force would be left. I knew all of those things would take care of themselves, whether it was through the air campaign that basically made a land campaign quick with very few casualties. I knew that at day's end, to be able to get that land army out of Kuwait, we were going to destroy approximately half of it or at least a lot of it. Even the Republican Guard didn't concern me as much as trying to deal with the NBC facilities and trying to get Saddam.

No matter how hard I worked, we just could never get our arms around it. We could never get inside of the decision cycle from an intelligence standpoint to figure out where Saddam was and what he was going to do next. A few times we came close, but not close enough. I felt that our failure to achieve those objectives went back to the decimation of intelligence that occurred in the CIA as the result of dismantling the CIA human intelligence network in favor of all the technology and overheads that were going to do everything. In fact, we're still trying to recover from that to this day.

I was frustrated because I wanted to hit Tikrit now, and Schwarzkopf couldn't get clearance from Powell. I believed Saddam Hussein was spending more time in Tikrit that anyone thought. Sudairy told me Saddam was going back and forth to Tikrit, but I could never get a handle on how often he went there. I requested that McConnell use his capabilities to give us better watch over the Tikrit area.

Ground War Start

We were well on track to get Schwarzkopf where he wanted to be for Phase IV. Yet his deputy, Waller, was on my case. He sent over the CENT-COM Joint Combined Target List—the daily list—on February 17 with a personal note hand-written on the last page.

"Buster, you attack these targets before you hit anything else in the KTO." He signed it "CW."

Iraqi artillery batteries were all over the list. If I let Baptiste schedule them, we'd be violating Schwarzkopf's guidance. This was no time to take out the Medina's artillery—they'd have plenty of time to get more artillery batteries in time for the ground war. The timing of the memo was significant because Yeosock had been sent back to Germany for a medical operation. Waller was now Third Army commander as well as the DCINC.

There was no way I could let this stand. I had to remind him of the CINC's guidance. "He was misinformed," I wrote on his memo. I kept a copy just for the record.

On February 18, I met with Lewis to review the progress in ground campaign support. The tally recorded the Republican Guard was at 73 percent strength. Other Iraqi units in the ARCENT area were at 56 percent, with most of the front line infantry much lower. MARCENT was at 81 percent. It was time to send them some help. The results were superior. I was encouraged to see it. Plus, Lewis had no personal agenda. 'How refreshing,' I noted.

That evening the ground war dominated the CINC's meeting.

"We haven't used the B-52s very much in front of the Marines," Schwarzkopf said.

There was deep irony in Schwarzkopf's comment. The Marines had tried several times to disengage from JFACC control and use their aircraft only to support Marine Expeditionary Force concepts of operation. For example, we'd sent Marine air to hit a Scud rocket motor plant near Baghdad—a high-threat area but a vital mission. The Marine commander promptly informed us their planes weren't available to hit targets in central Iraq, and indeed, it was the only time the Marines attacked near Baghdad. Early in the campaign, they'd also asked to have their "contribution" to the air war limited to three packages a day, keeping their precision-capable A-6Es to themselves. After weeks of stepping back from the Coalition campaign, the Marines had on Day 23—February 8—given up their "participation" in the offensive air campaign altogether so they could concentrate on targets in their own sector in Kuwait.[5]

After the war Marine Colonel Manfred Reitch reiterated his view that, "Marine combat planes should not be assigned to drop a single bomb on a target in Iraq until the Marine ground forces had successfully launched their ground offensive in Kuwait."[6]

That's just the way Marines thought. It went against everything airmen believed, against Schwarzkopf's plan, and against the whole principle of joint command. Horner didn't want to fight it, and I didn't need

5. *The Generals' War*, p. 320.
6. Ibid., p. 311.

the Marine planes. It was not an issue worth my time and effort. However, I did strike an understanding with Royal Moore, the Marine Air Commander. The Marines let us use the A-6s, their EA-6B jammers and half their number of F/A-18s, some of which were HARM-shooters and quite useful. They kept the other half of their fleet of F/A-18s and all their short-range AV-8B Harrier jump jets. At this point I had Coalition airmen like the Saudis begging to go to harder targets, the British sacrificing aircraft for low-level attacks, and the other allies flying wherever I needed them. But the Marines never were total, joint, team players, a fact that is sad but true. I hoped that would be corrected before the next war.

In Operation Desert Storm, it wasn't working out for the Marines to handle their own sector. They hadn't been able to get near Schwarzkopf's 50-percent attrition goals on the Iraqi units in their sector. After Boomer finally confessed he needed help, we sent over JFACC-controlled aircraft, F-111s, F-16s and F-15Es, and the attrition numbers improved, dropping from February 11's 89 percent to February 15's 82 percent to an average strength of 75 percent for MARCENT's area of operations by G-Day. For the frontline forces that worried Boomer most, the results were even better. The eight committed Iraqi divisions in MARCENT averaged 83-percent strength on February 11, 71 percent on February 15, and 66 percent on February 23.

For all the focus on attrition, I couldn't get over the feeling that my Army and Marine colleagues were ignoring the big lesson of the war to date—Khafji. On February 15, I wrote, 'Army and marines are ignoring Khafji lessons. Almost a Gestapo line mentality. Actually fighting technology changes unless ground warfare is at hand. Sad.'

In other words, the land warriors were treating what happened in Khafji as a simple incursion that was dealt with and then forgotten. They ignored the devastation that occurred when the Iraqis tried to move those tanks and not leave them in dug-in positions. We had destroyed them like they were popcorn. But many in the Army and Marines were just unwilling to accept the improvement that technology had made in the ability of air forces to deal with armor, especially armor on the move.

To help correct this, I had another deep background discussion with the *New York Times.* Once again I repeated to reporter Eric Schmitt my deep conviction phrase—"rarely does an informed citizenry make a bad decision." I wanted them to know how hard we were hitting the Iraqi army.

The clock was counting down to the start of the ground war. The real driver in the timetable was how long it would take to reposition the two corps for the flanking attack.

The only person who did not want to talk about the start date for the ground campaign was Sudairy. He came to my office on February 18 to discuss air support for the ground campaign. I reviewed the close-air-support plans he brought with him and although he paid attention, he did not seem too concerned with the details.

"The Royal Saudi Air Force will continue to fly missions during this time?" he asked. That was all he cared about. He wanted the Saudis to remain integral to the action especially as Khalid led off the ground advance in the Joint Forces Command East sector. I assured my friend the Saudis would by flying their pants off like everyone else in the Coalition. To wrap up the discussion, I started to brief him on our proposed start date.

"No, no, do not tell me in advance," Sudairy interjected.

Once again, I thought, the unique Saudi culture raised its head. If I'd told Sudairy, he would have been obliged to pass the word along. It would be improper for the brigadier general to hold onto information unknown to the King.

"Just let it begin," he said.

STARTING THE GROUND WAR

The Iraqi army was "about to come unglued," as Schwarzkopf said. Did that mean we could accomplish all the objectives in Kuwait separately or independently without any use of ground forces?

I always believed this was a possibility. When you attrit a land army at 2 percent to 3 percent per day, eventually there will be nothing remaining to continue the fight. You always have the potential if you have the military strength and the will to bring a nation-state to its knees using air, land or sea forces separately. This works if you don't care how long it takes or what it costs in civilian casualties or your own casualties.

Certainly with the air superiority we had and the Navy choking any movement in the Straits we could have gone on indefinitely using the F-117s and TLAM missiles and just bombing Baghdad targets. Or we could have driven B-52s in to level the place.

But my own conviction was that our society would not tolerate that. I did not think we would ever see another situation like the fire-bombing of Dresden in World War II, where the RAF bombers leveled the city. The combination of an air campaign followed by a land campaign was simply more efficient.

Generally speaking, the combination of air, land and sea will almost always be more efficient. We all hoped Saddam would be killed. Everyone agreed that would end the war quickly and save many lives, especially on the Iraqi side. Worded differently, we hoped for the best but always planned for the worst. The problem was we could not locate him. We all knew the land campaign was a risk with potential for high loss of life, even after the air campaign, if the Iraqis used chemical or biological weapons. McConnell estimated there was a 50-50 chance the Iraqis would use chemical weapons on our ground troops as they advanced, and this was a prospect that deeply worried Schwarzkopf.

But remember, our whole purpose was to *win*. I'm positive that Schwarzkopf was hoping that a land campaign would not be necessary.

Schwarzkopf and I discussed our sincere hope that the air campaign would so weaken Iraq's military capability that the Army could deliver the final blow in short order and without great risk of loss of life. Fifty percent attrition was all about creating those conditions.

Peace Plan

As the countdown to the ground war began, the Soviets mounted a major diplomatic offensive aimed at brokering an end to the war in Moscow before any land forces got moving.

Gorbachev sent Foreign Minister Yevgeni Primakov to meet with Saddam Hussein in Baghdad and offer him one possible chance to avoid defeat on the ground. Primakov could not exactly hop in a Soviet transport and fly through the Coalition-owned skies. To get there, he flew to Tehran and then drove to the border and into Iraq to a meeting in a small house outside Baghdad. With the power and heat off, the meeting took place in light provided by a noisy electric generator hauled in just for the meeting. Saddam was willing to deal and he sent Tariq Aziz to Moscow on February 18, where he frustrated Gorbachev by asking for at least six weeks to withdraw from Kuwait.[1] The Soviets were still putting a peace plan on the table and it had the attention of two major allies. French President Francois Mitterand and Egyptian President Hosni Mubarak both made it known privately that they might favor delaying the land campaign to explore a settlement. France's brigade and Egypt's corps were both part of the land offensive plan, so their objections could have real impact.

We took the peace plan seriously because it could mean avoiding a ground war. Schwarzkopf talked it over at a staff meeting on February 19. "If it had been up to the veteran military men in that war room, they'd have been thrilled to see Saddam accept a cease-fire and walk off the bat-

1. Ibid, pp. 333–334

tlefield—not that anyone believed he would," Schwarzkopf said later.[2] "At bottom, neither Powell nor I wanted a ground war," he added.

But the Iraqi forces weren't moving and the situation in Kuwait itself was growing worse while the diplomats talked. We'd hear reports of torture, and rumors of plans the Iraqis might trash Kuwait.

Then came a chilling warning from Sudairy on February 19.

"You need to keep the prisoners of war away from the Ba'ath Party Intelligence Service Headquarters," Sudairy warned. The Ba'ath headquarters was Baghdad's equivalent of Moscow's Lyublyanka prison under Stalin. Torture was its specialty, and many who entered the building did not come out. Sudairy had learned from his contacts in the Kuwaiti resistance that the POWs were about to be moved.

"If the POWs go there, they will be treated brutally. They will interrogate them and some of them will die," Sudairy said.

"Please push your contacts hard for more information," I told Sudairy.

I was worried. Sudairy's information came from a very senior Iraqi military officer in Kuwait and I did not doubt that the prisoners were in serious danger. After he left, I called McConnell, but he had no fresh news on the prisoners. With Sudairy's excellent contacts, we almost knew more about the status of the prisoners than Washington did.

I immediately called for Lewis to review all probable locations of the prisoners, while Deptula contacted Checkmate to get Warden's bunch working to see what else they could find out about the prisoners through our intelligence channels.

Over the next few days, we'd be keeping an eye on both the POW situation and the Soviet peace plan. Meanwhile for me, the final days of air attacks before the ground campaign overshadowed everything else.

That night the CINC's staff meeting homed in on ground war preparations.

"Why is every sortie not preparing the battlefield?" Schwarzkopf asked on February 19. That night for the first time, Schwarzkopf would not approve the targets in Baghdad I wanted to strike in the next ATO cycle. He made an exception for bridges and any NBC facilities, but that was it. In fact, it was the first time Schwarzkopf failed to approve what I wanted to do.

After the meeting adjourned, I sought him out privately.

2. *It Doesn't Take a Hero*, p. 442.

"We had three targets in the plans," I told him. "Two of them I can let pass, but we must bomb the AT&T building."

McConnell had informed me the Iraqis were still using the lower floors of the telephone exchange we'd hit in the first week of the war. The first two strikes totally took the international and domestic lines down, lines we were monitoring, so we assumed it had been 100 percent successful. What we didn't know until February 18 was that underneath this rubble, the second and third floor still had military communications and intelligence lines still in use!

Naturally this target was right in the middle of downtown Baghdad. I told Schwarzkopf we had some new intelligence from McConnell on the AT&T building. The Iraqis redundancy in the building, meant that they could still have leadership and intelligence communications down on the bottom floors. I needed to take that out.

"Fine," he said.

We sent the F-117s back to the AT&T building to put four GBU-27s on this facility again. They put one GBU-27 right through the top with a maximum-delay fuse on it, and then they put two on one side and one on the other side, so we hit three different sides of the building. That put them out of business.

Schwarzkopf then said, "We'll go on the 24th for the ground war if the weather's good."

That was interesting news. Later, I went back to my office and directed Deptula to massively bomb the whole Tikrit area, including bridges, railroads, police, etc. so we could get at Saddam's base. Then to make myself feel better I talked to McPeak in Washington. "The options aren't being intellectually discussed," I grumbled. "Everyone is following Powell's lead." The Chief let me blow off steam. Then he said, "I think it is time to end the war as quick as possible, and I believe the ground campaign will only last a few days." I could not disagree with his logic or conclusion.

The POWs

The next morning, February 20, I had a personal concern of my own. In walked Sudairy. "Be careful," he said. "The Iraqis are watching you."

"Who?" I demanded.

"The Iraqis who have been holding up in the embassy. They're going to try to take you out," Sudairy reported calmly.

"Thanks," I said. "A little more information would be helpful, like how."

"I don't know," Sudairy replied. "But I'm hearing from our people that they've targeted you and it is a high priority."

"Thank you," I said to him, and promised to be careful. I really did not have time to worry and McConnell had warned me a couple of times before on the same issue. *En Shalah*. I did what all pilots do well during a war and put it out of my mind. Sudairy made this easy with his next remark.

"My sources say the treatment of the prisoners is getting progressively worse." Sudairy believed the prisoners were now in the Ba'ath Party Security Regional Headquarters facility and were all in one building, a very crucial detail. By this time, we had 20 U.S. service members—including two women—being held as prisoners.[3] They were a mix of aviators from all services plus others, like two Army soldiers who'd been captured with their truck during the attack at Khafji. Also held prisoner was Bob Simon, the CBS News reporter.

After Sudairy departed, I tried to confirm the information once again with McConnell. He said he'd try to focus assets and help.

This was a big decision for me. We had only anecdotal comments, but if Sudairy was right, we were now in the worst of all worlds because the prisoners were exactly where he had warned me a couple of days earlier they'd go. His words echoed in my mind. *"They will interrogate them and some of them will die."*

I couldn't sit back and do nothing. What were the options? The CINC would never send special ops into downtown Baghdad this close to the start of the ground campaign. It just wasn't going to happen. My options were very limited. I could drop bombs close to their location to try to force the Iraqis to move them, or I could ignore it.

"Go look at the regional headquarters intel facility and security service facility," I said to Deptula. He could not believe I was directing him to consider a Baghdad target. McConnell would send over photos.

Yet by the next day, there was still no new information on the POWs. *'Tough, tough,'* I noted down. But Sudairy had always been reliable. I had to make a decision and I had to do it myself. I opted not to discuss it with

---

3. Prisoner of War number from DoD, Conduct of the Persian Gulf War, p. 317. One more POW, Capt Andrews, was captured after this date, on February 26, bringing the final total to 21 POWs.

Horner or Schwarzkopf. That would only complicate a decision that was hard enough already. If something went wrong, I didn't see any sense in tarnishing Horner and Schwarzkopf. There would be no value added in their input. This was the type of decision that you could discuss all day, yet it was still going to be a subjective call in the end. It was just that simple.

Although it moves ahead a few days, I want to tell this story all at once. Here was the problem: my intent was to bomb the building complex to compel the Iraqis to relocate the prisoners, who were of value to them. I got a picture of the facility and Sudairy came over so we could look at it. Four buildings grouped with a parking lot showed on the overhead photo. I asked Sudairy to get more information.

The pictures of these buildings showed that they appeared to be very strong structures indeed. A short while later Sudairy came back to tell me the prisoners were in the building the longest distance from the car parking area and I jotted that down in my diary notes.

Naturally, I did not want to hit the building they were actually in. I planned the mission for the F-117s to hit the other three buildings; then on second thought, altered the guidance so we hit just one building: to be safe, the one closest to the parking lot.

Only Tolin, Lewis and I knew that the prisoners were in the Ba'ath Party building. I wrote it down in my diary to document it and confine the damage if the worst happened. Sudairy and the Kuwaiti resistance were the only ones who were certain the prisoners were in there. Neither McConnell nor Bill Wrattan, through his British sources, was able to tell me anymore. McConnell agreed that this building complex was where they'd taken people to torture them. That had been a pattern, and our sources told us that a significant number of people, foreigners or Iraqis, went into that building and never came out, just as Sudairy had warned. McConnell confirmed that although he could not confirm that the POWs were there.

Deciding to attack was the toughest decision of the war for me, a decision I really had to wrestle with.

You first ask yourself, what is the right thing to do from our nation's perspective? That had several sides to it. And then you say, how about the people you are endangering? I was caught between having to risk one, two or three POWs being tortured to death, or, heaven forbid, killing one or all of them in an attack if it went awry.

Right or wrong, after praying over this and getting every ounce of information available, I came to the conclusion that I could live with the results if I inadvertently killed several of the POWs. I decided I could *not* live with the results if I let them get tortured to death and did nothing.

I micromanaged this strike to the *n*th degree. On February 22, strategic target L-42, the Ba'ath headquarters, came up for the CINC's approval at the nightly staff meeting. It was briefed as an intelligence facility and security forces headquarters target. *'I did not discuss POWs,'* I logged in my diary.

With target approval in hand, Deptula added it to the list for strike prior to 2100 local time the next night, February 23. I picked the time because Sudairy had told me we might catch some of the security forces at work in the building if we attacked before 10 PM.

Four F-117s were scheduled for the target. I called the wing and told them their aimpoint was the building nearest the parking lot. "And make sure you DO NOT put delayed fuses on those bombs. I want to blow out the tops of these buildings," I added.

The plan was in motion. Was it a prudent risk or was I just too caught up in it?

On the afternoon of February 22, I sat down with Rick and I told him where I was on this issue.

"What do your instincts tell you?" I asked him.

"I'm not sure that if I was making the decision, I would decide to bomb. But, I can certainly understand why you would make the decision to bomb, and I could support that," Lewis said.

I then went down the hall and had a much briefer conversation with Tolin.

"I made the decision," I said. "I'm going to do it. Do you think that's wrong?"

Tolin said, "This is a question we can't answer until after the fact. No matter how we try to think it through or project what's going to happen, if you do nothing, and two or three get tortured to death, you'll never forgive yourself. Likewise, if we bomb and you kill four or five of them, you'll still never forgive yourself. You're in a no-win situation. There is no right answer."

That's when command gets lonely, but my decision was made—I was going to do it. I just could not come to grips with the thought of one or more of them being tortured to death. I even convinced myself that if they got killed from a bomb, at least it'd be quick.

Of course, I felt the likelihood of them getting killed from a bomb was almost zero. I felt that I had a sure way of trying to get them moved out of those facilities. I wasn't going to get them killed.

As it turned out, I almost did.

When I got to work around noon on February 23 I called Whitley to get him to confirm the aimpoint that had been passed to the F-117s for that night's strike. "That's the only acceptable aimpoint. Bring the bombs home if you don't drop on that aim point for any reason."

"God, I pray your guiding hand will protect the POWs," I wrote in my notes.

Then I also had Tolin make the same call to the wing so they could confirm to him what I had said. Tolin instructed them to make sure—hit only the building nearest the parking lot. I checked with Sudairy but he still had no news. With the strike now just hours away, I checked with McConnell one last time and was sorely tempted to ask his opinion. *'Not fair question,'* I wrote in my diary, underlining it, and kept my mouth shut.

Toward nine o'clock, I thought about it again and said one last prayer. Greg Feest was leading the strike. *"God I pray you will guide his bombs!"*

How I needed that prayer. We had targeted the wrong building. We should have been bombing the building the *farthest* from the parking lot. The POWs were in the nearest one—but we didn't know it. I was playing the odds with the strike I'd planned, but this was a major screw-up.

The F-117s strikes hit the headquarters' entrance and blew up unoccupied cells. Water pipes broke, walls buckled and the doors of the cells of several where the prisoners were held sprang open. Instantaneous fuses on the GBU-27s confined damage to the upper levels; in the process, it spared the prisoners' lives. In the darkness, the prisoners were probably scared to death by the attack, but miraculously,—I would later learn—no POWs were hurt.

And, another miracle, the Iraqis rounded up the prisoners and moved them by bus to another building. The prisoners were jailed in groups, instead of alone, and entrusted to the Iraqi army, instead of the security forces. The prisoners had been beaten and poorly fed over the past several weeks and ended up better off out of the torture building.

We so often hear about fog and friction in war but now and then there are miracles, too.

Assessing the Iraqi Army

The ordeal of the prisoners pointed out why Schwarzkopf wanted to bring this campaign to an end. We were increasingly concerned about what the Iraqis might do when they pulled out of Kuwait. On February 22, Sudairy stopped by to say his people were saying the Iraqis were planning to leave Kuwait in a hurry very soon.

But we couldn't launch the ground war until Schwarzkopf deemed all was ready. As he later explained to reporters, "They really outnumbered us about 3-to-2—as far as fighting troops, we were really outnumbered 2-to-1. In addition to that, they had about 4,700 tanks versus our 3,500 when the buildup was complete, and they had a great deal more artillery than we did. I think any student of military strategy would tell you that in order to attack a position, you should have a ratio of 3-to-1 in favor of the attacker, and in order to attack a position that was heavily dug in and barricaded such as we had here, you should have a ratio of 5-to-1 of troops in favor of the attacker." Schwarzkopf said we, "had to come up with some way to make up the difference. What we did, of course, was start an extensive air campaign."[4]

Was it enough? Only Schwarzkopf could decide. The meeting on February 20 was tense—"a bloody meeting," as Lewis termed it, due largely to a confrontation with Waller.

Just before the meeting began, Waller came over to me in the briefing room.

"Buster, I want you to hit targets across these two divisions," he said.

I looked at the map. "They're both at less than 50-percent strength," I told him.

"I don't give a damn if it's less than 50 percent, I want you to hit it anyway."

"That's in violation of the CINC's guidance," I replied.

"I'll take responsibility for that," Waller said. "And I will clear it with the CINC."

"Okay," I said. "I am going to make sure at the staff meeting that the CINC approves this."

Waller and I parted. I stepped out into the hallway to see if I could intercept Schwarzkopf.

---

4. From Schwarzkopf's end-of-war briefing, televised February 27, 1991.

I stopped him and said, "Sir, Waller has asked me to hit two divisions that are below 50 percent. You said not to do that. This would be the only time we have violated that."

"I'll take care of it," Schwarzkopf said.

During the meeting, Waller stood up and briefed how the air would now attack the two divisions in question. Schwarzkopf let him go on, but then said, "Stop. We're not going to hit a division below 50 percent. Buster is not going to attack these divisions."

'Maybe he sees the light—Corps commanders can't direct air!' I wrote later.

The major issue hanging over his head was the level of destruction of the Iraqi forces. BDA continued to be a nightmare. At the CINC's meeting on February 21, we learned that the CIA, DIA and CENTCOM intelligence staffs could not agree on the number of tanks and other military vehicles destroyed. CIA Director William Webster had a briefing claiming CIA analysts could only confirm a fraction of the kills. Here was the count as briefed to President Bush on February 23, 1991.

Organization	Tanks	APCs	Artillery
CENTCOM	1688 (39%)	929 (32%)	1452 (47%)
CIA	524 (12%)	245 (9%)	255 (8%)
DIA	685 (16%)	373 (13%)	622 (20%)

You take the three intelligence organizations and that's the range they were giving the CINC. He was furious and I understood. I'd have been livid too if some idiot came in and told me, well maybe we've destroyed 400 but maybe we've destroyed 1,800. I mean, you have got to be kidding. No one ever has perfect information in war, but this was as ridiculous as TV comedy if it weren't such a serious matter, I thought.

The fact was that the CIA analysis was based on overhead images, some of which were more than two weeks old. Cheney, for one, dismissed the CIA conclusions outright.

"If we'd waited to convince the CIA, we'd still be in Saudi Arabia," Schwarzkopf wrote later.[5]

Still, as I entered in my diary, *'CINC not handling pressure well tonight.'* Schwarzkopf commented to the press that the Iraqi military was

5. *It Doesn't Take a Hero*, p. 432.

about to collapse. The Chairman had jumped all over him for it. *'Most truthful statement we have made concerning Iraqi capability since last August,'* I recorded in my notes.

Schwarzkopf believed the air campaign was having the impact he needed. The campaign was leveling the numerical disadvantage and softening the front lines so the Coalition could breach them fast. Still, Powell had jumped on Schwarzkopf's case about his remark to the press that the Iraqi army was on the verge of collapse.

Schwarzkopf was comfortable with his plan and held tight to his prerogative to start the ground war when he believed we'd degraded the Iraqi army sufficiently. The two Army corps commanders were the ones who had the gravest doubts. For Luck and Franks, every piece of intelligence and every cross-border foray convinced them they were facing a tough, unbowed opponent. The way the XVIII Corps plan looked, Luck thought he'd have to fight through two RGFC infantry divisions then face the heavy Hammurabi division.

Signs to the contrary were all but ignored. For example, 450 Iraqis surrendered en masse on February 20 while being mauled by A-10s. The Army whisked the Iraqi battalion commanders away for debriefing and learned that the air attacks and psychological operations had done their work on the group.

An ARCENT situation report dated the same day said, "Numerous reports indicate a serious morale problem as a direct result of coalition air attacks" and went on to cite "inadequate supply, disassociation with the Iraqi regime's policy toward Kuwait, poor training, and war weariness." By February 23, ARCENT had 972 Iraqi prisoners of war—this despite reports that deserters were shot in the back if caught in the act.[6]

In my opinion, Waller didn't help matters during his time as commander of Third Army. He was constantly a disruptive force. He briefed his staff on February 18 that the Army had estimated 20,000 casualties.[7] *'CINC made a critical mistake assigning Waller control of ground campaign,'* I wrote in my diary on February 21. *'Service biases render him ineffective . . . I will not permit his lack of understanding of air power to undermine the CINCs overall effort.'*

---

6. *Lucky War: Third Army in Desert Storm*, p. 204.
7. Ibid, p. 205

Strategic Targets

We were still trying to pursue major strategic targets, but with the heavy restrictions in place after the Al-Firdos incident, it was not easy. I felt the strategic campaign had reached a stage where we were not aggressively focusing on finding the targets that remained in Iraq and picking them off from the air. Any strategic targets we destroyed would be few and far between because Powell had such restrictions on strikes around Baghdad. We weren't going to accomplish much worthwhile, in my opinion, unless it was just a quirk of fate.

The one big exception to this was that Powell was very concerned about the remaining Iraqi communications.

There's been a misunderstanding about the objectives of targeting communications nodes in Desert Storm. People think that, as the authoritative Gulf War Air Power Survey put it, the objective was "to sever completely communications between Baghdad and Iraq's military forces in the Kuwait theater." Not true. In this age—or any other—no one can completely eliminate communications with a large army. They have their battlefield radios if nothing else. They have couriers. Maybe it's not efficient, but messages will get through.

The Iraqis had a redundant communications system of coaxial cable landlines, fixed and mobile microwave relays, and fiber optic lines. We knew where a lot of it was, but as with the fiber optic line that ran along the pipeline to Basra, it had taken us a while to figure some of it out. Other lines were strung under bridges, and there, we had restrictions.

On our side, we had many highly sophisticated ways of listening to an enemy army and its leaders. I didn't want them to stop talking. It was much more useful for us to control their communications, by destroying enough to route their communications and leave open a few lines so we could listen in. We wanted to wait until the last moment so the Iraqis wouldn't be able to repair landlines. Then they'd have to come up on radio so we could monitor them when the ground war started. Or, as the survey hinted, "it would not necessarily have been militarily advantageous to cut all communications links between Baghdad and the Kuwait theater, particularly prior to the beginning of the ground war."[8] *Shack.*

McConnell and I were trying desperately to leave the Iraqis just two

8. GWAPS Vol II Part 2 p. 278.

routes of communications, routes that we'd tapped into and could monitor. We wanted to take everything else away from them. Then, if McConnell and I were right, and we really knew their communications paths, we would force them to use only the lines to which we had access. We'd know what their thought processes and intentions were. Powell was eager for us to seal up the plan. And for the most part, we did. We were finally able to cut the fiber optic cable that ran along the pipeline by taking out a routing station in Al Najif. That disrupted it, and for the most part forced communications back into the routes we preferred.

McConnell relayed to me on February 23 that Iraqi communications were the Chairman's number-one concern. This was ironic, since the Chairman still wouldn't approve destroying the Baghdad bridge that carried the fiber optic communications cable underneath it.

"Tell the Chairman not to worry. I guarantee they will use the lines you desire or they will not talk," I said to McConnell.

I understood Powell's concern perfectly. If we pulled it off, we could have access to the bulk of Iraq's military communications and listen to the orders that were being given. It would be a tremendous political and military advantage in what was to come.

One way or the other, either the Soviet peace plan or the ground war was going to bring the air campaign to a halt very soon. Had we met the President's full objectives, those that only the air campaign could achieve? Leading off my diary notes for February 22, I reminded myself to review the major targets left in Baghdad, especially the NBC sites. We had a short time remaining in this air campaign. I needed to plan so as to hedge against the war stopping any time now.

Later that afternoon, I directed Tolin, Lewis, Deptula and Rogers to develop a list of infrastructure that we still needed to destroy. I needed to make sure that I was hitting only what was most important, in case the war ended. Also, it was critical to get more photos of what remained on the list.

Meanwhile, Saddam "accepted" the Soviet offer to withdraw. McConnell and I talked about the Soviet peace initiatives. His view was that the administration could not afford to appear to stiff-arm Gorbachev.

"The Chairman recommended a limited bombing halt to the President," McConnell told me.

I was furious. A halt was the last thing we needed with both Iraqi armor and strategic targets still left to destroy. I couldn't believe it. Hadn't we learned anything from Vietnam? Bombing halts were one of the dumbest things we ever did during Vietnam and now here was the same bad idea floating up the chain.

Right after my conversation with McConnell, Sudairy came in.

"Will the President accept the Soviet offer?" he asked.

"No," I said, hoping that was true.

Sudairy was pleased. "We would wish a complete ending," he said meaningfully. He didn't want Saddam to get away with a withdrawal any more than I did.

"So would I," I replied. "But our political leaders must always have the final say on when to start or end wars."

"I know," Sudairy said. "But we don't want to have the same problem again in short order."

Iraqi War Crimes

One of the ways to ensure this was to hit the Iraqi forces hard as they exited Kuwait. Sudairy told me the Kuwaiti resistance was picking up signs that the Iraqis were preparing for a fast withdrawal from Kuwait City. In my notes for February 23, I jotted down, *'When withdrawal from Kuwait City occurs, F-15E only system with capability to significantly impact. Must destroy the maximum. Brutality in Kuwait City has been unreal.'*

I made a decision before the Iraqi forces in Kuwait even started their withdrawal that we were going to try to destroy as much as possible when they attempted to run. This was because of the brutality they had wreaked on the innocent people of Kuwait and the way that they had brutalized the city and the people for more than six months. I had never seen such total disregard for human life.

I told Lewis to track this and make sure that I knew as soon as we had any indication that any kind of break was happening inside Kuwait City because I didn't want to leave it up to the TACC. I knew they'd screw it up and I wanted to make sure that we killed as many of those Iraqi security and military thugs as we could and not give them the opportunity to repeat their brutality.

The war crimes carried out by the Iraqis in Kuwait were extensive. On a daily basis they were brutalizing and committing heinous crimes. We could not permit those security and military personnel to go back into their society because, if given the opportunity to do the same thing again, they would.

We had done all we could to destroy Saddam's military capability and degrade his forces. Working with restrictions, we'd try to hit remaining strategic targets. During the ground war, air power would support troops in contact and we'd also have our last chance to make sure the Iraqi army went home without its war-waging equipment.

Around this time I received one of numerous letters from Vicki written in standard blue ink on a piece of plain ruled paper. Nothing fancy, but the message and love were singular.

Hon, I just miss you so much. I try to push it out of my mind, so I don't get down. But sometimes I'm not as successful as others. You are such a treasure to me. I just want you here to protect and love you. God has truly blessed me, when he saw fit for you to fall in love with me. Your children are also very fortunate to have such a loving and caring father. You are truly the glue to this family. You are so special to all of us. Some of us may fall short sometimes, but I know how much you're loved. Take care, and always know I love you with all my heart and soul.

After I read it, I folded Vicki's letter and stapled it into the diary so I would always have it to read.

Green Light

"He has the green light for the ground war," McConnell told me on February 23.

The CINC's staff meeting on the evening of February 23 came at a critical decision point. Weather forecasts were still uncertain.

The real final decision to move to Phase IV hinged on weather. At the meeting that night, Schwarzkopf said, "I won't go without air support."

'Nor should he,' I jotted down.

"We'll look at it hour by hour. I'm not going to be rushed," Schwarzkopf told us.

Then Schwarzkopf asked his commanders if they had any final comments. General Sir Peter de la Billiere had a slide to show us. It said, "We tossed a coin. Saddam won. He elected to receive."

We could all relate to that, and we enjoyed that bit of well-timed British humor. To close the meeting, Schwarzkopf settled us back on a serious note, talking of prayer. It made an impact on me for it was the first time I'd heard Schwarzkopf talk about prayer in a solemn manner. His remarks were somber, well-intentioned and very appropriate.

Schwarzkopf was steadfast that he would not let Washington rush him, but there was another factor I thought he should know about. As we rose from the staff meeting, I walked over to Schwarzkopf for a quick private discussion.

"The Iraqis are getting ready to pull out of Kuwait City," I told him. McConnell, Sudairy and Sheikh Mohammed in the UAE all agreed this was their plan.

"I don't expect intel to confirm it for you, but I'm telling you, I've got it from three different sources, and I think it's about to happen," I said.

"Is there an air problem if we go early?" Schwarzkopf asked me.

"No. Weather's the only concern."

"Be ready after midnight," he said. "We're going if at all possible."

I immediately found Horner.

"He's made a decision he's going after midnight," I told him.

"That's what I thought he was going to do anyway," Horner said.

"Well, I can tell you for a fact now that's what we're going to do."

Back in the Black Hole, I called together Wrattan, Profitt, Caruana, Tolin, Deptula, Lewis, Rogers and Baptiste.

"Expect a ground campaign before sunrise, or at least the initial movement, unless the weather really turns to crap," I said to them. "I believe the weather's going to hold."

Air Support Plan

Our last-minute preparations for the ground war were to do nothing unusual to startle the Iraqis. For the last week we'd postured ourselves to continue our activity exactly as the Iraqis had seen it. I insisted that it appear that everything was happening in the usual way. We were grid-bombing in the killboxes and I wanted to continue that right up to the last moment so that there'd be no tip-off of what was about to happen so the Iraqis wouldn't accidentally stumble into the tail end of those crossing corps. We wanted to keep the Iraqis from moving for any reason.

Once the ground war began, we had air designated to support XVIIIth Corps, VIIth Corps, the Marines and the Arab corps over where the Khafji attack had been. I primarily let the Marines use their own indigenous air to support themselves, backed up with a reserve of F-16s and A-10s I designated as on-call to go help the Marines in case they needed it.

The concept was Push CAS. Horner had a lot of experience with CAS (Close-Air Support) from Vietnam and he wanted to do business differently. He briefed the Push CAS concept around CENTCOM long before Iraq invaded Kuwait. We'd use it in Desert Storm to provide responsive yet flexible support. Push CAS "pushed" close-air support sorties into the combat area on a regular basis, such as every ten minutes. The U.S.A.F. Tactical Air Control Parties (TACP) operating with the Army units could call on the aircraft for CAS strikes. If there were no targets for CAS, the aircraft went on to other targets deeper behind the lines. Then a few minutes later, another two-ship or four-ship was "pushed" into the area.

The support package for XVIIIth Corps out west and VIIth Corps in the middle were divided up between aircraft loaded with weapons for fixed targets, for pop-up targets and for close air support. The F-117s in particular were loaded to be able to attack fixed targets in each corps' operating area. The F-111s could attack fixed targets too, or moving targets (like tanks!) that were identified by JSTARS. Then the F-16s and the A-10s were tasked to provide close-air support as called for by the forward air controllers attached to ground force units.

Then I had what I always referred to as a strategic reserve made up of F-111s and F-15Es. I lowered the tasking on both systems during the initial onslaught of the ground campaign in case I needed them to divert in an emergency. We were very attuned to keeping that capability open to use as needed. The F-15Es were still busy out west trying to keep the Scud count down. The last thing we needed in Phase IV was more Scuds going into Israel and Riyadh or onto our airbases. However, I pulled other platforms off the Scud mission and kept the F-15Es focused on it. My plan was, if push came to shove, I knew we could divert all the F-15Es for whatever the ground forces needed.

The F-15E was by far the most capable airplane for bad weather. The forecasts pushed me into a situation where I had to almost totally rely on the F-15E if something went wrong in those first hours because I could put them under the weather no matter what.

I called Hal Hornburg to warn him they might get some unusual taskings in the next few days.

"Look, there's the possibility that your guys may fly outside of crew rest and everything else during the first few days of the ground campaign. I don't think it'll last very long," I said to him. "But for however long it lasts, I've got to lean on the F-15Es as a last resort to solve any problem I get. Because it doesn't matter what the problem is, the F-15E can solve it. And that's the way I've got to look at it. All of your guys may fly a five- or six-hour mission, and retire for the night. But I might be forced to put everybody back in the air two hours later," I warned him. I didn't know how prophetic that comment would be, because that's what happened when the Iraqis tried to run up the road to Basra and pull out of Kuwait. Hornburg's only comment was, "No problem sir. We will be ready." I was fortunate to have commanders like Hornburg: tough, loyal and can-do! The best of the best.

There are those that like to say supporting the land campaign was the most challenging part of the air campaign. Nothing could be further from the truth. In reality, it was the simplest part. The Iraqi forces were beat down and devastated by the time the land campaign started. It was really very simple to plan out because we had so much capability and so little to use it on. We had airplanes on call, stacked up six or eight flights high, waiting for JSTARS to use them or AWACS to use them or ABCCC to use them or somebody to use them. We were resource rich, not target rich.

The Coalition had three or four times as many ground forces as we needed to eject the Iraqi army from Kuwait. Friendly fire was my number-one concern. I didn't want airstrikes to inadvertently kill more people than the Iraqis were going to kill. I was close to paranoid that fratricide would be the biggest problem Americans and our allies faced on the battlefield. It sure wouldn't be the Iraqis.

Eve of the Ground War

I came into work on February 24 after a few hours of sleep and called McConnell. We were now in almost hourly contact.

Next I gathered Tolin, Lewis and Baptiste. "I want to sit down and table-fly the 24th and 25th on this ground campaign action," I told the three of them. That's what I'd done for the first few days in the air campaign back in January.

For some reason, on the land campaign, it kept gnawing at me that since there were so many moving parts, there was bound to be an opportunity for a massive screw-up. I couldn't get that out of my mind. The other thing on my mind was the fact American soldiers and Marines were going into harm's way. One soldier or Marine's life was the same to me as one fighter pilot's life. I wanted to go to whatever extreme necessary to make sure that one person, that one soldier, that one Marine did not unnecessarily lose his life or get injured. In all honesty, you never know exactly what makes you tick sometimes, but that obsession, if you want to call it that, drove me to do this review. For whatever reason, the good Lord was giving me a much-needed helping hand.

As we began the review around the little table, we got a big shock. The Egyptian Corps was not included in the pre-planned close air support.

The Egyptians were assigned an area between VIIth Corps and the Marines with some special operations forces. The Egyptian corps' American forward air controllers and everybody had seduced themselves into thinking that somehow the special operators were going to provide what they needed initially.

"I don't frappin' believe it," I said. We'd left out an entire allied corps. No airplanes were scheduled to provide CAS. Schwarzkopf had even made a point of it back in December. Personally, I'd rather we'd forgotten to support an American corps because they had the strength to recover. If the Egyptian corps had ever had the tide turn against them, just for a minute, it could have been devastating. *Devastating.*

I was irate. I had directed both Tolin and Lewis to review our support plan for the ground campaign about a week earlier. They did not offer any excuses. As for Baptiste, all the blood drained from his face. I'm sure he thought his involvement in the war was about to end.

I was so mad I got up from the table and walked away and told them all I'd be back in a minute. We were too close to execution and I didn't want this oversight to become larger than life. When I walked out of the room, my instincts reminded me that everyone is human, we all make mistakes. All three were as shocked and frustrated as I was.

Good as Baptiste had been, for him to make a mistake like this was mind-boggling to me. I just could not comprehend how a person that was responsible for that part of the planning on the ATO every day would have had an oversight like that.

Are there any other oversights, was the question I had for Tolin, Lewis and Baptiste when I walked back into the room. They all assured me there were no other surprises. Nevertheless, I directed Tolin and Lewis to make one final review.

As it turned out, there had not been enough direct contact between our people and the FACs assigned to the sector where the Egyptian corps was placed. Tolin and Lewis had not made the thorough review—I'd stretched them too thin. I told Lewis to put four A-10s per hour for the first six hours, then four F-16s or F-18s per hour in for the Egyptian Corps. "Your number-one responsibility for the first 24 hours of the ground campaign is to ensure the Egyptian Corps receives more support than they can possibly use," I told him.

Once again, thank God for intuition.

That just goes to show you that even though the war had been going on quite a while now and our decision-making process was as good as it was going to get, a big mistake almost bit us. I blame myself for letting it get so close to happening but I'm thankful that it didn't happen and I was able to catch it.

Aside from this, the weather piled on the stress. '*Weather. The devil to the end. F-117s in KTO very effective when weather permits,*' I wrote at this time.

We had two more delicate incidents that night. First, McConnell called to tell me the Baghdad Republican Guard headquarters building was no longer being used by the military.

"I'm nervous about who might be inside," he confided. We still had no word on where the POWs had been moved after the strike the day before. McConnell was warning us not to select the Republican Guard headquarters lest we hit the POWs again.

"I won't attack that target without your personal permission," I promised McConnell. Then I told Deptula, "The Republican Guard headquarters building is off limits. Don't use it as an alternate target or anything."

We also picked up some funny infrared temperature returns at the Kuwait international airport building. We were concerned that maybe there were some chemical or biological weapons that had been moved into the theater there. I put my hip-pocket F-111s on alert to take out the whole premises, everything around that area, if we had to.

Suddenly the entire RSAF building filled with the sounds of Muslim prayer call coming in over the loudspeakers. There we were, on the eve of the ground war, in the middle of a heated discussion on Baghdad targeting. '*Would never happen in a total American facility,*' I jotted down. It just wouldn't, and the irony struck me. We refer to ourselves as the world's Christian nation yet we also believe in separating church and state. The Saudis were far more diligent and more committed to the Koran and Islam, even in official life, even in the middle of a war, and they didn't let anything interrupt it.

Soon after we made the nightly journey to the CINC's staff meeting. Schwarzkopf was in an upbeat mood, trying to take the high road and instill confidence in everyone.

One more coordination issue needed to be checked: the location of the FSCL. The FSCL in the Army sector had lain quietly on the border during the air war. But, as the ground corps started moving, they planned to extend the FSCL out in front of them in pre-selected increments. The plan was to move it forward tomorrow north of Salam, west and parallel to the gulf. I wanted to make sure that it didn't get yanked around without my involvement. I made a note to myself. *'FSCL location movement. Potential problem. Must get CINC support.'*

I returned to my little office and with immaculate timing; Sudairy walked in at 15 minutes to midnight.

"The POWs are safe. They have been moved to another area," he said.

I was overjoyed. Needless to say, after that the CINC wasn't the only one who was upbeat.

I immediately called McConnell to needle him.

"Give me a status on the POWs," I said. I couldn't resist seeing if Sudairy had beaten him to the punch. Indeed, McConnell had not heard anything and I was able to give him the good news that the prisoners were safe.

Buoyed with sweet relief, I called Vicki. They were all doing well. I thought about Brad and Tanya, and reminded myself that tomorrow a lot of other people's children were going into harm's way. *God be with them,* I prayed.

PHASE IV

Schwarzkopf's plan for Phase IV was to roll up the Iraqi army occupying Kuwait with a movement of Coalition troops like swinging a door on its hinge as shown in Figure 8. The hinge was on the right in the Marine sector. Four corps were involved. Two corps moved almost due north, while two other corps were to move rapidly through Iraq then turn east to envelope the Republican Guard and other Iraqi forces.

The Marines under Boomer and the Saudis in the easternmost sector—the right of the line—would do two things. First, they'd threaten an amphibious invasion to the east, above Kuwait City. This would hold the Iraqi units in place. Meanwhile, the Marines would move up from the south, heading north through Kuwait and up to Kuwait City on the coast, where the Saudis, Qataris and other Arab forces would liberate Kuwait City.

To the left of the Marines the Egyptian Corps with other Coalition forces attached would also move north in Kuwait.

This "hinge" had to advance at the right pace and hold firm while the two Army-led corps swung northwest.

Next in line to the left was VII Corps. VII Corps under Fred Franks was a heavy corps—all armored divisions, with tanks—composed of U.S. and British forces. As an Army historian later put it, VII Corps was assigned a "force oriented" mission, to destroy the Republican Guard in its zone. For the Army, the corps commander had complete freedom of action in the corps' designated zone of operations but could not cross the

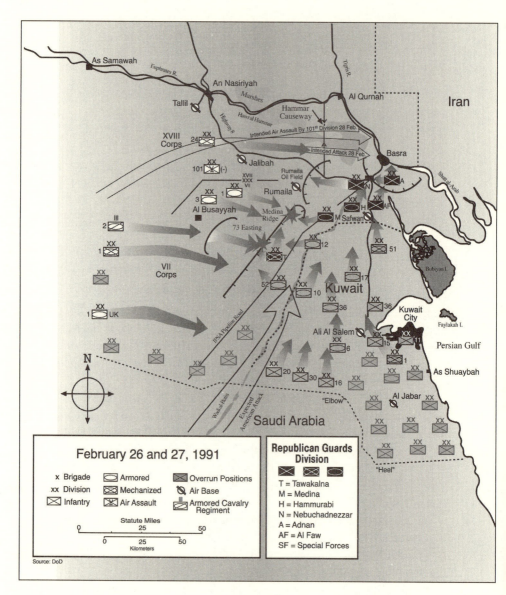

FIGURE 8

line without orders from higher headquarters. Franks, therefore, was responsible for engaging and destroying the two Republican Guard divisions in his zone. These were the Tawakalna, Medina and Hammurabi divisions.

XVIII Corps held the far left of the Coalition line. It combined medium, heavy and light forces from the U.S. and France. Its mission was "terrain oriented and designed to block the Iraqi routes of withdrawal or reinforcement" using the fast-moving light and medium forces. The farther west a unit was positioned in XVIII Corps, the faster they needed to go. Luck's corps would jump off like racehorses charging out of the starting gate at the Preakness.

The French light armored brigade next to VII Corps would take its objective while the U.S. 101st Division moved forward and sent its AH-64 Apaches ahead to destroy armor. They were heading for the Euphrates, as fast as possible. Then they'd link up with the heavy forces of the corps, which were positioned next to VII Corps on the left, and drive on to Basra.[1] On the way they'd engage and destroy the other three main Republican Guard divisions: the Al Faw and the Nebuchadnezzar, which were infantry divisions, and the Adnan division of motorized infantry.

Schwarzkopf's direction for weeks was to concentrate on the mechanized Republican Guard divisions. Coalition air attack left the Tawakalna at 58 percent strength; the Medina at 54 percent and the Hammurabi at 77 percent before the ground war began. The three infantry divisions were largely intact. Before the ground war their strength was assessed at 100 percent for the Al Faw, 88 percent for the Nebuchadnezzar and 83 percent for the Adnan.

Yeosock—who as commander of Third Army had both VII and XVIII Corps under him—sketched out his view of the overall offensive:

• Cross the line of departure as fast as possible, with as much as we can carry.

• Take on the Republican Guard Forces Command (RGFC) a battalion or brigade at a time; a war of attrition to deliberately destroy it.

• Operational pause to assess what is where and ignore that which does not matter.

• If he offers surrender, increase OPTEMPO and let NCA decide.[2]

1. *Lucky War: Third Army in Desert Storm*, p. 207.
2. Ibid., p. 197.

The offensive air campaign during Phase IV had two jobs: supply close air support, and plenty of it; and conduct air interdiction, like we'd been doing, by working deep to destroy Iraqi tanks and vehicles on the move—especially the Republican Guard forces. For weeks they'd been buried in sand but now they'd have to maneuver either to fight or retreat. Whatever armor was left, I wanted to herd it together and destroy it as they tried to pull back in the face of the Coalition advance.

If all went according to plan, the Saudis, other Coalition forces, Marines and the Egyptian Corps would end up in control of Kuwait. VII Corps would take out the Iraqi 12th Infantry, the Tawakalna and the Medina; XVIII Corps would close the loop and cut off the Republican Guard divisions positioned just north of Kuwait. These were the divisions hit least in the air campaign. Then, with the Iraqi army fixed in place, it could be destroyed at will from the air and on the ground. We weren't clear when we'd get the call to cease-fire. The essence of the plan was all about where forces ended up: in possession of Kuwait, and with the Republican Guard divisions sealed off.

What we did not know was this: How would Saddam and the Iraqi army react when Coalition troops started to move? For 38 days, we had pounded Iraqi forces from the air. We attacked tanks, APCs, and artillery. We hit their food, water and ammunition supplies. We destroyed fire trenches and disrupted communications. Overall, the Iraqi troops were at 64 percent strength after the air attacks. More important to Schwarzkopf, nine of the 14 Iraqi divisions manning the front lines were assessed at less than 50 percent strength. True, these weren't Iraq's best divisions. They were filled with conscripts. But these were the divisions that would be shooting at our Coalition soldiers. The divisions might collapse in place. Stronger units might put up a token fight. They might try an orderly retreat—but a good retreat under fire with a better army advancing on you is one of the hardest military maneuvers to pull off. The Iraqis might simply run. Tolin, Lewis and I had discussed all these possibilities and we thought putting up a token fight then running was the most likely Iraqi action.

H-Hour

The ground war commenced at 0400 on February 24.

Iraqi forces on the front lines started surrendering almost immediately. The POWs were in rough shape, many with lice and sores, the marks of deprivation. They were so broken that before 0900 Schwarz-kopf was talking to Yeosock about commencing the heavy attack early, which they did, at 1500 that afternoon. VII Corps started its breaching operations then paused for the night so they could start the advance synchronized in the morning.

By midnight, the ground war was already several hours old. *'No major glitches in ground campaign,'* was the first entry in my log for what the Army called "G+1."

There'd also been no reported contact with the Republican Guard yet, but very soon, that was old news. We ran over the divisions on the front lines too fast for them to do anything but surrender. However, across the theater, Iraq's second echelon forces and Republican Guard started to move to counter the Coalition.

The 12th Armored Division and the Tawakalna backed up by the RGFC Adnan Infantry and other Iraqi army elements pulled into a line on February 25 to try to oppose VII Corps. This "line" running southwest to northeast was really just a series of divisions starting with the 12th Armored, then the Tawakalna, the Medina and beyond it, the Hammurabi division. Of the Republican Guard's three heavy divisions, the Hammurabi was the one we'd hit least and it was pegged at 77 percent of its original strength. The connect-the-dots formation of the 12th, the Tawakalna and the Medina set up the terrain for most of VII Corps's engagements.[3]

The 12th and the Tawakalna reorganized between 40 and 60 tanks. JSTARS saw the movement, and we put the F-111s and F-15s on them. They were destroying tanks at a high rate—it totaled approximately 100 tanks during a six-hour period. This was just the response I wanted. *'I'm sure ground troops will take credit for these kills,'* I couldn't help noting down in my diary.

The reason we could pick up on the Tawakalna so fast was all due to JSTARS. JSTARS had the best picture of everything going on in the battle area. The JSTARS battle manager had the direction authority over the air-to-ground airplanes and could divert them anytime based on what they saw developing. This was all George Muellner. As the colonel in charge of JSTARS, he had nothing but a system that was still in test. Muellner was a genius in the way he employed JSTARS. Let there be no

3. Ibid., 244.

doubt. He absolutely saved lives because of his warfighting instincts and intellect. He all but flew the wings off his aircraft during the land campaign. "I'll take care of crew rest later," he told me. I didn't ask any questions.

As for combat air support, we weren't seeing as many requests because of the rapid movement and minimal resistance.

The CINC's staff meeting that night was quick and routine. The only off note was the CINC humorously comparing himself to Alexander the Great. In a more serious vein, Schwarzkopf was now concerned about the number of Iraqi POWs putting themselves in the hands of the Coalition's combat troops. First estimates that night put the number at 10,000 to 20,000, maybe more. It would turn out to be a lot more. The news from each corps on the move was good. The Egyptians had acquitted themselves well. One mistake was that Marine AV-8s under control of an Air Force FAC had bombed Saudi troops by accident. I headed back to my office to follow up on the incident. Saudi skirmishers had been out in front of the Saudi positions and the FAC hadn't known they were there— a gross mistake.

Checking in later at the TACC I found there was no sense of urgency. The Iraqi 12th was still trying to move south. We needed to increase the intensity of our air attacks on them, I urged Horner, and he directed JS-TARS to swing its coverage to concentrate on the activity of the 12th Infantry Division.

Other Targets

Even as the ground war rolled forward, we were still pursuing strategic targets hundreds of miles north of the front lines, with mixed methods and results. Five targets of interest became major issues that day.

First was one we'd already missed. In my first phone call back to McConnell, he told me a Boeing 737 airliner escorted by two MiG-23s had escaped to Iran. He thought the passengers were most likely some of Saddam's family members. We all wondered—was there an off chance Saddam was aboard? My instincts suggested Saddam was not on the airplane; it wasn't consistent with his personality, and if he left, he could never return. But I wasn't 100 percent sure.

To make matters worse, it turned out that we'd left the airspace uncovered for a time when Navy F-14s assigned to the CAP returned to their

ship without notification.[4] I warned them I'd take them off the CAPs altogether if it happened again.

I kicked myself for failing to follow my instincts. A few days earlier,
I'd thought about going back to circling F-15s over Baghdad to catch any
aircraft coming out. Then I'd dropped the thought without taking any
action. After this news, I did bring F-15s down from Turkey. As the
CENTAF directive put it, they'd orbit Baghdad until the war ended. Their
instructions: Shoot down anything in the air north of 35 degrees latitude
unless I tell you it's coming. Although I put the plan in motion immediately I was afraid that I had gone to it a day late and a dollar short.

The second strategic target was one I did *not* want to attack: the Basra
water purification plant. Schwarzkopf pulled me aside for quick private
discussion after the staff meeting. Some of his people wanted to take out
the plant on the grounds that it was supplying water to the Iraqi ground
troops.

To me, this was just like Saddam blowing up the Kuwait pumping station.

"We don't want to do this," I said. "We can't lower ourselves to his
level."

"My view exactly," Schwarzkopf said. While I had his ear, I gave him
an alternative target group: the presidential palace VIP facility, security
services, Ba'ath Party facilities and that statue of Saddam's hands leading
down the parade route they sometimes used.

"Let's level them all," I suggested. "We will put two bombs each from
the F-117s on those facilities." I just wanted to make sure they knew the
war was still going on in Baghdad—just as a psychological thing, more
than anything else. Schwarzkopf approved it, but he still had to work the
targets back via the Chairman for his approval. McConnell passed on the
word a few hours later that the Chairman's lawyer said no to bombing
the statue.

You could make an argument that they were right. If you look at the
Geneva Convention, it says not to go out of your way to destroy artifacts
and history. No way would we try to destroy the wall of Babylon near the
museum, or similar archaeological sites. But a statue of Saddam? I would
have taken it down because I wanted to destroy anything that enhanced
Saddam's image in the eyes of the people of Iraq. But it wasn't that big a
deal to me.

4. GWAPS, Volume V, p. 234, cites TACC current ops Log

Case four was a direct request from the CINC: Drop leaflets on Baghdad, which I did.

Case five came in the same phone call.

"I want the Rangers to go in and take out a microwave tower," he said. "They'd need air support to accomplish the mission. Downing will work out the details with you." Deptula had moved around the strategic campaign to insert SOF teams numerous times in preceding weeks. This time, I had a better idea.

"I can take that target out with one bomb," I told the CINC.

"No," he said, "SOF forces are already out there. Let them take care of it. Give them the support they need."

Downing and I worked out the details following the CINC's direction, but it took a lot more effort to support the Rangers than it would have to send one F-117 to do the job. This was, in all truthfulness, the first and only time during the war that I saw a decision made strictly for political reasons. To me, this was a "get the Rangers involved" mission and nothing more.

The next day, Schwarzkopf asked me, "You remember those targets I approved last night? I don't want to strike them." Evidently the Chairman was giving him a hard time. But 24 hours had passed; these missions were planned for tonight. Once the F-117s passed a certain point there was no turning them back.

"I'm not sure I can call them off," I said. "The bombs may already be falling."

"I understand," he said. One of the targets was going to be hit within five minutes of when he made that statement. On two of the others, the F-117s had already passed the point of no return. I probably could have stopped one of the missions, even at that late date. Bottom line, I did not take any action.

The Highway of Death

Now came the first chance to trap and strike fleeing Iraqi forces. Moving faster than anyone expected, the Marines in their sector pushed closer to Kuwait City. Along with VII Corps, the Marines stopped for the night on G-Day, February 24, after their 0400 start. The Iraqi Third Corps commander, General Mahmoud, managed to pull together some resistance. Out of the burning Burqan oilfields on the morning of February 25 came an Iraqi counterattack. The Marines were ready, and they beat back the first attack and a second counterattack with artillery, anti-tank missiles, small arms fire and Cobra helicopters flying in the inky smudge. Later that day, they took Al-Jaber air base, the Kuwait International Airport, and cut the major highway south of Kuwait City. The Iraqis were out of options. JSTARS reports all that day indicated they were starting to retreat in small groups.

Later that evening, McConnell intercepted a communication from the commanders of the 3rd and 5th Corps telling Baghdad they could not fight anymore and must surrender. McConnell's call to me came about 9 PM. "You make sure that the President or SecDef, if they go on TV, they say that retreating combat forces will be attacked," I told McConnell as we finished our conversation. "Because we are going to try to stop or destroy all the Iraqi security and military forces coming out of Kuwait City."

Ninety minutes later Mahmoud began moving out the Iraqi III Corps at around 2230. At 0135 local time on what was now February 26, Radio Baghdad broadcast orders for a retreat from Kuwait.[5]

The initiative was in my hands. Neither the Marines, the Coalition forces, nor VII Corps's forces were in position to encircle and stop the Iraqis. These were the troops who had taken Kuwait by force and then brutalized and murdered Kuwaitis for seven months. I could reach them with air, and I wanted to destroy these units if I could. This was a decision I had made in advance. Those Iraqi security and military cowards were not going to mutilate people in Kuwait and then cut and run when the Marines and the Coalition forces rushed into town. The Iraqis wanted to haul ass back to Basra and then be on television talking about what all they did and didn't do. Horner called them "plunderers." I called them ruthless thugs and killers and I intended to ensure they never had the opportunity to totally disregard human life again.

My first priority was Highway 6. This was the main route almost due north through Safwan toward Basra. Before midnight local time on February 25, JSTARS had reported to the TACC that columns were moving north from Kuwait City. JSTARS moving target indicators made up a detailed picture of the whole retreat with each dot of light representing moving vehicles. Iraqis coming out of Kuwait City first had to head east on the highway for about 35 kilometers. They held a slim buffer around that highway and would hold it through February 27. Then the fleeing

5. *Lucky War: Third Army in Desert Storm*, p. 250.

Iraqis turned north up the highway toward Safwan, just over the Kuwait-Iraq border, another 100 kilometers up the road.

I wanted aircraft moving into those killboxes to destroy everything heading north up that highway. Sudairy's contacts in the Kuwaiti resistance told us that the cars and trucks mixed in with military vehicles headed north contained the Iraqis who'd done the brutal killings in Kuwait. Horner had another input—that there might be Kuwaitis taken as hostages in those vehicles—and he overruled me, instructing aircraft to bomb only armored vehicles on the road. That was a mistake, as later intelligence reports confirmed.

It was up to me to do something. From the TACC, I called Bull Baker, Hornburg's Deputy for Operations, and directed twelve F-15Es to get in the air and check in with JSTARS to be routed to the Iraqi columns they were monitoring.

"I know they've flown six to seven hours already today," I told Bull. "Get them out of bed. No delays. I don't want them to pre-brief. Get their flight suits on and get them in the cockpit. I wanted these convoys stopped and I don't care about the weather. I'll accept responsibility for any losses."

I knew these pilots and their weapon systems officers knew this territory well. They could do it. It was going to be tough on Baker at first, though.

"You put in a memo for the record that you are acting on my direct orders," I told Baker. That way he couldn't be blamed.

But Baker wasn't worried about that. "Sir, if I felt that way, I'd have to take the uniform off," he told me.

A-6s, F/A-18s and AV-8s also worked the killboxes AH6 and AG5 covering Highway 6. I ordered the F-16s to continue to attack for 36 hours straight, flying the crews 18 hours at a stretch. Twenty-four F-16s moved up to KKMC airfield right on the Saudi border so they could "double-turn" and fly a mission, land to take on more bombs and gas, and go right back out.

At Al-Minhad, I swung 12 more F-16s into the fight and waived all crew rest. They'd fly as long as the ceiling was above 2,000 feet. I wasn't putting up with any crap about the weather being too low. The day before I'd chewed out a Guard unit that wanted to cancel its missions because the ceiling was 6,000 feet over their targets.

'*Ground forces will have total support!*' I noted down, and underlined.

Only the F-117s were spared from the double-turn. Besides, Whitley had 42 F-117s now and didn't need to do that.

In 30 minutes at the TACC we were able to change things around. My intent was to destroy everything going north, whatever it took. We succeeded partly. We didn't succeed 100 percent, but we sure stopped them from going up the road. If they wanted to go north they'd have to make their way out in the desert if they could.

Throughout the wee hours and on into the morning of February 26, air power pounded the vehicles on that highway. Later, back at the RSAF headquarters building, we watched President Bush's news conference live on television. I liked the President's message. "Saddam claims he is retreating," Bush said. "He refuses to accept responsibility. Retreating combat forces will be attacked."

"That's right. They're going to be," I said out loud. I can't be sure, but I always thought that maybe McConnell had something to do with the President making that statement.

For February 26, the air component surged 350 sorties to destroy artillery and armored vehicles as the Iraqi forces tried to maneuver. The F-15Es worked Highway 6 and a cluster of Iraqi forces around Tallil. We didn't lose any of them and they stopped or distroyed major elements of the security units leaving Kuwait City. Aircraft flowing into the schedule for Push CAS either hit targets directed by forward air controllers, or diverted to attack Republican Guard forces to the south and west of Basra. I didn't mind stacking up airplanes and having them unable to drop weapons. It was the best way to ensure ground forces wouldn't get in trouble; and I planned to use the extra Push CAS sorties on the back side, across the FSCL, to bomb targets of opportunity like they'd been doing for weeks. The F-16s logged 158 sorties in the killboxes. Including other platforms, the four killboxes along Highway 6 absorbed 309 strike sorties that day, the lion's share of the 574 total we flew in the killbox area.

Fifty-two packages plus 22 B-52 strikes attacked fixed sites. Our rough battle damage count for the day listed 128 tanks, 38 armored personnel carriers, and 401 trucks.[6]

I also wanted to destroy as much as I could of the Republican Guard, and other Iraqi divisions that were just starting to pull out. I took cockpit videotapes of the F-111 and F-15E strikes over to show Schwarzkopf. Later, we had a private discussion after his staff meeting.

6. GWAPS, Volume V, entry for 26 Feb, which cites USCINCCENT Sitrep.

"We need to keep pressure on Saddam in Baghdad," I told him. "CNN needs to continue to report that Baghdad is being attacked." In my view, it would take both internal and external pressure to force Saddam out.

"I agree with you Buster, but Powell is only interested in the war ending," Schwarzkopf said. "He has no interest in more attacks on Baghdad."

I knew not to push it. In essence, whatever we could do that night would be the end of it. Yet we were still fighting the weather.

'Deptula, Glock, Tolin, Lewis, Baptiste, Rogers . . . all showing frustration with the weather,' I wrote in my notes. *'I'm sure my raw edges are also showing.'*

I also wrote: *'As we near day's end, must stay focused.*

- *Saving lives.*
- *Saddam not escaping.*
- *Saddam being ousted.*
- *Long-term threat NBC.'*

These were four things still on my mind. Unless I do something, nothing happens, but I was reminding myself as much as anything that these were the four things to zero in on, and forget all the rest of the stuff.

Several times during the war I'd thought about what to do if it all ended in a few days; now, that ending looked very near. The Iraqis were running. And I was still trying my best to rid the world of Saddam.

The only way we could kill Saddam was if McConnell would provide the information and we could do it quickly and, God bless him, McConnell tried, he was just unable to do it. Sometimes he was just 30 minutes or an hour off when we were attacking things and it was frustrating. Saddam was cagey. Among other things, he had at least two look-a-likes. When he moved, if he was going to move by helicopter himself, he'd have a look-alike moving by car or by military convoy or something else. He was a very paranoid guy, and rightfully so. I wished we could have made him even *more* paranoid.

The fate of Saddam was a huge, black cloud hanging over the operation. I had thought from Day One that no matter how successful we were, if we did not take Saddam out of power, our success would ultimately be questioned. Two things kept gnawing at me throughout the campaign. First and foremost was that Saddam had things and we didn't know where they were and our intelligence was not good enough to be able to give us the information we needed to destroy it.

The second thing was that Saddam would survive this whole thing. Then, our culture being what it is, five years later everybody basically would have forgotten his atrocities and he would be at it again. I had no doubt that a person trying to develop a nuclear weapon, who was right on the verge of it, and had used chemical and biological weapons on the Iranians as well as his own people, if he stayed in power five or 10 years down the road, he would reconstitute and he'd try to do something else again. You had to be totally oblivious to the culture of the region and to human nature to think otherwise, and that was what was so frustrating to me.

The FSCL

My other most intense frustration of Phase IV lay just ahead, although I did not know it yet. My plans to lure the fleeing Iraqis into a cauldron where they could be decimated from the air were about to fall victim to Army coordination problems.

The most difficult period of time in a war is when you're trying to bring it to closure. The position of your forces and your opponent's forces can dictate half the terms of the peace.

Here's what happened. Phase IV went well at the start. XVIII Corps had lead elements at the Euphrates by the end of the day on February 26.[7] VII Corps drew battle with the two Republican Guard divisions we'd hit hardest in the air campaign, the Tawakalna and the Medina, both of which were assessed at 50- to 74-percent strength when the CINC made his decision to start the ground war. VII Corps' 2nd Armored Cavalry Regiment (ACR) overran the lead elements of Tawakalna on February 26. After one fierce, short battle, later named the Battle of 73 Easting, the Tawakalna was finished.

The Battle of 73 Easting in the late afternoon on February 26 showed that even when the Iraqis fought ferociously they were no match for the Army's precision firepower on the ground. The tank battle that obliterated the Tawakalna began as part of VII Corps' deep attack. As VII Corps pushed forward, a sandstorm kicked up in the afternoon. The Tawakalna was waiting but they were surprised to hear the U.S. 2nd Armored Cavalry Regiment advancing out of the sandstorm. Two of the Tawakalna's three brigades, the 9th Armored and the 18th Mechanized, were in

7. *Certain Victory,* p. 302.

bivouac while the 29th Mechanized, off to the northeast, was trying to reposition.

Three troops of the ACR tangled with the 18th Brigade, which had 12 of its 18 tanks still intact after the air war. The M1A1 tanks destroyed Iraqi T-72s at ranges over three kilometers. Precise U.S. counter-battery fire silenced Iraqi artillery. The Tawakalna was a smoking ruin. Captain H.R. McMaster, leading Eagle Troop, reached the line 70 easting, where he was supposed to stop. "We are still in heavy contact, advancing to the 73," McMaster radioed back. "Tell them I'm sorry."[8]

This famous little engagement got the name the Battle of 73 Easting. After the battle was over, aerial reconnaissance would show the Iraqis left over 200 destroyed armored vehicles. That's what precision forces—air or ground—could do.

Elsewhere that day, the intense fighting in VII Corps area lasted several hours. The order to withdraw was already out. By fighting hard, the Tawakalna and Medina "essentially bought the rest of the Iraqi army one more day," a CIA report said later.

The combination of massive front-line collapse, followed by the delaying action, upset the Coalition's timetable. Here's where the fog of war closed in and caused all of us to miss the chance to destroy the Republican Guard.

The retreat seemed to sweep the Iraqis into a narrow area around Basra. In fact, although bruised and bloodied by the ground forces, they were doing their best to get into a defensive line. While we didn't fully comprehend it at the time, the Republican Guard was moving into a coordinated defensive screen to protect each other and their escape routes. To the northwest, the Hammurabi pulled out behind the Medina and got in position as a swing force while the two best remaining infantry divisions moved *westward* to prepared bulwarks. Saddam wanted his Republican Guard to make it across the border. XVIII Corps and VII Corps were moving fast but they were still well south and west of the turn points to drive east and cut off an Iraqi retreat. All the roads north to Baghdad remained in Iraqi hands.

It put Schwarzkopf's major objective—destroying the Republican Guard—in peril. Schwarzkopf's left hook ground attack strategy was about to come up short, as shown in Figure 8.

8. *The Generals' War*, p. 391.

FSCL Movements as of 1800L

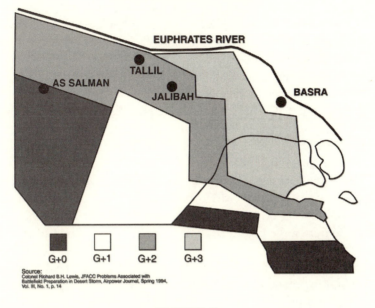

FIGURE 9

Just as the ground units should have been closing with the Iraqis, our strike sortie count was dropping. When the Republican Guard started to move into its defensive posture, it gave us a huge opportunity to truly finish them off as an effective fighting force and as an instrument of power for Saddam to use to keep himself in power.

The Army screwed it up by moving the FSCL prematurely.

When I came in on February 27, Lewis was waiting.

"They've moved the FSCL north of the river," he said.

"Oh bullshit," I retorted. "That can't be right."

"Yes, sir, they have," he said.

Before the ground war, we'd set up a series of preplanned Fire Support Coordination Lines (FSCL) based on what the Army thought their pro- jected rate of movement would be, as shown in Figure 9. It was logical—at least starting out, we all knew what we were going to do with the FSCL in- stead of just randomly placing it to suit somebody's whim. Since the Army had moved so fast they'd activated FSCLs far out of their positions—just at the point when they'd slowed down. Major General Barry McCaffrey in 24th Division ran out of fuel and had to stop for several hours. Franks needed to regroup, too. Now the FSCLs were way too far out.

I went immediately to the ops center.

"Where is the FSCL?" I demanded.

"North of the river," someone said.

I called up B.B. Bell. "You tell the CINC that the FSCL must be moved back or I can't guarantee people aren't going to be able to escape across the river," I said.

"I'll take care of it," Bell said.

For whatever reason, the FSCL was moved out beyond Highway 8 and north of the Euphrates River. Somebody at XVIII Corps had moved it even before they got near Jalibah Airfield to turn east. They'd moved it sometime during the night of February 26. VII Corps' line had moved, too.

I'd always figured either ground or air forces could hit the Republican Guard. But in practical terms, the ground forces had to make contact to engage, and at the same time, circle behind to cut off the escape route. With air, we could hit deeper elements at will under direction of the Killer Scouts or flight leads; and hit forces up close, as long as ground or airborne FACs with the army units directed the strike aircraft into their targets. Now all my sorties that weren't needed in the Push CAS were blocked off from the most lucrative target areas because of that FSCL being in the wrong place. *'We cannot destroy the armor being abandoned by Iraqis,'* I noted.

It was 17 hours before Horner, who went to battle for it, got the line moved.

With the XVIII Corps FSCL pushed out in front, the control of the battlefield shifted. The FSCL—intended as a safety and coordination line—was now like a boundary marker. For the first day the FSCL moved in small, pre-arranged increments and kept pace with the breaching actions and positioning for the main thrust. But after the attack started in earnest on February 25, the two corps in the west moved so rapidly that two things happened. XVIII Corps lead elements got to the Euphrates. In VII Corps, the 1st Armored covered a stunning 144 kilometers in 16 hours. They sent their Apaches deep to work the next objectives and for that they decided they needed a big maneuver space and that meant pushing the FSCL way out.

Each of the four corps had its own FSCL (although the FSCL for the Egyptian Corps was set by VII Corps.) We'd been working an arrangement where we placed the "Horner Line" 30 nautical miles in front of the FSCL. FACs controlled air inside the FSCL. Our Killer Scouts worked the zone between the FSCL and the Horner Line. Beyond the Horner Line we flew air interdiction using the killbox system.

The Marines and the Egyptian Corps moved their FSCLs in measured increments tied to their ground movement. The FSCL in their sectors advanced mainly northward, as they did. But XVIII and VII Corps had a different idea. They put their FSCLs out far in front of their actual movement. It covered where they intended to end up, and left them room to use their AH-64 Apaches to strike the Iraqis, or as a blocking force.

What made me call Schwarzkopf on February 27 was that the FSCL had been staked out about 140 kilometers in front of XVIII Corps' position. The direction of advance was turning east with the XVIII Corps boundary essentially on top of VII Corps boundary line. Divisions from both corps were stacked up facing east from the British 1st Armored above Wadi al Batin, parallel to Kuwait City, to the U.S. 101st Airborne, barely below Tallil Airfield, about 175 kilometers north. Still the FSCLs for the two corps were pushed in front of that line. The XVIII Corps sector was out beyond an objective they called EA Thomas, a box north of Basra. At the time this was about 140 kilometers in front of their positions.[9]

Picture this as a box about 17,000 square kilometers.[10]

Inside that box are five Republican Guard divisions and anything that could still move from the Tawakalna.

Because of the FSCL locations, every sortie inside that area needed FAC control. Unfortunately, the FSCL was so far forward of XVIII and VII Corps actual troops that there weren't even any FACs in most of the area, because the troops hadn't gotten there yet, and the FACs stayed with the troops.

XVIII Corps had its reasons and one was so they could push attack helicopters out to deep attack EA Thomas, which they did mid-afternoon on February 27. They set up Forward Operating Base Viper complete with fuel and supplies and sent four battalions of Apaches out to hunt the Republican Guard on roads north of Basra, 145 kilometers away.

9. *Lucky War: Third Army in Desert Storm*, p. 253.
10. Ibid., p. 253.

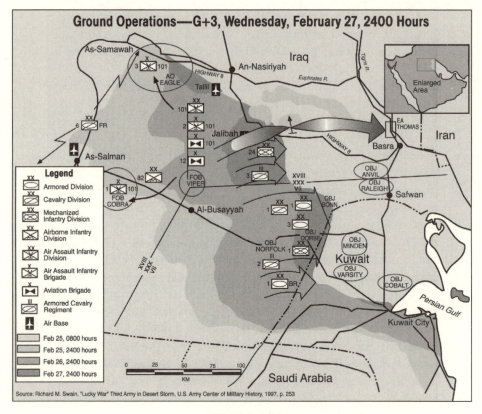

FIGURE 10

Apaches could be devastating against tanks—but in four hours of operations, they didn't see a single tank in EA Thomas.[11]

The Iraqis weren't there yet. They were still to the south in that 17,000 square kilometer area where I couldn't fly my F-111s, F-15Es, or my prime CAS assets like the A-10s and F-16s, because the FACs weren't calling us in. The Iraqi forces we needed to hit were in between XVIII Corps' ground forces and where they'd sent the Apaches.

We could have told them the Apaches would find it target-poor up there. We'd already attacked everything we saw on those roads north of the Euphrates.

This wouldn't have mattered as much if the ground units were close in with the Iraqis, but they weren't yet, as shown in Figure 10. On the

11. *Certain Victory*, p. 305.

ground, the 24th Infantry was just leaving Tallil and Jalibah on the afternoon of February 27. They went fast and rolled up part of the Nebuchadnezzar division, but stopped around Phase Line Knife at 1800 on the 27th. VII Corps steamrollered the Medina in another firefight that began about 1130 on February 27, the Battle of Medina Ridge.[12] Here they did call for CAS and the A-10s and F-16s got into the fray. But for the most part, our Coalition air power was wasted that day.

Moving the FSCL out so far beyond their line of advance was a disaster for us. We allocated 1,200 sorties to support the ground forces operations directly. That was 50 sorties an hour. The flight leads got airborne, then checked in with ABCCC, the airborne control point. If a FAC wanted air he called ABCCC, they looked at flights available, threats in the area, and so forth, and handed the aircraft off to the FAC. If there were no FAC requests when the flight checked in, ABCCC relayed them to the Killer Scouts, out beyond the FSCL; then if the Killer Scouts had no targets for them, it was up to the flight lead to go on out farther and either find a target or head to the day's dump target to release bombs and go home. It was a great, flexible system: The army could use all 1,200 sorties for CAS if they wanted, or we could swing them off to targets of opportunity. But only if their FACs were in contact with the Iraqis. Now essentially the FSCL was marking out a zone for the Apaches to fly over. It was a disgrace this happened in Desert Storm. If it ever happens again someone should be held criminally accountable.

Meanwhile, on the ground, while the Medina division tangled with our 1st Armored Division, the Hammurabi sped up their retreat. Incidentally, they were moving across our corps boundary. XVIII Corps' 24th Infantry still had to fight its way past clusters of Iraqi soldiers and was unable to close fast enough to cut off the escape route to Basra as planned. A study after the war put it just right: "The Hammurabi appears to have used the Battle of Medina Ridge as a rearguard action to escape to the northeast in the direction of Basra." (Lieutenant Colonel William F. Andrews wrote the study—he also became the last U.S. POW, and the only one I didn't accidentally bomb, when he ejected from his F-16 on February 27 and was taken prisoner by the Republican Guard.)[13]

12. *Certain Victory,* p. 293 and 306.

13. William F. Andrews, *Air Power Against an Army: Challenge and Response in CENTAF's Duel with the Republican Guard,* (Maxwell AFB, AL: AU Press CADRE Papers, 1998), 64–66.

The bottom line was that all that day we couldn't attack the most lucrative areas because of where XVIII and VII Corps placed the FSCL. So our strike count plummeted. On Days One and Two of the ground war, even with bad weather, we'd logged 697 and 649 strike sorties respectively in the KTO killboxes. On Day Three, it was just 574 strikes, concentrating on Highway 6 out of Kuwait. For Day Four, February 27, the count was just 210 strike sorties in the killboxes, the lowest total of the whole war.[14]

It just didn't work if our FACs weren't in the same area where the Iraqis were—and if we'd pushed the Killer Scouts so far north they couldn't cover the target areas. Four Republican Guard divisions were now piled inside the XVIII Corps and VII Corps FSCLs below Highway 8. By the night of February 27, the three fleeing infantry divisions and remnants of the three heavy divisions were essentially trapped in this "Basra pocket" waiting to get across the causeway to the other side of the Euphrates.

It was absolutely unforgivable. We could have destroyed them all with air. Instead, our Killer Scouts were north of the Euphrates looking at sand and empty highways. There were a few key lines of communication, and we attacked them, but the Republican Guard was in a sanctuary to the south.

Ending the War

Time was running out on that strategic objective. McConnell and I talked mid-afternoon Riyadh time on February 27.

"The war will probably end within the next 12 hours," he told me.

It seemed that Powell was the main driver; he was afraid of the public reaction to the slaughter of Iraqi forces. *'The CINC is correct: "Chairman does not have backbone for war." We're killing the people that brutalized Kuwaiti men, women and children for six months. Yet chairman is concerned about public backlash. He grossly underestimates the American people.'*

McConnell's tip was right. While we were struggling with the FSCL and areas out to the west, television crews were in Kuwait filming the destruction we'd caused on Highway 6, which quickly got the nickname the "Highway of Death." Vehicles were piled everywhere. Many were trucks,

14. GWAPS, Vol. V, p. 467.

cars and buses looted from Kuwait by fleeing Iraqi soldiers and then abandoned. In fact there was an intelligence photo showing dozens of tracks of footprints in the sand where Iraqis had fled from the roads.

The media coverage was having a negative effect. Powell had called Schwarzkopf about four in the afternoon Riyadh time—first thing in the morning in Washington, DC. The night before, the Kuwait Highway of Death was all over the television. Powell told Schwarzkopf he "sensed we were nearing endgame" and that he, Powell, "would have to give the President and the Secretary a recommendation soon as to when we could stop" because the television coverage now looked like "slaughter for slaughter's sake."[15]

Schwarzkopf was pleased with the way the war was going so far. He was "confident this war was going to end very soon" but he realized that until "we'd destroyed the Republican Guard forces, our job was only half done." On that score, he wrote in his memoirs that he'd asked Yeosock on the 27th how much longer it would take to finish off the Republican Guard. Yeosock told Schwarzkopf one more day: "They'll be done for by tomorrow night," was how Schwarzkopf recalled Yeosock phrased it.[16]

That was Schwarzkopf's state of mind when Powell called him. When Powell said they ought to start talking about a cease-fire, Schwarzkopf first asked, "What do you mean?" He was initially livid that Powell was in a hurry to get him to cease hostilities. I know this because I was sitting beside him when the call came in.

To Schwarzkopf, the Highway of Death was one of the miseries of war. Also, he knew it was a pile of looted vehicles, not Iraqi bodies. It "irritated" him that Washington was glued to the TV re-running footage of the Highway of Death and he said he thought to himself "the best thing the White House could do would be to turn off the damned TV in the situation room." But he didn't say this to Powell, and by the end of the conversation, they'd sold themselves on stopping in time to call Desert Storm the Five-Day War.

That night, at the staff meeting, the change was in the air. Schwarzkopf was very focused on his upcoming press conference and he was in a victory mood. He started talking about the war being four to five days long, or 100 hours. "That's less than the Israelis," he said, referring to their famous Six-Day War.

---

15. Colin L. Powell, *My American Journey* (New York: Random House, 1995), p. 505.
16. *It Doesn't Take a Hero*, pp. 465–67 for all quotes.

What was irritating to me was counting the days as though the air war had never taken place.

As soon as I got back from the meeting, I telephoned Whitley, Hornburg, and Lennon, in turn. "For your ears only," I told each of them. "Keep focus. Tonight may be the last night." I wanted them to know I didn't want them to risk losing anybody else at this late date. I didn't call the other units because they were still supporting the ground forces, so I didn't want them backing off any.

With that done, I tuned in for Schwarzkopf's famous press conference, later dubbed "the mother of all briefings." Schwarzkopf gave a masterly show as a Coalition commander with the dust of battle still on him but the scent of victory in the air. But something had changed. He started off well, talking about how waging an "extensive air campaign" got the force ratios right for the ground attack. But I could see now he was completely captured by the majesty of tanks moving across the desert. It disturbed me greatly.

Of the conference, I wrote: *'Overall very effective But . . . Attempting to rewrite history before it's printed. Why not be candid, 100% truthful with the American people? Their sons and daughter's lives were at risk. The ground campaign has been remarkably fought. The leadership, the weapons, the people, speed was historical. The air campaign impact on Iraqi infrastructure, telephone, bridges, railroad, C3, NBC, tanks, artillery, supply was massive. We had thousands of desertions during the air campaign that continued during the ground war. The Iraqi soldier's will to fight was missing.'*

His statement about air being very effective initially, and less so in recent weeks, really burned me. I vented in my diary. The facts were *'air destroyed over a thousand tanks. 90% of the ground C3, 500+ tubes of artillery during the last week. The troublesome point is he was aware of the air impact. We planned and strategized together the timely destruction of the command and control, artillery feed junctions and oil trenches. Therefore his comments were intentional.'*

The truth was, his remarks hurt and all the more so because I felt a special relationship with Schwarzkopf. That added to my disappointment that night. I'd never seen this side of him, or if I had, I'd ignored it. It hurt personally, but it hurt still more for the people that had done all of the flying, putting their lives into harm's way. It was the first time I ever really got irritated at the CINC because I didn't think he was being even-handed. What about all of those fighter pilots that flew all of those sorties and risked their lives on a daily basis for the last five weeks?

Although we had very few casualties. It just was not fair to their families to portray the air war the way he did that night.

Shortly after the press conference ended, McConnell called me.

"I would think you had trouble with the CINC's press conference," he said gingerly.

"You're correct about that," I said. "The size of the Army accomplishments got in the way of truth. You and I must make sure history is correctly written." McConnell listened to me a little more while I blew off steam.

But the real problem, as it turned out, was that the ground picture of the battle was not clear enough to indicate that it was still too soon to stop. The Iraqi forces were only partially encircled. Both Corps were regrouping for another push and, due to a chain of events driven by Powell and the ground commanders weren't going to get the chance to finish the job by cutting the Iraqis off before they escaped across the Euphrates.

While Schwarzkopf was giving his press conference in Riyadh, the timetable in Washington was moving even faster. Powell and Cheney met with Bush at the White House at about 2 p.m. Washington time (near midnight in Riyadh). Powell told him that the forces "had a specific objective, authorized by the UN, to liberate Kuwait, and we had achieved it."

Here's what Powell said in his memoirs that he told Bush:

"We don't want to be seen as killing for the sake of killing, Mr. President . . . We're within the window of success. I've talked to General Schwarzkopf. I expect by sometime tomorrow the job will be done, and I'll probably be bringing you a recommendation to stop the fighting." According to Powell, Bush surprised him by asking, "Why not end it today?"[17]

Powell called Schwarzkopf, who was just back from his press conference. Powell said to him, "I'm at the White House. We've been batting around your idea about ending the war at five days. The President is thinking about going on the air tonight at nine o'clock and announcing we're cutting it off. Would you have any problem with that?"

According to Schwarzkopf, he thought about it, especially the risk of getting a few more Coalition soldiers killed. He replied: "I don't have any problem with it . . . Our objective was the destruction of the enemy forces, and for all intents and purposes we've accomplished that objec-

17. *My American Journey*, p. 507.

tive. I'll check with my commanders, but unless they've hit some snag I don't know about, we can stop."[18]

By the time he got off the phone, Schwarzkopf had six hours and twenty-five minutes to stop Operation Desert Storm although Washington later gave him three more hours so it would be a 100-hour war.

At the time, what I heard was from McConnell. "The President's addressing the nation tonight," McConnell said. Unless there was a last-minute glitch, the plan was for Bush to announce the war was ending at 0500 local time on February 28—or midnight, Washington time.

It just didn't make sense to me. In my diary, I wrote: *'It appears the President's military advice is lacking . . . end game picture being portrayed is not accurate . . . Chairman misleading the President . . . history will judge.'*

Based on what McConnell was telling me, I could tell that Powell was painting a picture that was not totally accurate about what had been destroyed, what was locked in, what was not locked out. He was talking about everything south of the Euphrates River as either destroyed or under our control, and that was simply false. With this inaccurate report to the President, Powell initiated a chain reaction that resulted in a premature end to the war. Referring to the Republican Guard, Powell had told the American people, "First, we are going to cut it off, then we are going to kill it,"[19] It sounded tough on television. Where was that toughness now?

Powell's promise was turning into empty rhetoric and the significance can't be overstated. The Republican Guard waited for the cease-fire and then moved to safety across the Euphrates River where Saddam immediately used it to crush a rebellion against his regime in Basra.

Just as the FSCL placement deflated the air campaign for 17 precious hours, deciding to end the war at 100 hours pulled the rug out from under the ground attack. If Powell had not been in such a hurry, he'd have received a whole different picture within a few hours of where the war really stood.

Look at the reports later from different commanders—Waller, Peay, McCaffrey, Franks, and just about anybody who was asked about it—and you'll see that everyone was stunned that the war was going to end right then. We didn't want it to drag on needlessly. But all the immediate tactical commanders still had a mass of Iraqi forces right in front of their

18. *It Doesn't Take a Hero*, pp. 468–470.
19. Department of Defense news briefing, January 23, 1991.

faces. None of us thought we'd cut off and destroyed the Republican Guard. We were all planning engagements—on the ground or in the air—for the next day.

Here was the real situation.

For February 28, XVIII Corps' 24th Infantry was scheduled to resume its advance at 0400 and move southeast, along the Euphrates River valley, to attack and block off the Hammurabi Division. In their path was a newly formed defensive line with positions for two infantry divisions. The Nebuchadnezzar and the Adnan manned the line with perhaps two brigades from the Hammurabi behind them in support. The 24th Division's target was Objective Anvil, an area slightly southwest of where Highway 8 merged with Highway 6, and incidentally, the area where RGFC Adnan Infantry division had been when the ground war started. The Iraqis' new line was about 35 kilometers west—in front of—Objective Anvil. Given the pace they'd maintained, XVIII Corps would have had a big, successful battle probably on the afternoon of February 28 when they hit that line.

Indeed, while Bush was in Washington addressing the nation (and the world) XVIII Corps was trying to get its offensive restarted. They fired artillery barrages all night. U-2 photographs interpreted by the CIA later showed the pockmarked battlefield. They also launched attack helicopters in the early morning, but were still short of Objective Anvil at 0800 when the cease-fire took effect, though in the confusion, CENTCOM initially thought they were in possession of Objective Anvil.[20] The two infantry divisions and supporting Hammurabi elements were still lined up there.

A little to the south, VII Corps was gearing up for its chance to finish off the Republican Guard. From the VII Corps' point of view, the day's moves by XVIII Corps would finally fix the Hammurabi in place while VII Corps moved up to close with and destroy them. Franks had his division commanders in VII Corps hold their positions at 1800 on February 27 so they could regroup and prepare for the next phase the following morning. One option considered was for the 1st Armored Division to attack north toward Basra at 0500.[21] However, with warning about the cease-fire, "VII Corps ground forces were effectively stopped in place by 0130 on the 28th," according to an official Army history.

20. *Lucky War: Third Army in Desert Storm*, p. 289.
21. Ibid, p. 282.

So both corps were at least a day short of their objectives. We'd never planned to go farther up into Iraq or to fight around the city of Basra. The Republican Guard infantry divisions, or pieces of it, were mixed in there somewhere. Kuwait was liberated, the Republican Guard was in a tough spot, and they weren't mounting any more attempts at resistance. The Republican Guard was defeated but not encircled or destroyed. It got very easy to identify the Guardsmen a few days later when they started moving north again after the cease-fire. No one on our side had thought to tell the Iraqis that all forces must freeze in place as a condition of the cease-fire.

Getting the Planes Down

It was now just after midnight, in Riyadh—the last day of the war. As the clock advanced, I wrote in my diary, *'appears to be the last day of War—thank you, God.'*

I had a lot to do to get the airplanes down. B.B. Bell called from Schwarzkopf's headquarters.

"Do you have anything scheduled to happen after five o'clock local?" he asked.

"I do, but I'll cancel it," I told him.

What I really did was I backed it off to 0300 because I wanted everybody safely across the border before 0500. I told Tolin to call all my wing commanders with the orders. Not long after B.B. called, McConnell and Downing also checked in with me to make sure I had the stop order. Horner confirmed it. No bombing after 0500 local time, February 28— just a few hours away.

We still had a few major strikes that night. Ten F-117s hit the Ba'ath Party facilities in a wave. We also had two F-111s, Cardinal 71 and Cardinal 72, drop one GBU-28 on the hardened sector operations center at Taji Airfield. The GBU-28 was special 4,700-pound bomb developed and delivered to theater in less than 30 days for use on a deeply buried target. Once again the F-111s came up with an innovative stroke. The bomb penetrated for seven seconds before they saw a wisp of smoke come out of the air conditioning vent of the demolished bunker.

We watched President Bush announcing the war would end in three hours—0800 Riyadh time. I went down to the TACC to make certain everything stopped. My number-one priority now was to get everyone on the ground with no last-minute losses.

Tolin attended Horner's 0700 final staff meeting. He told me afterward it was a tour de force. Horner said to them, "You should have tremendous pride in your service, tremendous pride in your country, tremendous pride in mankind. We did what God wanted us to do. We really were magnificent. The world has never seen anything like it! *Thank you.*"

I felt a tremendous weight lift from my shoulders the morning of February 28. You always know that you're going to have loss of life, and loss of life troubles me. But now it was over and I was so grateful.

I went back to my quarters briefly to take a shower. It was near the end of the typical "day" for me but no way was I going to sleep.

Back at the RSAF Headquarters, I made a few more notes. *'Concerns . . . slightly premature ending . . . too much unmanned armor not destroyed . . . Saddam lives to threaten the World again . . . conditions of cease-fire not strong enough . . . too much wiggle room for Saddam.'*

Still, I felt that morning that we had been remarkably successful. We had done basically everything that I wanted to do—that I had the authority to do. We had revolutionized the way wars would be fought in the future. As for the failures or the shortcomings, I was really burdened by the fact that Saddam was still in power. I was really burdened by what NBC capabilities he might still have because of intelligence failures. The lack of human intelligence was so glaring during the Gulf War. But I also was very pleased at the success we enjoyed. I felt that we had been very, very successful in what we'd been asked to do. Certainly we had done everything that the President asked us to do. I was feeling relief that the war was over, satisfaction that it had been a low loss of life but with a realization that we certainly weren't anywhere close to a perfect ending.

I called my wing commanders in turn to thank them. I'd be out in a couple of days to visit and thank the aircrews personally. "Our nation is in your debt," I told each of them.

McConnell checked in to let me know everything was still on track. Lennon called up to crow about his F-111s, with justification. In 2,540 sorties, with 1,886 getting to targets, they'd recorded 2,189 hits through their VTR systems on everything from bridges to tanks to the oil manifold to the Taji bunker. Just one example of what we'd accomplished.

My primary thought I jotted down earlier in the day, and it still overrides everything else. I wrote: *'It is over . . . Thank You God for saving so many lives . . . thank you for guiding our every thought and action.'*

CONCLUSION / ENDING / CRITICAL LESSONS / FINAL THOUGHTS

By March 1, everyone was in the mood to go home. Still, we had a few more taskings. Schwarzkopf requested F-15s and F-111s over Baghdad to make sure Baghdad understood we could return very quickly if conditions of the cease-fire were violated. In response, Lennon pushed one flight of two aircraft to go supersonic over Iraq's capital city.

Over the next few days I visited all the 14th Air Division units. I wanted to thank them for putting "service before self" and for their professionalism across the board.

Here's what I told the aircrews:

"You have waged the most successful air campaign in the history of warfare, with unbelievable results. You saved thousands of lives.

"The nation is waiting to show you how much they appreciate what you have accomplished. Be appreciative, but humble. Remember also, our families paid the greatest price, not you and I. Make sure your families are included in the celebrations. Remember, family, family, family. The war is over!

"We fought aggressively, but while caring more about saving lives than most thought wise. We were willing to take risks, more than some thought safe.

"But at day's end, we expected and accomplished more than many thought possible.

"You made it happen. Our nation's thanks to you. God speed."

It was great to see the fighter pilots. Their eyes were tired, but clear. Their pride was tempered with humility. Several of them told me they were concerned that Saddam still remained in power. Their most immediate desire, of course, was to go home. *'God, I love them like Family,'* I wrote in my diary after the visits on March 4. *'Be with each and every one and keep them safe!'*

On March 6, I talked with McConnell about the firefight between McCaffrey's 24th Division and the Iraqi forces still below the causeway in Basra. He and I agreed there was too much attention on celebrating and too little to what was happening in Iraq.

"We need to write a book someday," he joked.

"That's right," I said. "You and I are the only two people who could tell the whole story."

As for Schwarzkopf, he seemed a changed man now that the war was over. We all were since we were free of the tension. He had some very sobering, kind words for me.

"You made this victory possible," Schwarzkopf said. "Our nation is in your debt. It is impossible for you to get enough credit."

He wanted to know what the Air Force had in mind for me. I told him my next assignment would be as the Director of Legislative Affairs on the Air Staff—the primary contact point with Congress.

"Why don't they work you toward being Horner's replacement?" Schwarzkopf asked. Great idea, I thought, but I'd need a couple more promotions first. But it is always special when you are referred to as a commander or a warfighter. I appreciated the CINC's comments.

For now, I wanted to go home, too. Horner thought Schwarzkopf would never approve it, but he did. My plane would leave on March 13.

Before then I wanted to produce our lessons learned; at least a short, immediate look so we wouldn't forget. Top of the list, of course, was that the JFACC concept worked. It was the only way for air power to realize its total potential. Without it, you do not have an overall strategy and plan to support CINC objectives. You will just service targets and support land or sea operations, and ultimately waste billions of dollars buying weapon systems you don't need, while risking American sons and daughters in combat. That was the bottom line.

Tolin and Deptula took on the task of putting together the lessons learned. While they got started, I arranged an F-15E flight for myself over

Kuwait and Iraq. Since Schwarzkopf would not permit me to fly in the war, I desperately wanted a look at the battlefield. With an instructor pilot in the back seat, I took off from Al Kharj for a memorable flight. Oil fields were burning. We had to fly below 100 feet to get under the billowing smoke. Highway 6 north from Kuwait City to Iraq was a disaster area. Up north, at Tallil, the damage was incredible. Intelligence had really underestimated what we'd done.

From Tallil I turned and followed the river north toward Baghdad. There was no widespread destruction. This wasn't devastated Germany in the spring of 1945. We'd hit only selected facilities, and hit them hard, but we'd caused Iraq, as a nation, no lasting damage. *'God, I thank you for low casualties on both sides,'* I wrote later.

Back from my flight, I entered some "lessons learned" notes on March 9. It was right to attack the centers of gravity, and to base the war plan around the precision of the F-117, F-15E and F-111. The F-117 was a home run. The mistake though, was to split the campaign in four phases. There were really only two phases: the strategic air campaign and the tactical support of the land campaign. Instead of finishing Phase I, we'd worked it right up to the last day.

As for the battlefield prep and air support during the ground offensive, the A-10 was the workhorse. Enemy prisoners of war stated it was the most feared aircraft of the war. They called it the "Black Jet." Wherever it pointed its nose, death and destruction were soon to follow. B-52s had a tremendous psychological impact on the Iraqi troops, as did the constant attacks by F-16s and Killer Scouts. Although the Army only counted tanks, APCs and artillery for their BDA, the sheer number of other military supply vehicles destroyed led to critical shortages throughout the KTO. The fighting force that invaded Iraq was not the same as the one facing our troops on the eve of the ground campaign.

Special operations forces provided key support. The biggest challenge was ensuring their operations were integrated and supported properly throughout the campaign.

Our successes were also directly attributable to the airborne command and control resources that allowed us to execute over 2,000 sorties a day. AWACS, JSTARS, ABCCC, Rivet Joint, TR-1 and tankers were the backbone of the operations. They gave us the real-time capability to divert fighters and bombers to where they were needed most.

There were a few other issues with the planning. I could not forget, of course, how weak our tanker planning was because we hadn't paid enough attention to its complexity. My planning staff was undermanned by 50 percent when the war started. On the other hand, involving the wings in the planning worked out great.

With proper intelligence, we'd seen the problems during the planning but could not correct them without moving McConnell to Saudi Arabia, which was not an option. Relying on Band-Aid intelligence solutions really hurt us during the execution phase. We'd used too many stubby pencils instead of making the most of available computer technology. Likewise, we didn't have enough effort in advance on quick reaction alerts for Phases I, II, and III. Not enough emphasis on tracking success and failures during the execution, so we could restrike more quickly. All our Phase IV support was planned around fluid reactions but we needed that before ground troops engaged, too.

Weather. Not enough back-up options. Who could forget January 19 and 20 with 188 and 177 weather aborts respectively.[1] Certainly I had not put enough emphasis on getting the senior leadership—from Schwarzkopf to Bush—to understand the impact of weather on the pace of the campaign. As a result, we'd set expectations too high and could not deliver the quick results when weather closed in.

Weather, of course, hurt us most on strategic targets such as the all-important NBC set. All together, we'd flown 969 strikes against NBC targets and had done a lot of damage. But the technical information and location intelligence was not available to facilitate optimum planning. It made "prudent risk" tough to define. Eventually, as the UN weapons inspectors did their work in Iraq over the next several years, they discovered weapons production and storage sites we hadn't even known about during Desert Storm. The Scud hunt was a similar story: 1,459 strikes and not enough intelligence to plan effectively.[2]

I also wished we'd had an airman at the Safwan negotiations to point out that the Iraqis should not be allowed to fly their helicopters. We were just getting the first reports that they were using them to suppress rebellions against Saddam.

Overall, as I wrote these notes, I rated the strategy as outstanding, planning as excellent, and execution as good—definitely a lower grade.

1. GWAPS, 389.
2. GWAPS, Vol. 5, 418.

'All three could and should be improved,' I noted. However my number-one message for the next person who'd plan and execute an offensive air campaign was this: We won, we focused on very low casualties, we delivered very low casualties, and again, we won!

There was no doubt in my mind, however, that air power's future was bright. Stealth was a must. Speed, an ever-present virtue. Standoff weapons were needed, more of them, new types, with penetration capability. We also needed three-meter accuracy in all weather. I wanted the next director of campaign plans to be able to target in a fog bank if he had to. Combine all that, stick with the JFACC concept, and air power would be as it was in Desert Storm, the most oft-used and decisive force in our military arsenal.

On March 12, I went to say goodbye to Schwarzkopf. It started with light conversation. Then, as we attempted to say goodbye, the talk stopped and tears suddenly filled both our eyes. We knew we had been called by our country to help in a time of need, and we'd been phenomenally successful. We both knew we would never be the same again, and that others would never totally understand. We recognized we were two of the most fortunate people on the face of the earth. He looked at my face and I looked at his. But we spoke not one word as we parted.

By March 13, the heroes who got all the publicity were on their way home but I had some unsung heroes I needed to take care of. Tolin and I wrote letters of commendation for all our Black Hole officers, so their commanders would know how well they'd done. The letters went out March 13. Many also received Bronze Stars and other decorations for their service.

March 13, 1991, was my final diary entry. The diary now filled three 80-page blue spiral notebooks plus a 100-page, hardbound, green record book. The last entry read: *'The war is over . . . we won! I pray for the families that lost loved ones . . . it is now history . . . let the historians sort it out . . . thank you God for your guiding hand!'*

Ending

For air power, the Gulf War was a turning point. Bush said it best during a speech at the U.S. Air Force Academy in June 1991: *"Gulf War lesson number one was the value of air power."*

Part of the reason was that the Gulf pointed out the value of precision *to the Air Force.* Precision technology—both laser-guided bombs and autonomous guidance—wasn't really anything new in 1991. We just did not have much of it spread through the force. We were lucky to have what we did. For example, the sensor-fused weapon was a concept I worked on when I was the squadron commander at the fighter weapons school in the 1980s. There I was, in the Gulf in the year 1990 as a general officer running the air campaign, and the Air Force still did not have that weapon fielded.

It was criminal. A sensor-fused weapon would have been just ideal for the masses of Iraqi tanks. But then, I had to fight hard to build the strategic campaign around the F-117. We all had to scramble to roll the F-111s and F-15Es into tank-plinking.

So the one thing the Gulf war did: the tank-plinking made everybody understand the importance of precise delivery of weapons for hitting a fielded enemy army. In other words, it showed that air power could very methodically and rapidly decimate a ground force if it had the accuracy on fairly small and conventional weapons.

This was a significant turning point. Nobody had ever looked at it from that standpoint before. They always looked at air power taking away the capability of an enemy army by destroying the logistics base of the division, interdicting them and impeding their ability to move in daylight, cutting off the supplies and all that crap. This is good, it's necessary, but nobody had ever looked at actually destroying the division itself and halting its maneuver in short order. At night. As proven at Khafji.

So once we did that, it became obvious to everybody how important having one- to three-meter accuracy was. And we needed it in all types of weather.

When the war was over, Secretary Cheney asked me, "What is the one thing that you believe from a technology standpoint that we should be working on the hardest?"

I said, "Be able to drop a conventional weapon of at least 500 pounds with one meter accuracy in any kind of weather." And that's true. I really believe it. JDAM became that weapon. Kosovo, Afghanistan and other operations have proven that in spades. By the end of the 1990s, the Air Force had gone through a precision revolution (with the Navy and Marines in the act, too.) They had far more precision-capable aircraft than I did. In fact, they retired the F-111s and A-6s and put precision on the newer fighters, including the F-16. What a change.

Notwithstanding all the good work in technology and tactics, we in the Air Force shortchanged ourselves. We did not completely document the innovations of the Gulf War and teach those lessons to our younger officers. I'm as responsible as anyone for letting that opportunity slip by. As a result, we've had to live with the consequences of people actually debating whether air power could be a decisive force. That stance got even more difficult after Kosovo, where NATO ground forces were not involved. And it sure is more difficult to say after Afghanistan, when air power enabled the Northern Alliance to make breakthroughs in a few weeks that they had not made in a few years. The public sees it straight. Air power dominates our joint military operations.

Yet airmen didn't do anything in Kosovo or Afghanistan that we didn't do, in some form, in the Gulf war. We should have insisted that joint warfighting doctrine takes that on board, studies it, embraces it, and improves on it. The Coalition air campaign—and the effect air power, properly executed, can have on armies and nation-states—that is the true operational lesson of Desert Storm.

Critical Lessons

I consider the Gulf War to be the base line of modern warfare. All objectives were achieved with minimum loss of life. The Gulf War was not a paradigm, because technology is always improving and lessons learned should assist future planning. Simply put, in war, strategy must evolve with technology and the repetition of historical errors is unacceptable.

War changes with technology. But war also has an enduring nature, for it reflects our own human nature. That's why its worth the time of the next generation of young warriors to study what we did in the past, both right and wrong.

Early on, I got into the habit of studying the great airmen of the past and their successes and failures; men such as General Billy Mitchell, Air Marshall Hugh Trenchard, General "Tooey" Spaatz, General Pete Quesada, General George Kenney, and General Bill Kirk. The Gulf War, like all other past wars, provided successes and failures that should not be ignored.

Here are my Gulf War critical lessons, with the hope that they may be useful to a combat commander in our Nation's future:

1. **Winning—there is no substitute; minimum loss of life—there is no compromise.**

2. Support of the American people must always be a prerequisite for any war.

3. The most important decision during a war is how and when to end it.

4. Professional relationships between the CINC and his component commanders will decide if the best strategies and tactics see the light of day.

5. Combat leadership based on intellect, courage, aggressiveness and flexibility will always result in the quickest victory with minimum loss of life. The Goldwater-Nichols legislation provides the authority for the warfighting commander to have the flexibility and control that has been missing in the past. The CINC must have the courage to use the new authority.

6. Massive and overwhelming force are effective political terms. However, to a warfighting leader, decisive force is the only one that matters.

7. Strategy should always be air and special operations first – followed by ground operations as necessary to reach political and military objectives.

8. All strategy, planning and execution should focus on minimum loss of life. Fighting wars otherwise with our technology and war-fighting asymmetrical advantage is criminal. Two sure ways to court disaster are:

    a. Rushing airpower by not waiting for its full impact, and

    b. Using a Roman legion approach to ground warfare.

9. Air-to-ground precision weapons with three-meter accuracy in all weather conditions is essential in any future war.

10. "Stealth" provided the surprise in the Gulf war – the follow-on to stealth must be developed so we always have surprise.

12. JFACC must be strengthened. He must be a true Joint Forces Air Component Commander—there is not an alternative.

12. A rogue nation-state must not enjoy any sanctuary! Their leaders should only be permitted to select the location of their death! Political leadership of a country and the force that permits it to govern must be destroyed. All other centers of gravity become insignificant unless the central "cog" is destroyed.

As I look at these lessons, the most critical will always be WINNING WITH MINIMUM LOSS OF LIFE. However, there are two other lessons that deserve more discussion. The first is leadership. I believe our country has been lucky to have the right individual appear at the right time so often in our history. Whether that was Abraham Lincoln, George C. Marshall, General Dwight Eisenhower, or Ronald Reagan—somehow, the right man came along. Schwarzkopf was such a man.

What's sometimes forgotten is how crippling it can be to have the wrong person in a leadership position. Military organizations are loath to do the kind of pruning that often desperately needs to be done when the shooting starts. We end up with people who don't like to make decisions, a condition that can prove fatal in time of war. A combat leader must be willing to stand his ground. In the weeks leading up to the Gulf War, many people tried to convince me that the F-117 would not perform as I expected. I heard them out but still held firm to my belief in the effectiveness of this new technology, even though it had yet to be tested in high-threat combat. I built the air war around the F-117 and it proved to be all that I anticipated, and more.

The second point I want to re-emphasize is that military leaders should not permit their thought processes to get preoccupied with "massive and overwhelming force." Instead, their focus should be on "decisive force." There's a political correctness about massive force that would have us believe that we are shortchanging the American fighting man if we send over anything less than massive force. No one wants to leave soldiers or airmen who get there first, alone and outnumbered. But there's too much confusion about massive force and it makes our nation's military jump through hoops for no reason. Additionally, it wastes hundreds of millions of tax-payer dollars!

Massive and overwhelming force is the term of choice for those who attempt to play political games with our precious military sons and daughters. For a time, such as during some battles of the American Civil War, decisive force did involve massive force—but not today. Success in battle will always be dependent upon decisive force—which may or may not be massive.

People who talk about massive force run the risk of archaic strategic thinking. If one Navy SEAL team is enough to win the war, they should go do it. I don't care about deploying all the fighter wings or ground divisions to produce a massive show of force. The only thing that matters is what will get the job done with minimal loss of life. Most often, you will find that the job does not take massive force. There's no need to risk all those lives in a combat theater just due to some obsolete force-ratio calculation. Air power combined with special forces can often do much more, providing *decisive* force without *massive or overwhelming* force.

Those are my "critical lessons" which I would like to pass on to anyone who may find himself or herself in a leadership role as combat approaches.

Final Thoughts

I put this story down for three reasons: first, to honor those who placed service before self and especially the families of those who paid the ultimate sacrifice; second, to ensure that those planning and executing future wars learn from our experience; and third, to shine sunlight on the numerous half-truths and attempts to rewrite the Gulf War history.

For me, the chance to serve my nation in the Gulf War will always stand out as the greatest honor and piece of good luck that came to me in my professional life. We fought well, we saved lives, and we did what skeptics said air power could never do.

I am proud of my accomplishments

I am proud of my family

I am proud of my country

I am proud to be an American!

MAXIMS

There's no corner on good ideas . . . There is a better way.
　　　　　　　—Commander, 414th Fighter Weapons Squadron
　　　　　　　Nellis AFB, NV, 1980

Hamburger is hamburger . . . No matter how you package it!
　　　　　　　—Commander, 414th Fighter Weapons Squadron
　　　　　　　Nellis AFB, NV, 1981

Class is difficult to define but easy to recognize
　　　　　　　—347th Tactical Fighter Wing Commander
　　　　　　　Moody AFB, GA, 1985

A military leader is responsible for everything his people do or don't do.
　　　　　　　—347th Tactical Fighter Wing Commander
　　　　　　　Moody AFB, GA, 1986

Achieving excellence is a journey not a destination.
　　　　　　　—1st Tactical Fighter Wing Commander
　　　　　　　Langley AFB, VA, 1986

The first rule of leadership: help others be all they can be, all they should be, and all they will be.
　　　　　　　—1st Tactical Fighter Wing Commander
　　　　　　　Langley AFB, VA, 1987

The shortest way home is through Baghdad.
　　　　　　　—Director of Air Campaign Plans
　　　　　　　Riyadh, Saudi Arabia, 1990

There are three levels for any operation: standard, prudent risks, and gamble—they all have their place . . . We must be sure we know which one we are selecting.

—Commander, 14th Air Division
Director of Air Campaign Plans
Riyadh, Saudi Arabia, 1991

We can accomplish the unbelievable if we don't care who gets the credit.

—Director of Legislative Liaison
Washington, D.C., 1991

Integrity and loyalty must be 100% or it doesn't exist.

—Director of Legislative Liaison
Washington, D.C., 1991

The number one Pentagon problem . . . People confused about what's urgent versus what's important.

—DCS Operations and Plans
Washington, D.C., 1993

GLOSSARY

AAA	Anti-Aircraft Artillery
ABCCC	Airborne Command, Control, Communications
ACE	Airborne Command Element
AETACS	Airborne Elements of Theater Air Control System
AFB	Air Force Base
AFLDS	Airfields
ALCM	Air-Launched Cruise Missile
AOR	Area of Responsibility
APC	Armored Personnel Carrier
ARCENT	U.S. Army Forces Central Command
ATACMS	Army Tactical Missile System
ATO	Air Tasking Order
AWACS	Airborne Warning and Control System
BAI	Battlefield Air Interdiction
BCE	Battlefield Control Element
BDA	Bomb Damage Assessment
C3	Command, Control, Communications
CAFMS	Computer Aided Force Management System
CALCM	Conventional, Air-Launched Cruise Missile
CAP	Combat Air Patrol
CAS	Close Air Support
CENTAF	U.S. Central Command Air Forces
CENTCOM	U.S. Central Command
CINC	Commander In Chief
FAC	Forward Air Controller
FRAG	Fragmentary Order
FSCL	Fire Support Coordination Line
GAT	Guidance Apportionment and Targeting
GBU	Guided Bomb Unit
HARM	High-speed Anti-Radiation Missile

IADS	Integrated Air Defense System
JCS	Joint Chiefs of Staff
JFACC	Joint Forces Air Component Commander
JSTARS	Joint Surveillance Target Attack Radar System
KTO	Kuwait Theater of Operations
LANTIRN	Low Altitude Navigation and Targeting Infrared for Night
LGB	Laser-Guided Bomb
LOC	Line of Communication
MARCENT	U.S. Marine Forces Central Command
MLRS	Multiple Launch Rocket System
MSS	Mission Support System
NAVCENT	U.S. Naval Forces Central Command
NBC	Nuclear, Biological, Chemical
NCA	National Command Authority
NSC	National Security Council
NSD	National Security Directive
OPTEMPO	Operations Tempo
PGM	Precision-Guided Munition
RAF	Royal Air Force
RGFC	Republican Guard Forces Command
ROE	Rules of Engagement
RSAF	Royal Saudi Air Force
SAC	Strategic Air Command
SAM	Surface-to-Air Missile
SEAD	Suppression of Enemy Air Defenses
SOF	Special Operations Forces
TAC	Tactical Air Command
TACC	Tactical Air Command and Control
TACP	Tactical Air Control Party
TACS	Theater Air Control System
TLAM	Tomahawk Land Attack Missile
TOW	Tube-launched, Optically tracked, Wire-guided

INDEX